THREE DECADES OF ASIAN TRAVEL AND ADVENTURE

THREE DECADES OF ASIAN TRAVEL AND ADVENTURE

by

Harold Stephens
Correspondent for the Bangkok Post

Post Books

Published by Post Books,
A division of The Post Publishing Public Co.,Ltd.
136 Na Ranong Road, off Sunthorn Kosa Road,
Klong Toey, Bangkok 10110, Thailand.

First published in Thailand in 1996

Proofread by Deborah L. Leenutaphong
Cover design by Watchara Ritmahan
Cover picture: Author Harold Stephens
in Northern Thailand 31 years ago

ISBN:974-202-041-8
Printed in Thailand by Allied Printers, Bangkok

TABLE OF CONTENTS

Foreward

I will always remember the morning over 20 years ago when Harold Stephens stopped by at my desk at the *Bangkok Post* while I was Features Editor in the early 1970s to ask if we would be interested in publishing an article about a schooner he was having outfitted here in Bangkok in our Sunday section, then called the *Sunday Extra*.

In a most unassuming way, he went on to describe how the ferro-cement hull of the schooner had been cast in Singapore, and how he had motored it to a boatyard in Phra Pradaeng, and he thought that this might make a good feature story.

This was my first meeting with Steve, as I later learned to call him. In Bangkok, one hears a lot of "travellers' tales", but here was a writer who was building and outfitting his own yacht and he had photographs to back this up. He also casually mentioned the possibility of the *Bangkok Post* being interested in other travel stories: several of which you will read in these pages.

As you can see from this book, I was most happy to publish these highly-readable and observant accounts of Steve's exploits in Russia, China, and indeed throughout Asia and the south and southwestern Pacific.

For Steve was indeed a writer after my own heart.

There was I, tethered to my desk with deadlines looming daily, while he was preparing to sail the world; and as I would quickly learn, Steve then had almost 30 years of tramping the jungles and sailing the high seas, while closely observing the arts, customs and cultures he encountered already behind him.

Harold Stephens is the first to admit that his wanderlust was kindled by reading novels by Joseph Conrad, Somerset Maugham and Rudyard Kipling, and I am certain that the power of the prose of a good travel and adventure writer is capable of inspiring others to follow in their footsteps.

I had also read many of the same books in my youth, and other books like this one you are about to read that described life in distant and colourful lands — distant from my damp and usually dismal native England, that is.

I believe that this compendium of short stories, in similar way, should broaden the horizons of every reader, and stimulate others to share in some of the experiences that the author describes in this book.

For this is more than a book about travel in Asia, and more than collection of tales of adventure; it is a wealth of candid observations about different customs and cultures from the pen of Harold Stephens the Philosopher.

And while some of the chapters offer practical advice on what to do when in a certain city: be it a particular bar to visit, a hotel to stay in or describing the ascent of Mount Kinabalu, other chapters provide powerful insights about the importance of recognising and appreciating different cultures.

This is in addition to vividly describing them in the context of friends who live there. Friends such as renowned artists Theo Meier and Han Snel who made their homes in Bali, or Khun Pornsri Luhphaiboon, when she was public relations officer of the Oriental Hotel.

There is also the wisdom in these pages that comes with having been a quiet but tenacious adventurer for almost 50 years, which all began when Steve exaggerated his age in order to be able to join the Marines so that he could fight in the Pacific, which ended up with the writer in China at the end of World War II. However, I'll let him share his experiences about China "then and now" with you as he recounts them in this book.

In addition the writer's perceptions and often amusing anecdotes, these articles present an excellent historical perspective, conveying how different it might have been to have travelled in Asia just 100 years ago, as well as vividly bringing alive the World War II battles for Corregidor in the Philippines as well as how life in South India might have been in the 17th Century in a Danish Settlement.

For anyone who travels to Asia, this collection of stories should enrich their experience by conveying a greater awareness of many places that the author describes, often in fine detail.

Suffice to say, I did get my touch of adventure with Steve.

I took up an offer he had made to pitch in and help out on my days off, sanding down the deck of his Schooner, to be named the *Third Sea*, while it was being outfitted in Phra Pradaeng, and I was aboard for the maiden voyage up the Chao Phraya and later under full sail to Pattaya.

A few days later we sailed down to Koh Samui, where reluctantly I had to wave Steve goodbye after he had rowed me ashore: he was to sail for distant ports and islands, but for me it would be the overnight train back to Bangkok and more deadlines.

But, as Steve told me the other day, true adventure still lurks in this day and age in Asia, and he explained that he had just returned from a trip to the far north of Burma where the local tribes people had never seen a White person before.

The best part of Steve's exploits is that the author shares his experiences with a wide audience, as you will find in these pages.

Might I suggest that you let your imagination be your guide — for a true adventure might be as close to Bangkok as Samut Prakarn, the fishing port to the south of the city on the mouth of the Chao Phraya River, as the writer points out, were you to pay your way to travel on a fishing trawler for a few days at sea in the Gulf of Thailand.

Tony Waltham, Editor
Post Database, Bangkok Post
March 1996

Harold Stephens launches his schooner *Third Sea.*

INTRODUCTION

TAKING THE CHALLENGE

The cocktail party and reception was held in the old wing of The Oriental Hotel. I can't remember who gave it, nor why it was given, but I was invited. What I do remember quite clearly, however, is the date and the events that followed. It was November 12, 1965. That morning on the front page of the *Bangkok Post* my photograph appeared, along with a story about my rescue from the war in East Pakistan, or what is Bangladesh today. At the time, I was leading a motor expedition around the world and unfortunately we crossed the border from India into Pakistan the very day war broke out between the two countries. Fortunately I was able to reach the security of the U.S. Embassy and parked my vehicles in the basement. The U.S. Military flew transport planes into Dacca to rescue stranded Americans who were caught in the war. I was among them. The C-147 brought me to Bangkok where I was met by the press.

I knew no one in Bangkok, nor did I know much about the city. I had been a visitor a few years before but had spent only a few days here. Now at The Oriental Hotel I found myself confronted with all kinds of questions from people I had never met. "When do you think you will get your vehicles back?" "Will you continue with your expedition?" "How do you like Bangkok?"

Then came a question that completely threw me off guard. "What do you think of our *Bangkok World* newspaper?" No doubt what prompted the question was that I had a copy of the *World* tucked under my arm. I read it through before coming to the reception and remembered seeing a women's column about fur coats. It struck me odd that such a column would appear in a newspaper geared for tropical Southeast Asia. I made the mistake of criticizing the column to the man who asked it. "Very interesting," he said with a chuckle. "I am the editor." He extended his hand and we shook. He introduced himself, Bob Udick.

"No apologies," I said. "It just seemed odd."

"None needed," he replied. "You're a writer. What would you write about?"

Before coming to Bangkok, I had been writing regular travel articles for the *Washington Post*, and I knew a little about travel writing and what readers like to read. "Maybe travel," I said. "Some off-beat travel, something different, interviews with people in the travel business, interesting personalities." He listened with keen interest.

"I wish I could ask you to do some stories for us while you're waiting to get your vehicles back," he said, "but unfortunately we don't have a budget like the *Washington Post*." He put down his drink and continued. "But maybe we can work something out." He asked if I could meet him for lunch the next day at Mizu's Kitchen in Patpong. I agreed.

Mizu's Kitchen back then was Bangkok's unofficial foreign correspondents' club. Reporters, editors, writers, PR people, they all met there for lunch and drinks. When I arrived, Bob was seated with another man. They stood up and he made the introductions. "Meet Roy Howard," he said. "Roy is the Advertising Manager for Thai Airways International." When we were seated and ordered, Roy came straight to the point. He had a proposition for me.

The proposal was clear cut. Thai International would sponsor me on a three-month trial basis to write weekly travel articles for the newspaper. I quickly ran it over in my mind—twelve articles. It would mean a great deal of travelling around Southeast

Asia—Singapore, Hong Kong, Manila, even to Calcutta where THAI flew. It could be interesting, but twelve articles. Could I do it? It could be months before the war between India and Pakistan ended. I decided to give it a try. The next day at the Thai International office on New Road I signed the contract with THAI. My articles would run every Wednesday under the title "Discover the Orient with Harold Stephens, Travel Correspondent for Thai International." For the next three months I travelled around Southeast Asia

When the three months ended, Roy Howard renewed my contract, for a year this time. The India-Pakistan war finally ended and I flew to Dacca to get my equipment after which I completed the motor trip around the world. The newspaper continued to run my articles, expanding my horizons to Australia, New Zealand and the South Pacific. In New York I did the publicity that was required by Toyota Motors, collected my check, wrote a book called *Who Needs A Road* for a New York publisher and returned to Bangkok as soon as I could. The *Bangkok Post* eventually bought the *Bangkok World*, and now I found myself writing for two newspapers. After nearly thirty years the number of articles rose from the original twelve to over 3,500. It didn't take long to discover that in Asia the material for a writer is endless.

The excitement of travelling in Asia has not diminished down through the years. I began looking for the off-beat, and soon I found myself trekking in the Malay jungles with Malaysia Chief Game Warden Mohammed Khan and going on archaeological digs with Kuala Lumpur's Director of Museums Dato Shahrun. I travelled every place Thai International flew, and then to places they didn't fly. I was soon at home in the jungles, climbing mountains, cave exploring, diving on wrecks, exploring rivers and sailing Asian waters. I discovered that Asia is more than good shopping and temples. For Thai International, I explored their new destinations. I went to Bali and Kathmandu before they had international airports, and stood at the end of the fields and watched the first Caravels land—and pop chutes from their tails to slow them down.

Often even more exciting than the places I visited were the people I met. Interesting people. Exciting people. People doing things. There were Legong dancers and painters on Bali, rubber planters in Malaysia, cargo boat captains on the Rejang in Sarawak, Iban chiefs in Sabah, stone-age natives on Mindanao in the Philippines, holy men on the Ganges, negritos in the tropical rain forests of Malaysia.

I came to know many wonderful people like Chitdee Rangareva who ran the public relations department for Thai International, and Connie Manscau who was without doubt Bangkok's most famous hostess. Then there were the hotel managers—Franz Schutzman, Kurt Wachtveitl, Axel Gorelach and scores of others.

A great help and good friend was Pornsri Luphaiboon, the Public Relations Director at The Oriental. She often invited me to lunch but she never told me who the other guests might be. Once it was the world-famous writer Han Su-yin. I was excited beyond words, and when we were introduced, I wished I had brought one of her books for her to autograph. Then, unexpectedly, when we were seated in Lord Jim's Restaurant, she reached into her bag and said, "Pornsri has been telling me all about you. What an exciting life you lead. I wonder if you would autograph your book for me." At that she withdrew a copy of my book *Asian Portraits* from her bag that Pornsri had given her. Here I was, talking to one of the great writers of our times, and she was asking me to autograph my book. Only Pornsri would do something like that to me.

And there were others at those lunches—Mary Martin, Bea Arthur, Peter Ustinov and Michael Landon. Through being invited to the SEA Write Awards, I met a host of writers—James Michener, Gore Vidal, William Golding, Paul Theroux, Barbara

Cartland. They were all good story material.

But the rich and the famous weren't always the most interesting. Not so famous were a pirate chieftain from the Sulu Sea; Muda, a dark Negrito from the Malay jungles; Colonel Firbank from the old Sam Brown's Regiment in India; an honest-to-goodness hit man named Alex; mountain climbers Norkay Tensing and Sir Edmund Hillary, the first two men to climb Mount Everest, and Reinhold Messner, an Italian who climbed Everest alone and made it to the summit.

Thai International sponsored four of my books on Asia, and the *Bangkok Post* published my stories.

The year 1975 brought about a big change in my life. I began building a 71-foot schooner that would take me to those places that were even harder to get to. Tony Waltham at the *Post* began publishing my stories every Sunday, and every Monday I went to the accountant to collect my check. Every baht I earned went into the construction of my schooner. In every respect, the *Bangkok Post* was a big contributor in the building my schooner. When I began to sail Asian waters and the South Pacific, including many of the great rivers of Asia, Tony published those stories too. These included diving on the *HMS Repulse*, the mighty British battleship sunk by Japanese bombers in the early days of World War II, and John F. Kennedy's PT-109, visiting a hermit who lived 21 years on a lonely island in the South Pacific, and meeting cannibals in the jungles of New Guinea and headhunters in the wilds of Borneo. I wrote about the wonderful charms of the women on Tahiti and about the black pearls of Tongareva. I wrote about typhoons, monsoons, lost islands and about being attacked by pirates on the high seas, and about the tragic loss of my schooner in a hurricane in the Hawaiian Islands.

In 1986, Mr. Theh, the editor-in-chief, began a new section in the *Bangkok Post* called "Outlook." I was asked, along with Mitch Srivorakul, to write the Monday travel page. Mitch and I had married a few years before, and we took on the assignment with zest. We became a travel writing team, and we took the travel business seriously. It wasn't only Southeast Asia now that I covered but every corner of the world. Mitch proved to be a splendid traveller. She put up with sleeping in airport lounges, on trains and in the cramped front seats of rented cars—I took the back seats. One week we would be aboard a bush plane flying over the jungles of the remote New Hebrides in the Western Pacific and the next week we would be walking with our cameras up dizzy flights of stairs on the Eiffel Tower in Paris. We brought to our readers the exciting cities of the world—Paris, Madrid, Stockholm, Sydney, Papeete, Sandakan and Zamboanga.

What follows are fifty articles that I had written for the *Bangkok Post* over the past thirty years. Except for the first article, they are not presented in any chronological order. I chose them to give readers a look at another side of Asia, the Asia that I came to know and love. And I chose them as a storyteller might choose a story to amuse an audience, and not for any moral or righteous message that I want to convey.

Chapter 1
THE LURE OF TRAVEL

This article, the author's first in a series that was to continue for 30 years, outlines his philosophy on travel and adventure. It appeared on January 19, 1966.

There is within the nature of everyone a longing to see strange places and people. Call it romance, or a dream, but it awakens at the sight of a white sail upon the sea, at the sound of a horn of an ocean steamer leaving port, or the thunder of a jet plane taking off for a distant land. Somewhere beyond lies adventure and romance, and every heart yearns to go and find it. To prove my point, you might ask a friend, "What would you do if you had all the money you wanted?" One of the first things he is certain to tell you is that he would travel. Ask someone, and you will see.

But why? Why does man want to travel?

Because man is a searcher, an explorer, an adventurer. By his very nature he is all these things. He craves discovery in every form. He craves to find something new, either for himself or for the world. It was this same urge for discovery that drew him from the darkness of the cave. It is discovery that takes him to the edges of the universe. Without discovery life would be static and empty. Man would not progress. And, indeed, life would be dull.

Discovery, however, need not be a new continent or a lost savage tribe or a search for the rainbow's end. We have all come to realize that forbidden seas are no more, barbarous coasts have long been tamed, the greatest mountain peaks have been scaled. No, discovery can be something else. It can be a personal achievement: a curio shop in Hong Kong, a secluded beach in Penang, a small restaurant in a back street in Singapore. It can be a sunrise over Bali, or a sun-flecked trail along a Malaysian beach. It can be many things.

Fortunately the days when one had to be either a seaman before the mast or have great wealth to travel have passed. Travel today is within the reach of us all, and the traveller who must watch where and how he spends his money can have experiences as great, if not greater, than the traveller going first class. Necessity may force him to seek out the less expensive hotels, to shun guided tours, to search out restaurants not in the guidebooks. The flavour is with the traveller with a budget as well as the traveller going first class: either can make his trip as intoxicating as he wishes.

I use the word 'traveller' as a separate identity from a 'tourist'. The distinction between the two is keen. The tourist generally has his itinerary planned, his bookings arranged, his schedules set by guided tours. The traveller on the other hand has no fixed schedules and he acts as his own guide. Both have their advantages and disadvantages, their good and bad sides.

Most of us dislike being tagged as tourists, and quite often we try to conceal that fact even when we are. But what is wrong with being a tourist? When we arrive in a city for the first time—unless we have friends living there—doing the tourist bit has all the advantages. I find that a guided tour aboard a comfortable, air-conditioned bus is the quickest and easiest way to get to know a city. In the long run it can also save me money. I obtain an overall picture and return at my leisure, as the traveller, to the spots that interested me most.

A number of excellent guide-books which list hotels, restaurants and places of interest are on the market. They have their value and are a definite must, and the wise visitor should select a good one, preferably one with a historical background of the country he intends to visit. This volume is not intended to be such a guidebook. Its only purpose is to introduce you to the Orient. Many of the trips I have taken and written about here I would not expect the traveller to try to duplicate although this is possible. It is possible in our modern twentieth century to find that adventure and romance are not dead. Being aware of this is sometimes satisfying enough. Sitting in a bungalow in the Cameron Highlands can be exhilarating when you know that only a few yards away there begins a jungle so dense that parts of it are virtually unexplored.

As I enjoyed the hardships, so I enjoyed the luxuries, and I have selected stories about both. I have tried to avoid the political issue of each country but that is not always possible. What I have seen and written about are my own viewpoints and opinions, and I hope the reader forgives any apparent inaccuracies he may find. For instance I have written Singapore is the fourth largest port in the world, but after this is published it might be the third.

Through my friend Khia Fatt Tan in Singapore you will have a glimpse of Asia through Asian eyes. You will travel with Willy Mettler, a Swiss photographer. There are rickshaw drivers, men of the arts, businessmen and jungle explorers. They each have an interesting story to tell, and they all are part of Asia today. It is very likely you will meet some of them.

My own discoveries of the Orient began almost twenty-five years ago, when at the end of World War II, I went to Peking where I studied Chinese. They began at the Great Wall of China; they have carried me across the China Sea and the Malay Straits aboard a junk and on jet planes; they have taken me through the jungles of East Pakistan and Indonesia. And yet I find there is still so much to discover. Like a dream they never end.

Stephens arriving back in the U.S. after completing his record-breaking motor trip around the world..

Chapter 2
AROUND THE WORLD IN A JEEP

A question everyone always asks is "What brought you to Asia?" The answer in part is explained in the following article that appeared on July 24, 1977.

A brand new Toyota Landcruiser appeared outside my door. It was all mine. Free! All I had to do was drive it around the world. Around the world! What a romantic thought. The only trouble was that all I wanted to do was to drive from Europe to Asia over the Asian Highway, not around the world.

That was a little more than 20 years ago. In 1965, mind you, driving from Europe to Asia was not that unusual. Travellers were making the trip in reconverted buses, Mini Mokes, jeeps, bicycles, and two Frenchmen even tried it on skate boards.

My reason for the drive was to do some out-of-the-way exploring on the way, and have my own vehicle when I arrived in Asia. A six-month trip at the most, I calculated. One destination I had in mind was the Soviet Union.

The plan at first seemed to be working. I bought a new jeep in America and shipped it aboard the *Queen Elizabeth* across the Atlantic to France. In Paris I found a back-alley travel agent who boasted he could arrange a visa anywhere. In three weeks, with a couple of hundred dollars less in my bank account, I had a visa to motor across the Soviet Union. Two months later while making an exit from Russia, I was arrested on the border. I never did know the charges but after another two months, without explanation, I was freed. But now I was also broke. I had to leave my jeep in Spain and return to America to raise more funds for my trip.

Several magazines were interested in my travels in Russia. Solvent again! Before returning I stopped to visit a friend, Al Podell, a New York editor. "You need a sponsor," he said.

"What for? I have all I need."

"Money?"

I listened. He had a few ideas, and asked that I wait around a month. A few weeks later he phoned. "It's all arranged," he said. "I have a new Toyota Landcruiser for you, plus a camper and a few other extras. Also—" he hesitated, "I'd like to go with you."

Toyota, camper, an extra body. I didn't want anyone tagging along. "But I already have a jeep waiting for me in Spain," I explained.

"I've raised $24,000!" he said.

The next day I was in New York, and soon to learn something about the promotion game. "There's only one catch," Al said.

"Your mother's going too," I said.

"No. I needed a peg to hitch it on."

"Hitch what on?" I didn't understand New York PR talk. Al explained. To sell the trip it had to be more than a drive to Asia. He had us booked for a motor trip around the world—the longest motor trip, non-repetitive miles, that is, ever to be attempted.

This wasn't what I had in mind. "What about your job?" I said. Surely Al wouldn't quit his job!

"Never mind," he said. "I quit."

He had quit, and I was stuck. I could hardly turn him down now.

And so began my motor trip around the world, some 42,500 non-repetitive miles. That same trip today—across North Africa, through the Middle East to Afghanistan, India, Pakistan and

Burma, and then from South America up through Central America to the US—would, of course, be quite impossible. But no one thought so then.

Toyota Motors was my sponsor, along with more than a dozen other companies, and for them I would prove the world was a safe place in which to live and sell their products. An idealistic dream! The tragedy is that instead of the world becoming better for the traveller over these past 25 years, as we all believed it would, conditions have grown worse. No longer can we hop in a car and drive from Europe to Asia but not even from one country to the next. Instead of announcing a new beginning to travel, my motor trip heralded the end of such overland travel.

Looking back, in spite of the difficulties, the trip did have its compensations; there were humorous moments, along with some very trying ones. Next year marks the 25th anniversary that I completed the journey, and it brings back all the memories. It's sad to know that it was also the last motor trip around the world.

And had it not been for Al Podell, the New York editor, it may not have happened at all.

When sponsorship for the trip was final, Al insisted that I move into his posh pad on 55th Street where I spent the next few weeks answering the doorbell and telephone. As I said, a new Toyota Landcruiser did appear on the sidewalk beneath my window, followed a few days later by a tent camper on two wheels. "It sleeps eight," Al said proudly.

The doorbell continued to ring. Delivery boys appeared. Firestone high-foliation tyres, plus an extra set. Picnic boxes. Gasoline stoves. Lanterns. Vacuum bottles. Two fast-erecting pop-up tents; they made a mess out the living room when they popped up and we couldn't get them down.

For our wearing comfort, the sponsors said, we had raincoats, jackets, sports shirts, knit-shirts, insulated underwear, regular underwear, socks, gloves, trousers. The Hat Corporation of

America came across with cowboy hats and desert hats, safari hats and rain hats, cold weather hats and tropical hats, and I swear, even a top hat.

But there was more, much more. Shoes, 44 pairs. Not for the expedition but 44 for each member. Then flashlight batteries, six cases. Seven flashlights; four lanterns. Over 100 aerosol cans with everything from shave cream to dog repellent. An archery company, with an assignment from a magazine, sent four bows and hundreds of arrows. An insect company sent 22 cases—repeat, 22 cases—of insect repellent, insecticide, disinfectant, car wax and shoe polish.

And still more: sun glasses and suntan oils, antifreeze and desert coolant for the radiator, floormats and mud guards, a year's supply of paper plates and cups, flashing rods and reels, a portable car massager and cigarette lighters that worked from solar energy. And a complete assortment of Pentax cameras and all the accessories to go with them.

There was a catch. We had to advertise each company's products. This meant taking along a photographer. Then a copy writer. Another journalist was added. We now had five, which meant we would need my jeep in Spain as a support vehicle.

Public relations representatives began to appear with stacks of typewritten sheets of instructions. One suntan lotion PR man had 500 mimeographed questionnaires for us to hand out, to see " what the natives use along the way for suntan oil." The press agent for a clothing company wanted photos taken at "photogenic waterholes, especially with crocodiles and elephants and interesting things like that." Another manufacturer wanted photos of us in woolen sweaters in front of the Taj Mahal. The Bourbon Institute of America arranged for us to pick up cases of the Kentucky Bourbon at major cities around the world.

Imagine trying to drive with such a load. I couldn't put on the brakes and not worry about a raft of paper cups hitting me on the head or 100 flash light batteries falling out when I opened the glove box. In desperation, in Spain I unloaded a half ton of supplies upon a band of roaming Gypsies. They feared some evil motive and at first didn't want to accept a thing. Then in Jerez, the wine capital of Spain, the Gonzales Bodega, not wanting to be outdone by our New York sponsors, presented us with six cases of brandy and another six of sherry. Now when I threw on the brakes I was threatened by a couple cases of brandy sailing through the windscreen.

France and Spain flew by with little difficulty, except for a blockade on the British Colony of Gibraltar that delayed us a few days. Although such incidents at the time were worrisome, today it could have been far worse!

North Africa 25 years ago was exciting but not with the same excitement you find there today. As tourists we went to Marrakesh and walked through the crooked streets of the Casbah. We never did fear for our safety or our lives. We made friends with Arabs everywhere we went, in the days before terrorism. We were invited to great feasts of lamb and green tea with the bedouins, under huge tents; we watched breathtaking sunsets on the desert; and we could camp anywhere we chose along white sand beaches of the Mediterranean.

And exciting moments there were too, like the time in Algeria when we camped in an unmarked minefield left over from the feud with Morocco and almost blew ourselves to bits before being rescued. Also in Algeria we crossed the Sahara, hopping from oasis to oasis toward the Tunisian border, and played like Lawrence of Arabia.

We found Tripoli a delight, and in Tunisia, our photographer, dazed by the cruel desert sun, stepped out of the Landcruiser doing 35 m.p.h. and badly battered himself on the road. Four days after that we broke an axle on one trailer in the middle of the Libyan desert, hundreds of hot miles from anywhere. We managed to feed ourselves by bartering for food with some nomads who gave us some eggs and goat milk in exchange for two pairs of shoes and a case of OFF mosquito repellent.

In the Middle East we did have problems since Al is Jewish, although everyone took him to be Arab. Nevertheless, the Egyptians refused to allow us to cross the Sinai Peninsula because of their war with Israel. We were forced to make an expensive detour from Alexandria to Beirut by ship.

Beirut was one of the finest cities we visited in the Middle East. With its open street cafes it reminded me much of Paris. I can't imagine it being bombed out today.

Even back then the crossing from Lebanon into Syria was tricky business for the two countries were fending one another every other week. By the time we reached Baghdad the strain was begin to show on us. We took a week to rest. Baghdad was delightful.

We crossed into Iran. In Teheran we had to be careful, we were told. "Don't say anything against the Shah." His picture was everywhere. Teheran was truly a cosmopolitan city. The street cafes were packed in the evenings and there was gaiety in the restaurants. Everyone then seemed to be pro-American, and every young person we talked to wanted to study in America. "Can you help me get a visa?"

In Iran we crossed another desert, the Dash-i-Kavir to Afghanistan. The difficulty I had was not with the intense heat but with my fellow travellers. Between the border of Iran and Afghanistan I had a mutiny on my hands.

We discovered the Americans had built a modern road in Afghanistan from Herat to Kabul, the capital. But across the north near the Soviet border was a legendary route Marco Polo took seven centuries before. I announced we'd be taking the northern route. The others refused. I set out in the jeep across the north with an English hitchhiking seaman I met in town. The others took the new highway to Kabul.

It was indeed wild country in the north. There were no roads. We entered great valleys where nomads by the thousands were camped. At Mazar-i-Sharif we moved slowly with camel caravans entering this northern town. And a few days later we found ourselves in a cholera epidemic. And a bit further on we met Russians who, like the Americans, were building roads. One new road came down from the USSR over the Hindu Kush. Three weeks after we left Herat we arrived in Kabul, to read my obituary in the New York Times. We were reported as lost in the cholera epidemic. "What will I tell everyone now?" Al asked.

We got safely through the Khyber Pass but coming out we broke an axle on the trailer. At the same time the monsoons hit, our first rain in many months. Unable to make repairs in the raging downpour, we pitched camp for the night. In the night thieves stole our tools and pulled the jacks from another trailer sending it down on our campsite below.

All through India we were oppressed by the problems of that sprawling trouble-torn democracy, a forerunner of what was to erupt a decade later. Nevertheless, we were able to visit places like the Sikh Golden Temple. It would be impossible to visit today.

In India my team began to drop out one by one. They had enough. Al too had to get back to New York, although he agreed to see me through to Thailand. We drove the jeep to Kathmandu where I was able to sell it to the Rana family. From Calcutta Al and I set out in the Landcruiser for East Pakistan, which is Bangladesh today. We crossed the border on September 5th; the very next day war between India and Pakistan broke out. We were caught in the middle.

We were arrested twice in the first four days of the war. Both times the U.S. Consul secured our release but the police put a tail on us day and night. After two weeks of mounting tension we drove the Landcruiser into the basement of the U.S. Embassy and were evacuated by the U.S. Air Force to Bangkok. Al flew back to New York.

Four months passed before I was granted permission to return for my vehicle and equipment. During that time I began writing travel articles for the *Bangkok World*. Thai International was authorised to resume flights to East Pakistan. There was only one problem. The flights were filled; there was a two-month waiting list. Disillusioned, I went to the Bamboo Bar at the Oriental Hotel to console myself. The Bamboo was in the Author's Wing then.

I was sitting at the bar, half listening to an Aussie blond sing "I left my heart in San Francisco" when an American businessman next to me started a conversation. He sold fertilizer. "I hear Bangkok's an exciting place," he rambled. I mumbled something. I wasn't in the mood for idle talk. "Wouldn't mind seeing some sights," he continued. "Leaving tomorrow for Dacca, on the first Thai International flight."

I helped him with a half dozen more drinks at the Bamboo and then showed him the Starlight on New Road, and slipped a pretty hostess 200 baht to see that he had a good time. I went out to Don Muang the next morning. There was an empty seat and I was on my way to Dacca.

I loaded my Landcruiser and equipment aboard a freighter in Chittagong and flew ahead. It was an easy drive after Thailand down through Malaysia to Singapore where I shipped to Australia. I crossed the Australian continent, via the Outback. It was the first time Aussies had seen a Toyota. In Sydney I boarded a freighter with my Landcruiser and camper secured on deck, and two weeks later reached Tahiti. Another two weeks after that I was in Panama. Al was there to greet me.

Now began the final drive through Central America via the Pan American Highway. After Panama came Costa Rica, then Nicaragua, Honduras, Guatemala and Mexico to the US. When I read the newspapers today I can't help thinking about that drive. Cities that I admired are in ruin today. I camped on the shores of Lake Managua and learned how with pride to pronounce the name of the capital of Honduras—Tegucigalpa. The last foreign country, Mexico, and ten days later we were in New York City driving down Fifth Avenue—where it all started, 18 months before.

"It's amazing, absolutely amazing," Al kept muttering as we parked in front of the Public Library on Fifth Avenue, where the Press and TV were waiting.

"You mean that we made it?" I asked.

"No," he said, "amazing that we found a parking place."

Al was home in New York, and I returned to Asia, by jet this time.

When we recall any adventure, what always comes to mind are the hardships, and when we tell about these experience, it gives an unbalanced picture. We had our rewards as well. There had been moments of unsurpassing beauty and moments of pure poetry: the red sails of dhows on the blue-green waters of the Nile, the Taj Mahal by moonlight, the blazing Sahara sunsets, the majestic snow peaks of the Himalayas rising over the valley of Kathmandu, the strange feeling of sitting at the driver's wheel while the Landcruiser is lashed to the deck of a freighter and watching Tahiti come into view.

And there were light moments which were not often taken lightly at the time. In Sydney I got very nice press coverage, about the world's longest motor trip, and was promptly invited to lead a parade of racing cars around the track in the forthcoming races. It was a splendid feeling to be doing the circuit, with two-dozen supercharged speed machines lined up behind me for the starting signal, except I failed to get off the track when the flag came down. I almost wiped out half a dozen race cars. The next newspaper story wasn't so favourable.

But the worst experience of all was in Texas, USA. Dowell Chemical had placed a special coolant in our radiator, then sealed the cap on. We drove across five of the world's hottest deserts, over the highest road in the world and upon the lowest at the Dead Sea. Our reward, when we returned to New York, provided we didn't drain the radiator, was to be US$5,000.

We watched any maintenance on the Landcruiser like a hawk. Half the time Al drove the nose of the Landcruiser into our tent for fear someone would drain the radiator.

In Texas it happened. We stopped at a gas station early one morning, after coming out of a Holiday Inn. One of our sponsors had notified the hotel that we were coming, so they had a large welcoming sign a storey high. Evidently it impressed the gas station attendant.

"Fill it up and check the oil," we said and went into a cafe for our morning coffee. We returned and the man was beaming.

"It's a pleasure, a real pleasure," he said. "I checked your tyres too. And, oh yes..." he hesitated, "I flushed out your radiator. Had a devil of a time getting that cap off."

I think Al and I both cried. The man never did understand. But Dowell Chemical was nice about it, and understanding. They filled up our radiator again. But no check.

Chapter 3
TRAVELLING IN SOUTHEAST ASIA A HUNDRED YEARS AGO

People live in the past, and they long for yesterdays. They believe that yesterday was a better time to live, and a better time to travel. In this article, that appeared on May 12, 1986, I wanted to show that today, not yesterday, can be just as eventful.

We become angered—we get caught in a traffic jam, a flight we planned is overbooked, a clerk at the other end fouled up our reservations and we must settle for another hotel. When this happens, how many times have we heard it said, or have uttered it ourselves: "I should have been born a hundred years ago!"

Granted, travel a hundred years ago had a romance all of its own. How thrilling for someone living in London to book a cabin (port side going out) on a P&O liner and steam off to the Far East, through the Suez, with a stopover in Bombay, and then on to Singapore, up the Chao Phaya to Bangkok, across to Saigon and then on to Hong Kong or maybe Manila before reaching Yokohama. A five to six month trip. What excitement!

But we must be realistic. Such travel was not for everyone. Unless they were seamen before the mast, government civil servants, anthropologists working for big museums, or else very, very rich, people would not have come to Asia merely for a vacation. Nor would they have had the incentive a hundred years ago to travel half way around the world to reach the East. What did they know about Asia? Siam, Singapore, Hong Kong—they were no

The Singapore waterfront as it appeared about 1890 during Conrad's time.

more than exotic names in fancy gazetteers. There were no guides or travellers' hand books in those days that sold Asia. In fact, there was very little knowledge about the area in 1886. When Sir Clarke was appointed Governor of the Straits settlement in 1876, he requested maps and information of any kind of the Malay Peninsula where he was going and was told there was absolutely no information of any kind available.

And those places that are so popular today—Bali and Kathmandu—a hundred years ago weren't known even in Asia. The great ruins of Angkor Wat were undiscovered. Kuala Lumpur, the present capital of Malaysia, was little more than a jungle outpost, less than 20 years old. Taiwan was a coaling station in the South China Sea, and Phuket, visited by Captain Light a century before, was only a mark on sailing charts. Pattaya was a fishing village.

Nevertheless, visitors did come east. We have the accounts of many of these early travellers. Joseph Conrad wrote volumes about Asia, Anna Leonowens told us in her book about her life in Bangkok, Alfred Wallace explored the eastern jungles and reported on them, and many lesser-known travellers, like Isabella Bird, an English woman who passed through Southeast Asia in 1874, have handed down their stories which fortunately are in print today. Many of these travellers' tales are fascinating and informative, and they give us a clear picture of what travelling in this part of the world was like in their day. And from what they had to tell, it wasn't all that romantic, not as we imagine it to have been.

So let's suppose, for one reason or another, perhaps a rich uncle died or a museum agreed to back you, you did decide to come to Asia. How would you get here, and once you did come, where would you stay? Hotels were few. What about the sights, what could you see and do, and how would you get around? There were no buses taxis or trains. There weren't even roads. What, then, was it like travelling in Asia?

To have reached Asia, of course you would have had to come by sea. Travel by land then was impossible. (It took Marco Polo 17 years to make the round trip.) There were, however, some fine shipping lines then, the P&O Line and the Messageries Maritimes, but the bulk of the travellers came by steerage class on merchant vessels. It was a tough way to travel, far below deck in airless cabins jammed with bunks. Furthermore, first class or steerage, you could expect the voyage to last six weeks from London- five weeks from San Francisco. The big boon to travel to Asia came in 1869 with the opening of the Suez Canal. Travel time was cut in half.

What we also tend to forget today is that those travellers who did manage to reach Asia back then made it a-once-in-a-lifetime trip. There were no repeat journeys. There simply wasn't enough time when travel was so slow. I often think about this when I meet someone today, and they announce in one breath how nice it would have been to visit Asia a hundred years ago, and in the next breath they say that on their vacation next year they might take in Phuket instead of Pattaya. Visits to Asia today can be yearly events; they weren't in 1886.

Our steamer arrives in Singapore. We disembark and after a fortnight we will travel up to Bangkok and then to Hong Kong and Manila. Where will we stay?

Finding accommodations presented problems for early travellers in Asia before the turn of the century. For civil servants and people travelling on official business, government rest houses were provided. They became institutions, spread out across the Indian subcontinent all the way to Burma and down the Malay Peninsula to Singapore. They averaged twenty miles apart, the distance a bullock cart loaded with luggage could travel in a day.

At the end of the day, after journeying by elephant or horseback, weary travellers would search eagerly in the darkness for the glow of a hurricane lamp lighting the verandah of the local rest house.

And there on the verandah steps the traveller was certain to be greeted by a white-coated Hindu or Malay house boy and led to his quarters. The sight was always welcoming—a spacious, high ceiling room, with shutters opened on the verandah, a mosquito net draped over the bed, a flowered porcelain Shanghai jar filled with fresh water and a dipper, and sticks of smoldering incense burning in a pot beside the bed to keep the mosquitoes at bay.

Air-conditioning then was a turbaned youth who sat in a far corner. In a slow rhythmic motion he would pull the cord of the punkah, causing the enormous rattan fan suspended from the ceiling to swing in pendulum motion back and forth. A few old rest houses still have their punkahs and every time I see one today, I wonder how honeymoon couples who checked into a rest-house managed. Turning on the air conditioner is so much easier, and less inhibiting.

But we are not government servants and we need to find a hotel. In Singapore there were several adequate establishments. Passengers from the P&O liners unloaded at Hotel de l'Europe. Conrad remarked in one of his novels that passengers came to the hotel with their luggage plastered with hotel labels to prove "they are well travelled." Even in those days tourists were the brunt of sarcasm.

If you were a seaman in 1886, you could have checked into the Seaman's Home on south Bridge Road, or into Raffles Hotel which opened that year. The Sarkies brothers bought the Raffles Girls Board School and converted it into the famous Raffles Hotel that it is today, and they opened two other properties, the E&O in Penang and the Strand in Rangoon. Rumour has it that Conrad was one of Raffles's first guests, also a 23-year-old journalist named Rudyard Kipling. Kipling commented that the food was great at Raffles but the place to stay was at the Hotel de l'Europe. The old Hotel de l'Europe remained standing until 1936, when it was demolished to make room for the Supreme Court.

Aside from Raffles opening her doors as a hotel, two other events took place that year. Singapore celebrated Queen Victoria's Golden Jubilee with parades and band concerts on the Padang, and the colony erected a statue of their founding father Sir Stamford Raffles. Had you been there, when the dark bronze statue of Raffles was unveiled, you would have heard the excited comments made by the Malays: "Why, he's a black man just like ourselves!"

Travellers who did arrive in Singapore a hundred years ago witnessed an atmosphere we could never know today. I felt it in part when I first arrived in Singapore 25 years ago, but that was nothing compared to what Isabella Bird found. She was enthralled with Singapore, especially the bazaars "the continuous rows of open shops which create for themselves perpetual twilight by hanging tatties forming long shady alleys." She tells of crowds of buyers and sellers, the bustle and noise, the ringing of bells and rapid beating of drums and tom-toms. She called it "an intensely heathenish sound. And heathenish this city is. How I wish I could convey an idea, however faint, of this huge, mingled, colourful Oriental city." That city disappeared fifteen years ago, when the Government decided to modernise.

It's 1886 and we've spent two weeks in Singapore and decide to visit Malaya to the north before continuing to Bangkok. There are no roads, and less than two dozen miles of rail lines. Towns on the Malay Peninsula were only pockets of civilisation, each one living in isolation. The only means of communication was by way of narrow jungle tracks. Goods had to be carried by bullock cart or elephant back.

The first rail line in Malaysia was opened on June 1, 1885, connecting Port Weld with Taiping, covering a distance of eight-and-a-half miles. The following years, in 1886, the year we decided to take our imaginary trip, another line was opened, from

Bukit Kuda to Kuala Lumpur, a grand distance of 20 miles. The news made headlines. It was no less important than our present day landing on the moon. It truly must have been exciting to have been there at the time.

The Straits Times, dated September 22, 1886, called it a momentous occasion, with brass and royalty aboard, from His Excellency the Governor and Lady Weld to His Highness the Sultan of Selangor and his hundred attendants. "It started at twenty to ten," the reporter wrote "and at quarter past eleven the train steamed into Kuala Lumpur, the run of about twenty miles having been done in ninety minutes."

The article goes on to tell how "as the train neared K.L. the speed was greatly accelerated and we were then going about thirty miles an hour." The reporter concluded by saying "the motion was very pleasant."

What did the arrival of the iron horse mean? Another reporter saw it merely as a tourist promotion scheme. In the same issue of *The Straits Time* he wrote: "The train will mean an increase in foreigners and strangers who will come, much to the profit of the country."

Since overland travel to the Malay states was impossible, the only way to visit was by steamer, as Isabella Bird had done. She left Singapore by local steamer and sailed to Malacca, Port Klang, Lumut and Penang. She described the voyage: "The mercury was 90 in my little cabin, and it swarmed not only with mosquitos but with cockroaches, which in the dim light looked as large as mice." It doesn't sound very much like a romantic way to travel.

Travel then did have its discomforts. One of these was mosquitos. There was no escaping them. "I am dreadfully bitten on the ankles, feet and arms, which are so swollen I can hardly put on my clothes," wrote Miss Bird from her room in Klang. "I have to sew my feet up daily in linen." She also remarked that a tiger which "had devoured six men" was killed in the forest nearby.

Tigers in Singapore at the same time were killing on average 600 workers a year. One did not venture away from the towns. Jungle walks were out and early morning joggers of today would have to have been beware back then.

Piracy was another threat. When Miss Bird arrived in Lumut, the ink on the Pangkor Treaty was not yet dry. The treaty gave Britain control over the Dindings, a strip of land along the Malay mainland where pirates hid in small coves and in the mangrove swamps. Pirates raided a town on the coast and slaughtered a dozen people the month before Miss Bird arrived.

But, in 1886, if you were a big game hunter you would have enjoyed Malaya and most Southeast Asian countries. In fact, in Malaya you could have made money at it. There was a $15 bounty on tigers, five for rhinos and five for crocodiles.

From Singapore to Bangkok it took five days by steamer. Conrad described sailing up the Chao Phaya to reach this eastern capital: "One morning early we crossed the bar, and while the sun was rising splendidly over-the flat spaces of land we steamed up the innumerable bends, passed the shadow of the great gilt pagoda, and reached the outskirts of the town." Anyone who sails up the same stretch today will find little has changed.

Conrad continues with his description with his arrival in Bangkok: "There it was, spread largely on both banks, the Oriental capital which has yet suffered no white conqueror." The author was truly moved by Bangkok, as we can see in the following lines. "Here and there in the distance, above the crowded mob of low, brown roof ridges, towered great piles of masonry, king's palaces, temples, gorgeous and dilapidated, crumbling under the vertical sunlight, tremendous, overpowering, almost palpable, which seemed to enter one's breast with the breath of one's nostrils and soak into one's limbs through every pore of one's skin."

The Bangkok that Conrad found upon his arrival was certainly not what we find today, and yet aspects of his world are still here.

The City of Angels was going through some dramatic changes, under the reign of King Chulalongkorn.

Before he acceeded to the throne, King Chulalongkorn had travelled extensively throughout Southeast Asia and Europe. As a result of his travels, when he became King, he began to modernise Bangkok. One of his projects was to carve a wide avenue from the Grand Palace to the new Dusit Palace, patterned after the Champs Elysees in Paris. The avenue as we see it today is called Rajdamnern, or Royal Progress Avenue.

Conrad was witness to some of these changes. He tells us in detail about his travels through Bangkok by horse-drawn carriage and by sampan on the klongs. A third means of travel in those days was by rickshaw. Only a few years before Conrad arrived, a Chinese nobleman humbly presented a rickshaw to the King for his private use. By Conrad's time the vehicle was seen in such numbers that the government had to promulgate an act governing its use. The reason given was for public safety. In 1884, electricity was installed to light up the Grand Palace, and about this same time horse-drawn trams were introduced to Bangkok. Soon 800 ponies were pulling trams up and down New Road. Getting around in Bangkok a hundred years ago would not have been a problem, and maybe a bit easier then than it is today.

As for hotels in Bangkok back then, there were a few. Siam had been closed to the West for nearly two hundred years, and when the King granted trading rights to the British in the late 1850's, he also gave them a Rama Palace on the right bank of the Chao Phaya where ships' officers could stay ashore at night. It may have been the original Oriental Hotel, making it much older than the 110 years the management claims it to be. Whether it's the same hotel, we may don't know, but we do know it was there when Conrad arrived a hundred years ago.

There's talk that Conrad stayed at the Oriental, but in one of his short stories he tells us that he thought the hotel might be too expensive for his meagre sailor's wages. But he made frequent references to the Oriental. He mentioned upon his arrival there were ten or more ships anchored out front, with the *Otaga*, which he was to command, anchored a little upstream from the hotel.

Conrad had his first meal ashore at the Union Hotel located in New Road. It was depressingly empty. "A wagging punkah fanned twenty vacant cane-bottomed chairs and two rows of shiny plates. Three Chinamen in white jackets loafed with napkins in their hands around that desolation."

How was the Oriental Hotel, today's number one hotel in the world, a hundred years ago? Another writer at the time described his stay in Room Number One. The room, he said, consisted of a double-bed sleeping room, a parlor and a large wide verandah. there were two sheets on the bed, a real luxury in those days, and a "peace-maker," a long, narrow bolster covered with white linen and placed in the centre of the mattress from head to foot. "An, important feature on a double bed on a Bangkok night."

If we think there may have been romance sailing the South China Sea in Conrad's day, then follow his voyage to Singapore. When the *Otaga* crossed the bar at the mouth of the Chao Phaya and entered the open sea, there was little wind and it took him three weeks to sail the 800 miles to Singapore. Fever and sickness broke out again aboard ship and only Conrad and his first mate were on deck when they swung the ship into the wind and let the anchor and chain rattle through the hawser in the outer roads in Singapore. It wasn't a pleasant way to travel.

To reach Hong Kong from Bangkok in the 1880's, sailing ships had to wait for the right monsoon winds to take them there, but with steamers the distance could be covered in a week. Isabella Bird described her first view of Hong Kong. "By a narrow and picturesque channel we enter the harbour," she wrote, "with the scorched and arid peaks of Hong Kong on the one side, and on the other the yet redder and rockier mainland of China, without a tree or trace of civilisation, or even habitation."

Kowloon without a trace of civilisation! She should see it today. She noted that "the Hongkongese are attempting to create a suburb but it appears to be too arid."

Hotels in Hong Kong when Miss Bird arrived were a real problem. She was advised to stay aboard, as every hotel and rooming house in the colony was filled. She commented there were no plays or music halls, but once a week people could cross into Canton and see public executions there.

Manila a hundred years ago was a pulsating city under the Spanish and an exciting place to visit. The walled city of Intramuros with its magnificent gates and tiled plazas was certainly one of the most beautiful cities in Southeast Asia. Called the "Pearl of the Orient" Manila was linked to Europe by a direct monthly maritime service, and by four indirect lines through Hong Kong. There were weekly vessels sailing from Hong Kong to Manila and vice-versa.

And that was Southeast Asia, more or less, a hundred years ago. The political situation was uncertain and did not make travel easy. Both France and Great Britain were attempting to extend their colonial influence if not their rule, over the area. In 1886, Great Britain had incorporated Burma into the British Empire as a province of India. To the south of Siam, the king had expanded his territory over the Malay Peninsula as far north as Perak. The French had extended their power in Indochina to the banks of the Mekong River, from the northern point of Laos to the Cambodian frontier. Travellers were simply not welcome.

Mosquitos, diseases, cockroach-infested tramp steamers, wild animals ready to prey, savage pirates, lack of accommodation, border wars, a six-month voyage to get back home—that was Southeast Asia one hundred years ago. I am sure travellers find Asia much more enjoyable today, and we can, if we wish, make it as romantic as we want it to be.

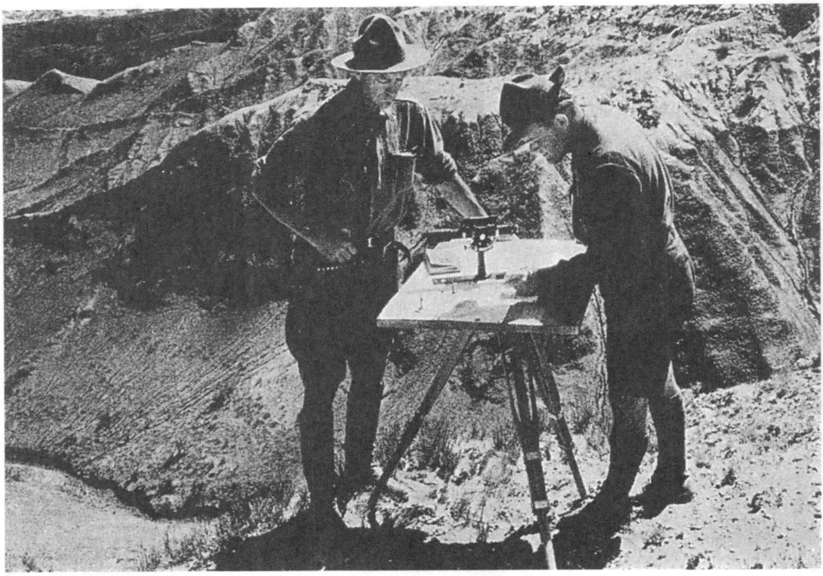

Roy Chapman Andrews crosses the Gobi Desert in Outer Mongolia in April 1922. Top, motorcars were used, the first time ever. Bottom, Andrews records the bearings of his discoveries.

Chapter 4
THE FIRST INDIANA JONES—ROY CHAPMAN ANDREWS

The following article appeared on June 1, 1992. Long before Hollywood created Indiana Jones, Asia had a real adventure writer named Roy Chapman Andrews.

There's a book I have on my library shelf at home that I've had so long I can't remember how I got it, except, I would imagine, my father gave it to me many years ago. I do remember when growing up, my father often talked about the author, a man I came to look upon with awe.

The book is *Heart of Asia,* and its author was Roy Chapman Andrews.

It's not a name you hear very often these days—Roy Chapman Andrews—but a few decades ago it was one name that everyone knew. During the ill-fated depression years of the late 1920s and early 30s, Andrews brought much needed adventure and romance to everyone's homes. He wrote dozens of adventure books, and his articles appeared in the pages of the *National Geographic* and other magazines.

People today may not remember the name but they are very much aware of what he left behind—a multi-billion dollar a year legacy to the travel industry. The boom we are witnessing in adventure travel today is deeply rooted in the exploits of the man with the wide-brimmed, felt hat and a pistol on his side. Roy Chapman Andrews is the prototype for today's movie character

Indiana Jones.

There's a photograph of Andrews that tells more about the man than the proverbial "thousand words" could ever possibly do. The picture was used on the frontispiece of his book, *Ends of the Earth,* published in 1929, and shows the author sitting on a rocky hillside. He is holding a bolt-action rifle in his right hand, and around his waist is a loaded cartridge belt. Tucked into the vest is his other gun, a revolver. His knee-high leather boots, and the sleeves of his work shirt are casually rolled up. His well-worn hat has just the right amount of tilt to it. Behind him rises a great eroded escarpment in the heart of the Gobi Desert.

If this description rings a bell, there's a good reason. Hollywood director Steven Spielberg denies it, but rumour has it that Ray Chapman Andrews was the real-life model for the film character Indiana Jones that Spielberg portrayed in three box-office hit films.

There's no question, Andrews was a macho man's man, the same type that Indiana Jones portrays so well on the silver screen. In real life, Andrews was a superb horseman and a crack shot with both pistol and rifle. He was an avid sportsman and hunted big game around the world. He recorded his hunting trips as well as his scientific expeditions in the many books and magazine articles he wrote. I read my first hunting tales in *Heart of Asia.*

Andrews loved the wild, untamed outdoors; he was deeply affected "by the vast open plains and the endless eroded badlands of Outer Mongolia." He recalls in *Heart of Asia* how he spent his adult life in the East and he relates with excitement his skirmishes with bandits and about being shot at by Chinese soldiers.

When reading his books one can't help wondering if his primary motive was actually the advancement of science or the discovery of fossils and not a meaningful yearning for adventure and remote, far-off places. Few anthropologists can make the task of dusting dinosaurs bones sound like an exciting adventure as well as he did

Whatever, Andrews was a product of his times, not unlike "rough riding" President Teddy Roosevelt, explorer William Beebe and "Bring 'em Back Alive" Frank Buck. In many ways, like Indiana Jones, he behaved as if he were invincible. He was a marvellous storyteller and some say he never let the facts get in the way of a good tale.

Andrews also happened to be at the right place at the right time. The world in the early 1900s had developed an interest in palaeontology, the study of fossils. Henry Fairfield Osborn, a noted palaeontologist at the American Museum of Natural History in New York, upset modern thinking when he proposed a daring new theory about where and how mammals arose. He predicted that "Central Asia would prove to be the dispersal point for mammalian life on the planet, including human beings." There," he said, "there is where the Missing Link would be found."

The theory was bold and speculative. Western scientists knew very little about the Central Asian plateau; a rhinoceros tooth, found by a Russian in the 1890s, was the only fossil from the Central Asian plateau ever to be recorded in Western scientific literature.

Since the mid-19th century, most anthropologists and men and women of science believed that either north Africa or the Fertile Crescent along the eastern Mediterranean was the site of human origins. Here in western Turkey, many claimed, is where mankind began. Andrews was sceptical. He pondered Osborn's theory. Could man have originated in Asia? The very thought was revolutionary.

In Andrew's opinion there was but one way to find out—go to Outer Mongolia and explore the far reaches of the Gobi Desert. He devised a plan. Twenty years after Osborn's announcement, Andrews, now himself a young curator at the American Museum of Natural History in New York, approached Osborn, by then the president of the museum. Andrew had lunch with Osborn, and at the end of the meal, while Osborn leaned back, he laid out his plan for the "biggest land expedition ever."

The purpose, he explained, was to explore Mongolia and prove Osborn's theory. How could Osborn not be interested! The expedition would try to reconstruct the whole past history of the Central Asian plateau—its geological structure, fossil life and its past climate. It would include an army of scientists, from palaeontologists to topographers.

Andrews further proposed that the expedition be conducted by motorcar, the first ever of this type. For fuel to run the motorcars, the expedition would be resupplied by a caravan of 75 camels.

Andrews convinced Osborn that the expedition would succeed. A few weeks later, when the final plans were formalised, the museum made the announcement. Immediately the press seized upon the story. The *New York Times* reported: "Today an anthropological expedition sponsored by the New York Museum of Natural History and led by scientist and explorer Roy Chapman Andrews left for Mongolia attempting to find traces of an early human type. Andrews feels that the earliest humans lived in Outer Mongolia hundreds of thousands of years ago and these forbearers may have migrated to Asia from Europe. They settled in an area of lakes and sand dunes now covered by the Gobi Desert."

It was a cold day in March 1922, when Andrews and his team departed for Peking, which is today Beijing. Osborn was there at the dock to see them off. A month later, on April 21, they sailed beneath the shadow of the summit of Wanchuan Pass outside of Kalgan (today Zhangjiakou), China. What lay ahead was Outer Mongolia and the Gobi Desert—one of the last scientifically unexplored areas on the globe. The maps the expedition carried showed little more than wavering dotted lines indicating ancient caravan routes, vague indications of mountain ranges and a few wrong landmarks and oases.

No Indiana Jones plot by Director Steven Spielberg could be more dramatic!

The expedition's caravan of motorcars started down the long, rough, boulder-strewn track into the great Asiatic interior basin that is Mongolia. For the first hundred miles they bumped and slid on a muddy road alongside the rolling, cultivated fields of Inner Mongolia, settled mostly by the Chinese. Slowly the fields gave way to a more arid landscape.

Here and there a low escarpment began to interrupt the monotonous horizon. Several expedition members stopped to inspect an outcrop of sedimentary rock while Andrews, in the lead car, continued on. A half mile west of the tiny settlement of Iren Dabasu, Andrews stopped to make camp. He had just finished pitching the tents when the last two cars that had been scouting the area roared into camp. Andrews hurried to meet them. In one car was Walter Granger, the chief palaeontologist.

"I knew that something unusual had happened," he wrote in his diary. "Granger's eyes were smiling and he was puffing violently at his pipe. Silently he dug into his pockets and produced a handful of bone fragments; out of his shirt came a rhino tooth, and the various folds of his upper garments yielded other fossils."

Andrews was stunned and could say nothing. "Well, Roy," Walter said. "We've done it. The stuff is here."

One can understand Andrews' excitement and relief on that day in April 1922 when Walter Granger literally poured fossils out of the folds of his shirt. They had conclusively proved there were fossils in Mongolia.

The Central Asiatic Expedition led by Roy Chapman Andrews explored Central Asia and China for eight years, from 1922 to 1930, spending most of the hot summers in Mongolia and the cold winters in China. The area they explored was huge: some 2,000 miles long by 1,000 miles wide. Camp life was hard and often dangerous. They were beset by violent windstorms and shot at by bandits; camels died by the dozen; their cars broke down. When it wasn't burning hot (they once recorded a temperature of 140 degrees F) it was freezing cold and snowing. But they had struck it rich. They made the first fossil discovery at what turned out to be one of the richest localities anywhere in the world. One skull, when returned to New York for study, proved to be a new species of dinosaur, which was later named for the expedition's leader. They also discovered the first specimens of eggs known to science, laid by dinosaurs some 75 million years ago.

The public back in America went wild over the discovery of dinosaur eggs. William Randolph Hearst, the newspaper magnet, offered Andrews $250,000 outright for the exclusive story on the eggs and the expedition's many other discoveries.

In the June 1933 issue of the *National Geographic*, Andrews wrote about discovering "one of the richest and most important fossil fields in all the world" in and article called "Explorations in the Gobi Desert."

Andrews discovered not just dinosaur eggs in Mongolia that he estimated to be ninety-five million years old, but also the skulls of tiny rat-size mammals that coexisted with the dinosaurs, and, among others, the thirty-million-year-old bones and "a huge tooth, nearly as large as an apple" from "the giant Baluchitherium...the largest land mammal that ever lived upon the earth...an aberrant browsing rhinoceros that stood about 17 feet high at the shoulders and was 24 feet long, and weighed many tons."

Andrews made some very astounding conclusions that scientists have been unable to dispute. He suggested that the many kinds of small mammals that had lived during the Age of Reptiles could be the answer to why the dinosaurs have become extinct: the small mammals ate their eggs.

For his findings Roy Chapman Andrews in 1931 was presented National Geographic Society's Hubbard Medal by its president, Gilbert H. Grosvenor, who stated such discoveries "have pushed back the horizons of life upon the earth and filled in gaps in the great ancestral tree of all that breathes."

Other than for scientific journals and *National Geographic,* Andrews wrote for other publications some very powerful, true-to-life adventure stories from his experiences, stories about summer desert heat and winter cold, about tribes people and bandits, and about savage sandstorms that swept down from the Siberian steppes, sometimes blowing for days. In the days before television and wide screen coloured movies, he kept his audience enthralled with his tales of adventure and exploration. Whether Steven Spielberg admits it or not, Roy Chapman Andrews was the first Indiana Jones.

Andrews realized, of course, that the world as he knew it would eventually change. Railroads and motorcars would gradually replace ancient caravans. "The romance and glamour of the desert will be destroyed," he sadly lamented. "Tourists will sit in heated cars, eating the food of Europe, reading week-old newspapers, and comprehending not at all the glorious history, the tragedy and the romance of the Gobi trails."

And as travel writers must face, Andrews had to suffer the same fate we all do. The very thing that he feared, he himself created. Within a short decade after he made his startling discoveries on the Gobi Desert, hundreds of such motor vehicles were making the same run, bringing not only scientists, news reporters and cameramen but tourists as well to the Gobi. The ancient Mongolian way of life was changed forever.

In 1934, Andrews accepted an appointment as director of the American Museum of Natural History, a desk job which he thought would grant him more opportunities for further explorations. Instead it proved to be a disaster. Like everything else, the museum was badly hit by the Depression: salaries were cut, publications curtailed and some jobs eliminated outright. No museum funds were available for field work or expeditions. The job would have been difficult for anyone, but on top of everything else, the board of trustees did not approve of the Andrews style of running things. In 1941 he resigned.

Roy Chapman Andrews spent the rest of his life at his home in Carmel, California, writing about his adventures. In 1960, at the age of 76, he died a forgotten man. His death was not even noted in the museum's annual report. But his legacy lives on, in the rich collections at the American Museum of Natural History in New York, which have done so much to help piece together the story of life on this planet, and finally, and as equally important, in the spirit of adventure that Roy Chapman Andrews fostered and which guides us all today.

Chapter 5
TRAVELLING THEIR WAY TO THE GUINNESS WORLD RECORD BOOK

A valuable reference for any travel writer is The Guinness Book of World Records. *I wrote this article to prove my point. It appeared on August 14, 1989.*

Some people travel for the fun of it, but there are others, according to The *Guinness Book of World Records*, who travel solely to make a name for themselves.

Parke G. Thompson of the United States is one of these people. He travelled to every country, possession, territory and island in the world, including both poles. He made 36 trips over 31 years to fulfil his goal. His reason for travelling is obvious—to set a world record.

But there are some who travel for one reason or another and make the record book without trying, like Francis Asbury, a Methodist preacher who travelled 264,000 miles around America on horseback to preach. He did it before there ever was a *Guinness Book of World Records*.

The Guinness Book, in fact, is not that old, having been first published in 1954. But 20 years later it did earn its own place in world records when it became the top-selling copyright book in publishing history. Today the total is 292 editions in 35 languages, including Thai. By the fall of last year the total global sales had risen to more than 60 million copies.

Much of the information in *Guinness* is trivial, like who has the longest fingernails or who can eat the most soft-boiled eggs in 30 seconds. My teenage son Paul, to whom I gave a *Guinness Book* for Christmas last year, is forever asking me such meaningless questions, such as, "Do you know who is the tallest man in the world, Dad?" Then he gets into things like "the strongest man," "the largest biceps," "the most push-ups?" And how can I be annoyed when he asks, "Are you stronger than him, Dad?"

But his questions are not always trivial. Sometimes he comes up with a question that causes me to go thumbing through the book when he puts it aside, without him knowing it, of course. And when I do, I'm stuck for the next hour or two. What's the biggest airline in the world? The fastest train? What city has the most taxis? Where's the best place to shop? When's the last time someone drove around the world? Sailed? Flew solo?

And so I've come to have a great respect for the *Guinness Book*. The pages of my son's book are earmarked, and I have lines drawn under those sections that most interest me. These, mostly, are related to travel, by every means—rail, motorcar, air, bicycle, lawnmower, go-cart. And foot.

So what does *Guinness* have to say about travel?

Naturally, in our modern age of jet travel, airplanes are on everyone's mind. And if my son were to ask the first question, it would be "what is the largest plane ever built?"

What immediately comes to mind is the B-747. First-flown in 1969, the B-747 is the highest-capacity jetliner which can carry more than 500 passengers at a speed of 600 miles an hour. The newest of these Boeing aircraft, which rolled out in January 1988 is the 747-400, with a wing span of 213 feet and which has a range of more than 8,000 miles and carries 422 passengers.

But the 747-400s are not the largest aircraft ever built. In 1947, multimillionaire aircraft manufacturer Howard Hughes built a wooden flying boat with a wing span of 319 feet, more than a hundred feet longer than the 747-400. It was made to carry a shipload of troops across the Atlantic during World War 11, but never did. The Spruce Goose, as it was jokingly called, made it's only flight well after the war's end, when, with Hughes at the controls, it took off to a height of 70 feet for less than a mile and landed barely a minute later—yet it was an experiment that laid the way for the jet age. The Spruce Goose was moved a decade ago to a giant geodesic dome in Long Beach, California, where tourists could look at it along with the retired steamship *Queen Mary,* the world's largest ocean liner from 1936 to 1940. Now the aircraft has been dismantled and moved once again, this time to an aviation museum on Oregon State where it will be the star.

Interesting as it might be, *Guinness* also lists the B-747 as the "world's heaviest glider." It's true; it is! A B-747 that was captained by Eric Moody had four engines stop at 37,000 feet, due to volcanic ash from an eruption on Java, Indonesia, on June 24,1982. Flight BA009 had 263 crew and passengers aboard. Captain Moody and his crew restarted the engines after 13 minutes and landed the plane safely in Jakarta.

The longest recorded scheduled nonstop flight today is a Qantas flight from Los Angeles to Sydney, covering 7,487 miles in 14 hours. United Airlines runs the shortest flight, from San Francisco to Oakland, California, averaging five minutes for the 12-mile hop.

The earliest round-the-world flight was made by a Douglas amphibian in 57 hops, from April to September 1924. Nine years later in 1933, Wiley Post, a famous American aviator, made the first solo flight around the world in 10 hops.

The first nonstop flight was made in 1947 by a B-50 Super Fortress in 94 hours. It refuelled four times in flight.

Boeing also holds for the fastest commercial flight around the world. In January 1988, the Boeing 747 Friendship One, with 141 passengers aboard, made it in 36 hours and 54 minutes. It refuelled twice, in Athens and Taipei.

But what's the fastest speed man has ever travelled? *Guinness* has the answer. The fastest speed at which humans have travelled is 24,791 m.p.h., and that was when the Command Module of *Apollo* X carrying Colonel Thomas Patten Stafford, USAF, and his two–man crew reached their maximum speed on their trans-earth return flight at an altitude of 40,000 ft. on May 26, 1969.

With all the air traffic we find in the world, what is the busiest airport? That position is held by Chicago's O'Hare International Airport, with a total of 795,026 flight movements and almost 55 million passengers in 1986. This represents a landing or takeoff every 40 seconds around the clock. Heathrow outside of London handles more international traffic than any other airport in the world.

Finally, what's the largest airline company in the world? Until the recent Soviet break-up, the USSR State Airline Aeroflot operated 1,650 aircraft over 650,000 miles of routes. The records show that in 1987, Aeroflot employed over 500,000 people and carried 119 million passengers. Maybe the new *Guinness Book* will come up with the latest Soviet figures.

When it comes to train travel we often think that the Bullet Train in Japan is the fastest train it the world. It's not. The fastest national rail system is not in Japan but in France. The French high-speed train TGV-PSE reached a speed of 236 m.p.h. in 1961. Today it runs from Paris to Lyon, a run of 264 miles, in two hours and 14 minutes, averaging 132 m.p.h..

Japan, however, does have the most crowded railways. The Japanese National Railways, which carry more than 19 million passengers daily, employ professional pushers, ex-Sumo wrestlers, before the doors can be closed.

The largest railway station in the world is the Grand Central Terminal in New York City. It covers an area of 42 acres on two levels, with 41 tracks on the upper level and 26 on the lower. Some 550 trains depart every day.

According to *Guinness,* the US has more rail lines than any other country in the world, 184,235 miles, but the longest line is the Trans-Siberian Line between Moscow and Nahodka in Siberia. It makes 97 stops and the journey takes a little more than eight days. It might sound like an exciting journey but on the contrary, it's quite boring. There is little to see, as conductors come through the train and pull the blinds down when the train arrives in restricted towns in Siberia.

The longest straight rail line in the world crosses the Nullarbor Plain in southern Australia. It runs in one section for 793 miles without a single curve. Having travelled both lines, I prefer the Nullarbor Plain journey. It's a reminder of the old American West.

If you are interested in train travel, here's a record to try to beat. One traveller who purchased a 30-day rail pass for US$299, travelled on Amtrak in the U.S. through 442 out of 498 stations, covering some 21,485 miles of unduplicated miles of track out of the 23,000 miles of tracks used by Amtrak.

One motor drive that I always enjoy making is across the United States. With the new super Interstate Highways as they are, you can leave San Francisco and arrive in New York without having to stop for a traffic light. If you could do it without refuelling, you could drive it nonstop.

But don't even consider making a drive across America in an attempt to make it to the *Guinness Book.* Every imaginable attempt to set a record has been made at some time or another, and by every means. Ben Garcia, for example, drove a lawnmower, a distance of 2,801 miles, from the state of Maine on the East Coast to Los Angeles. It took him 2 $\frac{1}{2}$ months.

If that doesn't sound a bit ridiculous, then consider Charles Creighton's record. He drove his Model A Ford Roadrunner across America in reverse, from New York City to Los Angeles, in 1930, without stopping the engine. If that wasn't enough, he drove back again in reverse to New York City. Both directions took him 42 days, and he clocked 7,180 miles. That was before superhighways.

Unfortunately, gone are the days when driving around the world is possible. In 1951, Australian Ben Carlin did it in an amphibious jeep. He completed his circumnavigation by covering 39,000 miles over land and 9,600 miles by sea.

The last land-driving record was made by Garry Sowerby in 1980 when he drove a Volvo 24,901 road miles across four continents and through 23 countries in 74 days, one hour and 11 minutes.

The same Garry Sowerby also drove the American north-south route, from the northern tip of Alaska to the southern tip of South America, in under 24 days, for a distance of 14,642. The only section he couldn't drive was Darien Gap between Panama and Colombia, a distance of 54 miles. A north-south route around the world, starting at North Cape in Norway to the tip of South Africa, was made in 86 days, totalling 17,500 miles.

One trip that wasn't intended to set records was made by a couple who travelled in a Volkswagen Camper 143,716 miles through 113 counties. It took them several years.

Unless we have our own transportation, when we arrive at our destination, we can either take a bus or a taxi to get around. Every city has its taxis, and they all differ. Bangkok's taxis differ from those we find in London and in New York. But what city in the world has the most taxis? *Guinness* says it's Mexico City with more than 60,000 taxis.

One of the longest taxi rides in Asia from airport to city is from Narita Airport in Japan to downtown Tokyo. The distance is 60 miles and costs in excess of US$150. But Guinness tells us that Stephen Tillyer stopped a taxi in London and set the record for the longest fare on record, through 10 countries, covering 7,533 miles. *Guinness* did not mention how much the fare cost when he returned to London.

Before the days of flight, records by sea were always sought after. Clipper ships could actually make better time on the Australia to Europe Fain run than our modern-day steamers can make. It was not uncommon to cover a thousand miles in three days. The record was 462 nautical miles in 24 hours under sail alone.

The fastest crossing of the Pacific Ocean in modern times (4,840 nautical miles) was six days, one hour and 45 minutes, by the container ship *Sea-Lane Commerce* from Yokohama, Japan, to Long Beach, California, from June 30 to July 6,1973, at a speed of 33.27 knots.

It used to be that a solo circumnavigation of the world by sail was top news. Joshua Slocum was the first man to complete the feat in 1898. It took him three years. Then Robin Knox-Johnson made history when he sailed solo, nonstop around the world in nine months. Both Slocum and Johnson wrote books about their adventures, but surprisingly, their names no not appear in *Guinness.* Another name does appear, however, in yachting annals, and he is Jon Sanders. He made not one but three solo circumnavigations in his 44-foot sailboat. The total time was 657 days.

Sergio Testa of Australia is also in the book. He sailed an 11-foot, 10-inch Bermudan sloop *Acrohc Australis* from Brisbane back to Brisbane in 500 days, from 1984 to 1987, to become the smallest boat to travel around the globe.

The earliest nonstop circumnavigation by a woman was made by Kay Cottee of Australia. She made the *Guinness Book* when she completed her trip aboard the 37-ft *First Lady* from Sydney to Sydney, via Cape Horn, in 1988.

But for all sailing records, here's one that's hard to beat. Hank Dekker, 42, sailed his 25-ft sloop, *Dark Star,* alone from San Francisco to Honolulu in August 1983. Hank Dekker is blind. He used Braille charts, a Braille compass, a talking clock, and a navigational system that reads the position aloud. A former race car driver, Dekker lost his sight in 1972.

Most travellers are interested in shopping. In fact, some people travel solely so they can shop. Where then is the best, the biggest and the best place to shop? Tokyo has some mighty large department stores, and both Hong Kong and Singapore are noted for their good shopping. But if it's the world's largest shopping centre you want to visit, then you have to travel to Alberta, Canada. The centre here is 110 acres in area and has 828 stores. But this is a record, I'm sure, that will be broken before too long.

And while still on shopping, what about the world's biggest toy store. It's Hamley's on Regent Street in London.

Airlines, ships, trains, taxis— what about cable cars? Asia has a few, although none are record setters. *Guinness Book* tells us the highest in the world is the Teleferico Merida in Venezuela that reaches the summit of Pico Espejo at 15,629 feet. The longest single span ropeway, or cable car, is the 13,500 foot span from the Coachella Valley to Mt. San Jacinto in California. The longest, the shortest, the first—let's not take the fun out of travel by trying to set records. Yet still, it is nice to know, every now and then, a few statistics about travel. *The Guinness Book of World Records* has them listed, that's for sure.

Chapter 6
IN SINGAPORE TAKE THE BKE TO THE PIE TO REACH THE EPC

Singapore is a city of laws, rules and regulations. For the visitor trying to find his way around, it can be frustrating, or hilarious, depending upon how you look at it. My interpretation of Singapore's jargon appeared in my weekly column on September 12, 1988. It's even more complicated today.

The next time you are in Singapore, pick up a copy of the *Straits Times.* You will read that the OCB is financing the HDB flats with CPF funds. Then ROV has new registration laws, and there's a warning that SAF will be holding live firing exercises at the offshore islands until midnight every night for the next month. You don't have a boat, so that's no problem.

But maybe you decide to rent a car and drive around town. Be prepared! Let's say you want to cross the Causeway and drive to Malaysia for the day. You ask directions. It's simple. Take the BKE and not the CTE to the PIE and get off at Woodland Hills. And, they will tell you, make sure your gas tank is filled up. You can't leave Singapore without a full tank of gas. They have gas tank checkers at the border.

Maybe you want to drive to Changi International Airport. The best bet, you'll hear, is to take the same BKE to the PIE and follow it until it intersects with the EPC and there you get off at the Changi exit. If you find that confusing, take the "green line" on the MRT. But it doesn't go all the way.

Singaporeans love to use initials, which may be well and good if you know what they are talking about, but if you are a newcomer to the island republic, it can be a bit baffling, especially if you are driving an automobile.

Other than following the signs BKE and PIE and ECP, driving in Singapore presents another set of problems. There are laws and rules, for example, that apply in the morning but not in the afternoon, and there are little police ladies hiding in the shadows who need only to jot down your license number to get you into trouble. Even if no police are around and you jump a traffic light, look out. Hidden high speed cameras are activated when the traffic light changes, catching law breakers on film.

Then there is the RZ and SLS. Don't forget them.

Between the hours of 7:30 am and 10:15 am, the CBD becomes the infamous RZ. An explanation is due. The CBD is the Central Business District, or the downtown area, while the RZ is the Restricted Zone, and the SLS is the Signal Light System.

What it means is that motorists cannot enter the RZ unless they purchase a monthly pass (for S$100) or else buy a disk for S$5 for a one-time entry and place it in the corner of the car windscreen. This enables them to drive into the RZ. Another way to gain entry is have four or more occupants in the vehicle.

What happens if you don't qualify and enter the RZ gates? Posted at each entry point are two to four meter maids. If they don't see the disk or four passengers, your license number is jotted down and the ROV adds a fine to your car rental bill.

If you live in Singapore and own a van or a pick-up truck, and you speed over 55 kph, you don't stand a chance. An amber light installed on top of the cab roof flashes when the driver exceeds the limit. Violators can expect a summons in their mailbox.

Maybe you don't want to drive and will settle for a taxis. If you think it's easier, don't kid yourself. You have to have a book of regulations to figure out the taxi rates. How's this for rules:

Two people pay normal fare; for three there is and extra charge. Luggage is extra. Coming from the airport there's a surcharge. If you catch a taxi outside the CBD, the driver must purchase a sticker to enter the RZ. The passenger pays. But if your are already in the RZ during the afternoon traffic rush and want to drive out of the zone, there's another change.

That's not all. If you try to catch a taxi before midnight, forget it. Twenty minutes before the hour they all seem to have stopped running. At the stroke of midnight they suddenly emerge from parking lots and side streets like ants after honey. At that bewitching hour taxis can add 50% to your normal fare.

And Singapore is the only place is the world where taxi rates increase rather than decrease the farther you travel. Instead of becoming cheaper it becomes more costly. It would be a savings to get out of a taxi and catch another one if you were driving from one side of the island to the other. And I've been told, if it's raining, you can be charged an additional fee.

If driving is too much, take the bus. Signs are posted at all bus stops. You can catch the SBS, the CBD 1, the CBD 2, Scheme B or the City Shuttle. Have the exact change when you climb aboard. Little machines take your money.

If it's just a matter of getting somewhere, and you don't care about a scenic view, then take the MRT, the underground railway, Singapore's latest Mass Rapid Transit System.

Singapore is a mass of rules and regulations but once you master the system it's a great place to live and visit. We must admit, it's the cleanest, greenest, neatest city in Asia.

For the record, PIE means Pan Island Express; MRT, Mass Rapid Transit; EPC, East Coast Parkway; BKE, Bukit Timah Expressway; SAF, Singapore Armed Forces; HDB, Housing Development Board; CPF, Central Providence Fund; OCB, Overseas Chinese Bank; and the ROV, it has something to do with automobiles. And I almost forgot. CTE, means the Central Expressway.

A photograph that Stephens sent home in 1947 showing him and a Chinese friend standing on the steps of the Temple of Heaven in Beijing.

Chapter 7
WHEN BEIJING WAS PEKING

In 1975, Editor Tony Waltham was interested in my tales about China. I wrote three articles about my experiences while serving there as a young U.S. Marine after World War II. When China reopened her doors I rewrote one of the articles and it appeared on July 14, 1985. A few years later I returned to China for the first time, something I thought I would never do. The China I write about here is not the same China we find today. And Peking is Beijing.

Whenever travellers return from China and begin talking about Beijing, my mind immediately races back to when I first saw that grand city. It was after World War II and I was a young, 17 year–old U.S. Marine sent to China to repatriate the Japanese forces.

I first arrived in Tsingtao, a port on southern coast of the Shantung Peninsula, and after a few months I was selected to attend the Chinese language school at Peking University. It's all so strange. That was more than 30 years ago, but it's a part of my life that is still very much alive. It is as though it happened not yesterday but only a few hours ago.

It was late fall when I left Tsingtao and arrived in Tiensin. I have never been to St. Louis, Missouri, but Tiensin fitted my impression of that middle American industrial town.

I certainly did not expect to find such a place on the Chinese Mainland: a modern pulsating city with highrises and glass front shops along busy thoroughfares. The port of Tiensin served as the main rail link between Peking and the sea. It wasn't my idea of China, and after a week I was glad to once again be en route to Peking.

The train was one of those ancient conveyances that must have served the marines before me during the Boxer Rebellion. A coal-burning engine buffed and puffed and sent out belches of steam and messy black soot. It left Tiensin and reached out for the outer edges of the great Gobi Desert.

The express, which really wasn't an express, carried both freight and passengers. Armed marines and Chinese guards stood watch in all the compartments.

The land was arid and dust-swept. Everything was brown and colourless. Farm lands were flat with the houses low and surrounded by mud walls. Much of the landscape was dominated by burial mounds of hard earth. The mounds seemed to be endless.

After the second day monotony set in, and being young and impatient, I was bored. I found it much more interesting to climb up the ladder between the coaches and sit on the roof with my legs hanging down. Since we moved slowly, there was not too much wind.

For hours every day, sitting on the roof I studied the unattainable horizon. The tracks before us unrolled like a black ribbon upon an endless waste, and behind us we left a finger of smoke that lingered motionless in the lacquered sky. And I became dust-covered—my eyelashes, my hair, my clothing.

Then I saw it.

First I saw the dust, a sky of dust, and then the outer walls. It was Peking. The great city loomed up like a picture in a child's storybook. Peking, the mighty and ancient capital of Cathay.

It seemed like hours to close the distance, and there was something so strange to it all. There appeared to be nothing else except a city surrounded by a wall. There was no hint of what might be beyond that wall. It was a bit frightening.

The track led into an arched opening, with barely enough room for the train to slip through, and certainly not enough for me sitting on top of the compartment. I leaped down on the platform between the coaches, but the conductor had locked the door. I came out of the tunnel coughing and covered with black soot.

But I soon forgot my discomfort. A new and fascinating world flashed before me, strange and unbelieving. Everything caught my attention. I wanted to stop the train then and there, as though once we passed, it might all have gone forever.

As we edged deeper into the city, I could catch the sounds and even the smells. Rickshaw drivers shouted warnings as they padded along, vendors clicked wooden blocks to gain attention, wood-burning lorries tooted their horns and there was the general clamour of an excited city.

Unexpected was the sudden opulence seen everywhere. Shops were bulging with wares; foodstuffs hung in the streets, meats and delicacies were displayed in glassless windows. Restaurants flew lively banners. Pedlars pushed heavy carts laden with vegetables and produce.

And there was the dress: men in long black robes, women in high necked silk gowns, and some with bound feet, moving in short choppy steps. School children in national uniforms carried their books in bags hung over their shoulders.

I remember that moment so well, my arrival by train at Peking. Now when I hear someone say they are going to China, I know it cannot be the same. I have read with great sadness that much of what I had seen after the war has changed.

Peking when I arrived had an estimated population of one and a half million, all living within the walls of the city. Today, there are over four million, and they have burst through the walls and spread out into every direction. Gates have been widened and sections of the 4,000–year–old wall torn down.

Even the name has been changed, again. In the twelfth century the city was called Chungtu. Genghis Khan and his mounted horde of 100,000 men captured the place, but it wasn't until years later that his grandson, Kublai Khan, rebuilt her and changed the name to Cambulac—The Great Capital. The emperors during the Ming Dynasty called her Peiping, which means "Northern Peace" in Mandarin.

For some reason in 1420 she became Peking or "Northern Capital." The name stuck until 1928 when General Chiang Kai-shek moved his capital to Nanking and the city reverted to its former name, Peiping. In October 1949, the Chinese People's Republic changed it again to Peking. And now it has become Beijing.

At the train station I was met by a staff member of the language school I was to attend and taken, via rickshaw, to my new home, called Hostel Number Three, in the very centre of the city. It was a grand old stone building with high ceiling hallways and rooms, with no plumbing. Wash basins and pitches of water. The communal W.C. down the hall. Meals were served at a given time only, and the food was awful, although they tried hard to reach Western standards. After a short time I was taking my meals in the local shops and stalls.

I guess Peking was the first time in my life that I was really alone. And when winter came the cold was almost unbearable. I dreaded the thought of returning to my room, where the only warmth came from heated bricks brought into the room by servants. I did all my studying in bed under the blankets.

Each morning I was awakened by a room boy with a bowl of hot water and lemon, and warm bricks to stand upon while I shaved and washed. A week had passed before I realised the hot water and lemon was to drink and not for shaving.

In spite of the loneliness, there was something exciting about becoming a student in a strange land. I exchanged my uniform for Chinese clothing, including wraparound trousers, and I was given a slate to write upon. I was now a bona fide student in Peking.

It was a bit terrifying at first. I was besieged by questions from fellow students. "In the West, why do you do everything backwards?" they asked.

"Backwards. Like what?"

"You read a book from the wrong end first."

Others would ask, "How can you tell one foreigner from another? You all look alike."

Oftentimes such questions left me empty inside. Were they, perhaps, not right? When I went back to my room at night, I would stand in front of the mirror and slant my eyes, and wonder why I had to look so different from everyone else.

At the language school there were requirements to which we had to adhere. Two or three evenings a week we had to attend local functions. Maybe attend a Chinese film, visit a "sing-song" cabaret or see an opera .... a Chinese opera, of course.

The Chinese films of those days were nothing like the ones showing in cinemas around Asia today. They produced some dandies 30 years ago. The players overacted and over-dramatised. Staging was totally without imagination. Scenes of a couple talking, for example, might be shot in an open field, with trees and hills for a background. Then came a close-up, shot in a studio, with white bed sheet for background. They didn't bother even to take the creases out of the sheets.

Sing-song cabaret was enjoyable for the first 10 minutes. The singers were always women accompanied by classical Chinese music, which was mainly one–string violins and gongs. The female vocalists were highly skilled. The audience, always well dressed, sat around tiny tables, drank pots of tea and ate sunflower seeds. After months I was still unable to understand a single word they sang, but I did develop a liking for tea and a dislike for sunflower seeds.

As part of my education in Peking, I was sent to live for the summer with a Chinese family in their summer home. The household was dominated by an elderly Chinese lady, Mrs. Djung. She was very wealthy and well educated.

Mrs. Djung was quite excited when it was confirmed that a foreign student was coming to live in her house. She held a feast the day I arrived. At the table, with the guests around, she said, "There is so much that I want to discuss with you." I thanked her, and said I would help in any way I could.

"How nice," she said. "Then maybe you can tell me. We have read so much about Western culture, and now we have a foreign student among us to explain it." I smiled. I liked Mrs. Djung.

She continued. "Tell me, do you think the philosophy of Kierkegaard had much influence on Christianity or led to the philosophical existentialism movement?"

"Huh?"

"Kierkegaard," she repeated. "You know, Jean-Paul Satre."

"Huh?"

Our conversations after that centred upon more basic topics. Years later, when I was actually studying philosophy at Georgetown University in Washington, D.C., I wished I could have talked to Mrs. Djung. But it was too late by then.

Life in Peking wasn't all studies, however. There was a marine garrison there, and any time I wanted some of my old Tsingtao excitement, I knew where to go.

Like in Tsingtao, there were the bars with swinging doors and the taxi dance halls that catered to the military. And there were the red light districts. One house was run by a mammoth Negro woman whom everyone called "Momma Georgia." And indeed, she had to be from Georgia. With her accent she could be from nowhere else.

She took a great delight in telling how she came to Peking many many years before. A southern colonel brought her, she said. He was assigned to the American legation and she came as governess to his children.

When the colonel's wife discovered her servant's duties appeared to have somewhat broader horizons than merely caring for the children, she up and left her husband, taking the children back home to the United States. The servant had little option but to fend for herself. "Momma Georgia's place" was born.

Peking was an exciting place to live after the war, if you liked living behind a wall or two. There was the massive, 12 metre-thick outer wall that I mentioned. But that was only the first wall. There was a second wall which enclosed the Tartar City, and within that a third wall around the Imperial City. And in the very centre of all these walls was another walled city. The most grand one of them all—the Forbidden City.

There were still other walls, like the Whispering Wall of China. It is a true masterpiece of masonry. You can stand with your ear to the wall and talk to a friend a half mile away. Another place I liked to visit was the Temple of Heaven. On the alter in a vast marble courtyard you could stand in one spot and hear your own echo while no one else could.

The language school was but a very small part of my education in Peking. There was so much to see and do, and things that I didn't understand. But the answers I found in reading and talks with my elders. Each day I grew a little more.

That first winter within the walls of Peking, I learned my way about the city along Hataman Boulevard (now called Chungwenmen) and gradually spread out into the maze of alleys called hutongs. They were great to explore. It was bitter cold that winter, and when the biting winds swept down from the Gobi they brought dust, which made day as dark as twilight. But even in a dust storm it was difficult to lose your way. There was always a wall to recognise and follow.

When spring came the Chinese took to the countryside, on hikes and long bicycle trips. Everyone hiked in those days. There was always much to see. During the week Mrs. Djung would fire up my imagination with stories about certain places and we would read the history books and on weekends set out on foot or by bicycle.

A short distance from the city there was another wall we visited, the walled Imperial Summer Palace. Within the palace was a lake, and upon the still waters was a magnificent boat. The boat in the Summer palace was constructed of solid marble. Naturally, it didn't float. The story is that when the Empress of China in 1911 was hounded by her advisers to build a powerful navy, she obliged them. She sank, literally, the entire treasury's purse into a marble boat.

A few hours farther on by motor car from the Summer Palace was the greatest discovery of all—the Great Wall of China. It has to be the greatest man-made structure of all times, ancient and modern. While places like Angkor Wat may astound one by its beauty, the Great Wall is a masterpiece of man's incredible determination to survive.

It was built in the Third Century B.C. when Rome was only a trading post. It varies from 4.5-metre to l5-metre high and in places is 7.6-metre wide. If it were relocated to America, it would stretch from New York to the Mississippi, or in Europe from Moscow to Paris.

I returned to the wall many times, once by jeep and followed it for nearly a hundred miles, on what was one of my first expeditions. My dream then, after my discharge, was to follow it from end to end. I have never really given up that dream.

I didn't finish out my complete year at the language school, for I was called back to duty. It wasn't a sudden thing. Little by little I was given more assignments as translator: a sudden trip to Port Arthur in Manchuria; to assist a Marine detachment in locating several planes which had lost their way and crashed near Wei

Hai Wei on the Shantung Peninsula; and to see what had happened to a convoy that never returned from a sightseeing trip to the Great Wall. Soon I was spending more time out of school than in it.

Slowly the military began to withdraw from Peking, and now speculations ran wild. Would China fall? My experiences in China have convinced me that the world governments should pay more attention to the advice of historians rather than to politicians. History does repeat itself. Events that were happening to China were to repeat themselves years later in Vietnam. The pattern was the same.

The dark shadow of gloom gradually began to spread across Peking. There were some table discussions at Mrs. Djung's that usually turned to other topics when I entered the room, and the Chinese who had once been my friends were now looking upon me with other eyes. It was only a matter of time. Peking's days were numbered, for me, and many others, foreigners and locals alike.

Finally my orders came to return to Tsingtao. I had to give up wearing my Chinese clothes and turn in my slate. And I had to leave a life that was very dear to me. With the People's Army ready to sweep down across the Gobi, I boarded a C-47 and flew back to Tsingtao.

Robin Dannhorn surrounded by monks at a lone monastery in Bhutan.

Chapter 8
SEVEN DAYS IN BHUTAN

Writing for the Bangkok Post *opened many doors for me, as this article on Bhutan will show. It appeared on May 9,1988.*

The pilot of the 16-seat Dornier 228 that flies from Calcutta to Bhutan has to search the high Himalayan valleys for an opening in the clouds to land at Paro, the only airfield in Bhutan. Sometimes, if he can't find an opening, he has to return to Calcutta.

Our pilot, Captain Blaggana, a retired Indian air force wing commander with 24 years' flying experience in the Himalayas, dips the starboard wing to the right and then to the left, searching for that opening. He can't seem to find it.

Everyone is tense. At a last attempt, he climbs to 16,000 feet, where the air is thin, and there, below, appears a break in the clouds and a valley beneath it. We drop through the skies and land at Paro.

A minibus, brand new, with driver and guide awaits us at the terminal. It's a two-hour drive from the landing field at Paro to Thimpu, the capital of Bhutan. We are still mystified by the whole experience. We can't believe we are in Bhutan, the most remote kingdom in the world.

We are a party of six who have come to explore the possibility of tourism for this fragile destination. Niels Lumholdt from the head office at Thai International, Khun Vivat, Thai International's area manager for India and Nepal, Tom Hackett from THAI in Seattle, hotelier Alex Goerlach, writer Robin Dannhorn and myself. We have no idea what to expect, and no idea what we will report.

Everything is new, and strange. An isolated mountain kingdom that has been independent for all its recorded history, more than two thousand years. And only a little more than 10 years ago, in 1974, did the monarchy open its doors to the outside world. Less than a hundred tourists arrived that year. Last year the number stood at about 2,000. Bangkok's Don Muang International Airport sees that many visitors within a few hours.

As we step from the plane at Paro we look around. A vast emptiness. High surrounding mountains that seal us in; a monastery with white walls perched on a cliff; we can almost feel the stillness. We wonder, when James Hilton wrote *Lost Horizon* and called the dream Shangri-La, did he have Bhutan in mind? It did, indeed, appear that way to us.

And where else but Bhutan? There isn't a television set in all the country. Newspapers—there's a weekly, but it can't be found readily outside the capital. Radio broadcast are limited to a few hours daily. There's no crime, no beggars, no prostitution, no suicides, and no threat of bombs, hijackings or terrorism. In fact, you don't even see policemen, except traffic cops in Thimpu. Nor are there juke boxes, pool halls or neon lights. There are but 2,000 kilometres of roads and less than 5,000 vehicles. The country's biggest expenditure is maintaining the roads.

Bhutan is a country that functions without the rest of the world. It's self-supporting, we were told.

Two things stood out most, aside from the mountainous, curving road, as we set out on our drive from Paro to Thimpu—the local dress and the architecture.

Everyone, even the mechanics who worked on refuelling the plane, wears the national dress. The men's costumes, called *khos,* are full-sleeved, long robes which come down to the knees and are tied with a belt. They don't wear trousers, only high stockings—Scottish plaid when they want to be stylish—and shoes. Women wear *kiras*, full–length dresses, tied with a belt at the waist and held up by a pair of brooches at the shoulder. We learned later it's possible to tell from which area of the country they come by the design of their skirts.

The national dress is appealing, for foreign eyes. You don't see local people in shabby, unsightly Western garments that have turned to rags. Even farmers in the field look neat.

The architecture is unlike any we have seen before. Houses are large, square buildings, made of tamped mud, stone, wood and clay. The outer walls are white-washed with raised roofs above the main structure. The roofs are shingled and are held in place by large stones evenly spaced apart. Our guide Loti tells us the stones prevent the shingles from being carried off by the strong winds which sometimes sweep through the valleys.

We stop to watch villagers build a house, a community effort. Women standing upon the high walls tamp the wet earth held in place in wooden forms, while the men carry baskets of mud up makeshift ladders. They chant as they work.

A valley widens and Thimpu appears ahead. It reminds me of Cameron Highlands in Malaysia, a one-street town, built on the slope of a hill (there is little flat land in Bhutan), except this place has much more drama than Cameron. Cameron doesn't have a royal palace built in the style of a vast monastery, where a young king and his family reside.

I am struck by the shops. They are open in front, and customers stand on the sidewalks outside to do their shopping. They turn to watch us pass.

Our minibus doesn't stop. It has a rendezvous elsewhere and whips us through town to the Motithan Hotel, which overlooks Thimpu.

The hotel, like the town, comes as a surprise. It sprawls, with wings and corridors and spacious bedrooms. Everything is neat and clean. The style of decor, characteristically Bhutanese, includes splashes of colour with hand-painted ceilings, eaves and beams all decorated with minuscule designs. There is an abundance of hanging banners and drapes of all sorts, fashioned from brightly coloured cloth. Framed black-and-white photographs from a past era hang on the walls.

Dinner is curry, Indian style, and it's early to bed. It's cold, and the blankets are thick and welcoming. Breakfast is scrambled eggs, and pots of coffee and tea.

We don't have time to linger: the bus is loaded and ready. But before we depart, the tourist office has sent a troupe of Bhutanese dancers to entertain us on the lawn of the Motithan. They perform their famous mask dance. Then we are off, without further delay. We have miles to go, across the backbone of Bhutan to the northeast. The names of places are complicated and elude me. They take on meaning later.

Loti, who speaks English with a commanding voice, tells us we are heading to places like Punakha, Tongsa and Bumthang. We will camp the first night by a river and stay in inns and lodges other nights. He has brought two casting rods for fly fishing.

The road is one curve after another, and at times it's treacherous, with sheer drops of hundreds of feet into deep canyons below. Or could it be thousands! It appears that way when we look out the window, especially when another vehicle approaches and our driver has to give way, for the road is only one-way without guard rails. We find it best not to look.

An army of Indian labourers work endlessly to keep the potholes filled and the landslides cleared. They do a remarkable job.

We cross a high pass, where great Mongol hordes once marched through this east-west passage on the first silk route. Now the pass is marked with hundreds of tall poles with white prayer flags fluttering in the breeze. These flags, seen on many distant hills, give the countryside an eerie animation.

Sheep, cows and even yaks feed along the roads. Their herders make no effort to shoo them away. At times we drive through the clouds. Villages are scattered, where old folk gaze and kids wave as we pass. The mountain sides are gardens of flowers; some trees in blossom look like exploding fireworks. Magnolias and rhododendrons predominate.

We arrive at the outskirts of Punakha to find a tent city has been set up, and that night, with a campfire to keeps us warm, we dine, among other things, on fresh trout Khun Vivat and Tom Hackett have caught in the river. Then, silently, out of the dark appear a dozen villagers, women and young girls. They have come to sing and entertain us. In gratitude, Khun Vivat leads our group in a *ramwong*. We are more amused with ourselves than the villagers are.

The next morning we drive into Punakha, the old capital, and visit the monastery, and that afternoon we reach Tongsa. The Tongsa monastery, dating back to 1543, is impressive, built on the bank of the Mangde River. The monasteries, or dzong as they are called, are closed to visitors, but we have permission to see the one at Tongsa. Here, cloistered behind thick walls, 700 monks live out their lives. Unlike in Thailand, Bhutanese monks are in the monkhood for life. Their robes are thick dark-red hand-woven cloth. They do not shave their heads, but their hair is clipped short, unparted and ruffled, like all the men's styles in Bhutan. The monks are as baffled by us as we are by them. They offer us salted yak butter tea. It's inhospitable to refuse them.

The monastery is as impressive inside as it is from the outside. We can feel its great age as we walk across stone courtyards and step upon wide plank floors. Trankar-like paintings, some quite ancient, adorn the inner walls. There are embroidered drapes hanging from lofty ceilings, altars with heavy silver trays and bowls flanked by ivory tusks cracked and yellowed with age. Pillars are square timbers painted red. Huge wooden doors swing not on hinges but on pins. Chambers are dark and ladders that connect the levels are steep and menacing to climb. Everywhere are large brass bells and gongs. In small hidden side rooms, monks chant, doing their pujas, and in the stone courtyards blackbirds and crows disrupt the silence with the heavy flapping of their wings and their mocking cries.

We spend the night in an inn overlooking the valley.

The road to Bumthang is even more thrilling and nerve shattering. After we pass a narrow section, the road collapses into the canyon. We know we have to return the way we came, and that night we sit around a log fire at the bar in our inn. We try to decide what drinks to have from the bottles behind the bar, all locally made—Pure Malt Whiskey, Bhutan Mist, Magpie Apple Brandy Khambu Spirits, Dragon XXX Rhum; Jachung Brandy. We try the rhum, and soon forget about the road.

The next day, as we return, we find an Indian work force has the road patched. But still we decide to walk and let the bus follow. It isn't so bad!

Eventually, after a week and a dozen monasteries (in one of which Robin and I got lost and couldn't find our way out), and an estimated 12,000 curves, we arrive back in Thimpu.

The town that first appeared so comically small now looms as big as Paris does to the farm boy seeing it for the first time. It's a welcoming sight.

This time we check into the Druk Hotel in the down town area. In two days, while our THAI delegation is in discussions with government officials, Robin and I visit the market, watch the Bhutanese at their national sport of archery, shop in all the shops, have coffee and pastry at the Swiss Bakery and meet the managing director of the Bhutan Tourism Corporation. And we are invited to dinner at the home of Lennie Dorji, uncle of the king and ex-prime minister.

We sit in his elaborately decorated house, with skins and tusks on the walls and elephant feet with red satin covers for stools to sit upon. Our host tells us about hunting wild boar and leopards and mountain thar and game we never heard of before. And he has fishing stories to tell, about trout bigger than New Zealand trout, giant carp, and mashseer which grow up to five feet in length. Then he laughed. "In the rivers in the lowlands you might snag a crocodile."

That night back in my hotel room I check my reference book on Bhutan for the facts. Lennie Dorji is right. There are crocodiles, and Bhutan is the home of the snow leopard, tiger, elephant, sambar, barking and swamp deer, rhino, wild boar, wild buffalo, gaur, thar and Himalayan bear. The index of birds in Bhutan goes on for pages. And there are cobra and mountain pit vipers, banded adders and coral snakes.

The next morning we hear that bears were spotted behind the Motithan Hotel on the hill where we stayed the first night.

After our visit to Lennie Dorji's we soon realise that parts of this grand world in which we live have not changed. There is still a Bhutan.

Back in Paro we wait for our flight. We hear an airplane engine above the clouds but it fades. Captain Blaggana has gone back. He couldn't find an opening. He may return in a few hours, then we can leave. Or maybe tomorrow, or the day after.

Loti tells us about a cliff-side monastery, the one seen in all the photos, a few hours up the Paro Valley. We go by horseback, Mongolian pony actually, to Taktsang, meaning Tiger's Nest. It is built around a cave and clings dizzily to a sheer precipice. We are tempted to take the daredevil challenge to reach the monastery but the skies clear and to the north Mount Chomolhari with its snow-covered peaks tells us it's time to leave.

We are right. Back in Paro the weather is clear; we hear the plane before we can see it. It lands and we bid our goodbyes. We roar down the runway, swerve to the left to miss a mountain ridge and turn south.

It's been quick, a short seven days, and as we look below we watch the sharp peaks of Bhutan turn into rolling hills and then into the flat plains of India. We look back and the snowcapped peaks of Bhutan vanish into the horizon. We wonder if it happened at all. Had we really discovered James Hilton's Shangri-La? Will we, too, turn old and wither away?

For many, Bhutan is just that, Shangri-La.

The scenery is overpowering not only the towering lofty mountain ranges but the wide valleys that open up like a cinerama screen as you cross over a pass. Each valley differs from the other.

The Bhutanese are a magnificent, proud and extremely friendly people. I had not seen one hostile person all the while I was there.

The monasteries, of course, are a main attraction. However, many are closed for fear visitors many disturb the monks. Special permission is needed to enter some. To visit one is truly an unforgettable experience.

There's good shopping for local crafts, and for the adventurer, the choices are river rafting, camping and canoeing, trout fishing and trekking to the borders of Tibet.

But perhaps, above everything else, the real appeal of Bhutan is that here is a land seen by so few outsiders. It is still, mainly, a closed land, access to it limited to only a few.

The government is considering, cautiously, raising the tourist quota from 2,000 to 10,000 a year. They want to keep tourists in groups that they can manage. No lone travellers.

The government is, with reason, deeply concerned about tourism. They are worried that it might bring the ills of Western civilisation with it. They want selected tourists under a carefully regulated programme. To preserve their lifestyle, they insist upon no tipping, and there are signs everywhere warning about the hazards of smoking, a Western influence. To preserve their tranquillity, other signs remind motorists not to blow their horns.

In preparation for tourist development, the tourist office is expanding operations. They have purchased new minibuses and cars, and have 20 English-speaking guides. They offer brochures and guidebooks to visitors. They have inns and cottages in most large towns, and they have marked a dozen trekking trails for excursions that last from three to 20 days.

Bhutan is not a large country, less that 47,000 sq. km. with fewer than 1.3 million inhabitants. The government is a constitutional monarchy and the religion is Mahayana Buddhism. With weather conditions the way they are, tourist travel is restricted to certain months. The peak periods are March, April and May and October and November. During the other months it's either wet or the country is snowbound.

Visitors with proper permits can enter overland from India or fly in from Calcutta on Druk Air. Both are exciting ways to reach Bhutan, an exciting country.

Harry's New York Bar in Paris, almost an institution, has been around since 1911. In Asia bars come and go overnight.

Chapter 9
GETTING INTO THE SPIRIT(S) OF TRAVEL

Part of the fun of travelling, as this article explains, can be sampling the spirits of the countries we visit. But it can have its downfalls if we are not careful. The articles appeared on February 12, 1990.

Ever had a cold Hinano while sitting at Vaima's Cafe in Papeete? Or a half-pint-size bottle of warm sake in one of those cubicle restaurants in Tokyo; what about a frosty tube of Tooheys in a pub in Alice Springs; or a bottle of Tanduay rum with coke chasers in a dingy bar in Zamboanga; maybe a margarita in Hussong's in Enseñada, Mexico; perhaps an Irish coffee in the Buena Vista in San Francisco; or a glass of Dry Sack sherry with a *tapa* in the Echegaray in old Madrid; could it be a cold Singha with your hot curry lunch at Lord Jim's in Bangkok's Oriental Hotel; by chance a *tuak* in a dirty glass in a longhouse up the Rejang in Sarawak?

These are the times worth remembering!

Bring a place to mind that you have visited, and what do you associate it with? Smells? Sounds? Colour? Or is it tastes? Whatever, it's part of our stream of conscious thought. Places bring specific thoughts to mind.

With me it's booze. I don't mean that alcohol is the first thought that comes to mind when I think of Madrid or Tahiti or Zamboanga, but when I dwell upon these places long enough, the drink I had there brings back a flood of memories. They may not all be good thoughts but nevertheless they are memories worth keeping.

Unless one is a confirmed teetotaller, or abstains from alcoholic beverages for health or religious reasons, one of the pleasures of travelling is sampling the refreshments, both alcoholic and nonalcoholic, of each place visited.

For example, I can hardly think of Spain without thinking of *tapas* and *copas.* Or if it's Greece, it's retsina wine. Someone can mention Colombia in South America and I don't think about the drug war there. I think about *aguaradiente,* which, when translated, means "fire water." Let them talk about the old days in China and I remember taxi dancers and Huba Huba vodka at the A.B.C. Bar in Tsingtao.

Let the name Mexico come up and I can taste tequila, and when I hear Japanese spoken I can feel the smoothness of sake, that is, providing it's warm sake. With the Philippines, it's rum, and in Singapore, Hennessy VO they serve at Chinese weddings. And so it goes.

But for the record, when one travels to new and different places I don't mean he or she should attempt to compete in the drinking habits with local citizens in each country visited. One may not get very far. In some countries they swill down drinks to get drunk; others savour them for the taste. For example, unless one has had training, one could never compete with the Aussies when it comes to drinking beer. Or if it's trying to distinguish the difference between an *oloroso* and an *amontillado,* don't challenge the Spanish.

And beware when you visit China and dine with a Chinese host. The Chinese believe that if a drink is strong and tastes like medicine, it's bound to be good for you. Whether it tastes good or not, drinking plays a large part of any traditional Chinese feast. And there is a special etiquette involved in drinking. If you accept to drink a toast, you can't stop. You have to go on drinking, toast after toast, no matter how many toasts there are, until everybody at the table calls it quits.

You must decide early in the game whether you are going to be a friendly social sort, or whether you're going to remain teetotal. Either you can refuse to touch a drop, or you can run the risk of winding up under the table. There's no halfway measure.

Chinese, of course, love to give toasts, and more formal toasts go on and on, never seeming to stop. Invariably everyone at your table toasts you, and you in return have to toast everyone else. Since eight guests are usually seated at a table, that makes 14 toasts for a start. And it isn't just a sip of wine that is required for a toast.The idea is to *gambay*—meaning bottoms up. Fortunately the cups are usually small.

Then in true Chinese function, where there are many tables with eight people at each, it becomes dangerous to *gambay* with someone you know at another table. You will have to do the round of toasts at that table once you begin. And there's always the possibility that those at that table may come to yours.

If you do get caught with too many *gambays*, it is no disgrace to have to be helped from your chair to a taxi at the end of the party.

Also beware of drinking games.The Chinese love them. And they too can be devastating.

If you are a beer drinker, you really can't go wrong when you travel.They make some pretty good brews around the world. And after all, the world has had a long experience in brewing beer. Drawings on temple walls in Anatolia show the early Sumerians entertaining themselves with beer at public functions.The Germans, we are told, perfected the technique and passed it on to the rest of the world.They even brought the trade to the Far East.

Before the First World War, Germany occupied Tsingtao on the Shantung Peninsula in China.Today Tsingtao beer is the best in China.The brewers learned the trade from the Germans.

And, for certain, every country around the world seems to boast about its own product. Some countries, like Mexico, a nation of 55 million souls, produces more than 25 brands of beer—Tecate, Corona, Carta Blanca and Dos Equis, to name a few. Which is the best? Ask four people and you get four different answers.

In the far South Pacific you can travel to the smallest coral atoll and chances are they will serve up their own brand of beer. Tahiti is famous for its Hinano, and indeed, it is good beer, made from mountain water. On Samoa it will be Vailima Beer; in Vanuatu, South Pacific Beer.

Singapore and Malaysia have their Tiger and Anchor, and Indonesia does well with Bintang.

The one country that receives a great deal of criticism for its bad beer is the US. I can understand why: they *do* produce, on purpose, some weak beer there. The reason, it's what the Americans like. American beer is a great thirst killer that doesn't get you very drunk very fast. It serves its purpose.

Many countries in Southeast Asia produce an illegal "poor man's" beer called toddy. It's sold in toddy shops where only the locals go. It's easy and inexpensive to produce. The fresh toddy is extracted from the central part of the young stem of a coconut palm. It ferments within a few hours. From this fermented sap they get palm beer. When they distil it, it becomes *arrack*, a potent liquor. The village of Tenganan on Bali is famous for its *tuk bayu,* or palm beer. In the Philippines there is hardly a small town where you can't buy toddy. In South America I have had the fortune, or misfortune, of having had to drink the local beer the Cuna Indians there make.

When I first arrived in the Cuna village, I watched the women sitting around chewing the roots of the guava plant, which they spit into a large communal wooden bowl. They then put the bowl out into the sun for the rest of the afternoon and the next morning. The contents bubbled like a volcano ready to explode. What

I didn't know was that the mixture was in my honour. It was fed to me and the other men in the village in half coconut shells to drink in one gulp. There was no refusing to drink. I was their guest.

Also, if you ever go up the Rejang River in Borneo and stay in a longhouse, be careful with the *tuak* they give you to drink. An Iban girl sits on the floor in front of you and puts the glass, always a dirty one, to your lips and begins pouring down your throat. You are not permitted to touch the glass with your hands. Tears come to your eyes, and you think you have finished when she refills the glass. The next morning I thought one of the heads hanging in the rafters above was my own. (Contrary to what some people say, some of the longhouses still keep human heads.)

But drinking can be sophisticated. In Spain it is a polished tradition.

In Spain, there are two words, the most important ones in the Spanish vocabulary—*tapa* and *copa.* A *tapa* is an appetizer, a kind of hors d'oeuvre, consisting of anything from fish to meat served on a thin slice of bread or cracker. A *tapa,* the Spanish say, prepares the palate for another *copa.* And a *copa,* in the traditional sense, is a glass of wine, usually a dry sherry.

Sherry comes in three types—*fino, oloroso* and *amontillado.* A *fino* is a dryer wine, the colour of straw. *Amontillado* is a lighter wine with a bit more bouquet and it's generally but not necessarily sweeter. *Oloroso* is a heavier, stronger wine, darker in colour.

The Echegaray, a street near the Puerta del Sol in Madrid, is where drinking achieves the perfection of an art. You wander from bar to bar. In all the bars customers stand two or three deep. Platters piled high with *tapa* line the counters; sausages and meats hang above the bars. The bars are simple but colourful. Most have wooden tables, great bullfight posters on white-washed walls and roving Gypsy guitarists. And the *copa* flows freely.

If you like to run the gauntlet and go hopping from place to place, then the Napa Valley in northern California is the place for you. The wine tasting there is free.

There are more than 100 wineries in the valley, but wine experts advise that no more than three be visited in one day. They also advise that wine tasters limit themselves to just one type of wine—normally white, red or rose—during a single tour; it's impossible, so they say, to assess wines adequately if the palate must skip from one to another. All wineries have a salesroom. Sometimes they offer discontinued stock at rock-bottom prices. At any rate, few visitors go home without buying at least a couple of bottles.

Most countries in the world have their own national drink. In Thailand, of course, it's Mekong, while in Russia it's vodka, France has her cognac and Germany, schnapps.

Some countries, like Mexico may have several, and yet all peculiar to that country alone. Mescal, tequila and pulque are three national drinks of Mexico. They are all made from the sap of the maguey plant, a plant which resembles a porcupine with long, wide, slightly curved spikes. Some say it even taste like the quills of a porcupine when you drink it.

Drinking tequila has a ritual that goes with it. The traditional steps are as follows: (1) lick the back of your hand and sprinkle salt on it, (2) lick the salt, (3) suck on a lime, (4) drink down the shot of tequila in one gulp and (5) lick more salt. Then make a face and snap your head to one side.

Mescal might be hard for some to take. In the bottom of each bottle is a fat, green worm which had been placed in the bottle before it was filled. When the bottle is emptied, the last person to fill his glass is supposed to eat the worm. But often, by the time you empty a bottle, you won't remember the worm, anyway.

Tequila and pulque, along with bourbon whisky, were the main drinks they served in those early cowboy saloons in America that we hear so much about. They also had other purposes—they could be used as an astringent for gunshot wounds, as insect repellent and for lighting hard-to-light campfires.

Many a barroom brawl started over bad whisky. Shootings often occurred when prospectors and cowboys of the day were not getting real Kentucky bourbon, but were being served "rotgut" that was flavoured with everything from chili peppers to tobacco juice.

For most foreigners not used to the potency of straight tequila, it is more popular to take it mixed in a drink called a margarita. It is made by adding lime juice and orange liqueur to the tequila in a salt-rimmed glass. It has a great taste, but it can be devastating.

Even tiny Bhutan, that remote mountain kingdom in the Himalayas, distils its own whisky, and when you look at bottles with their hand-painted labels—Pure Malt Whiskey, Bhutan Mist, Magpie Apple Brandy, Khumbu Spirits, Dragon XXX Rhum; Jachung Brandy—you may have doubts about the contents.

I was uncertain about the effects of Bhutan booze until one evening in Bumthang, a small village reached by way of a treacherous, single-lane mountain road. It had been a nerve-shattering drive. Just as we passed a particularly narrow section, a part of the road collapsed and tumbled hundreds of metres into the canyon below. That evening as we sat around a log fire at the bar in our inn, we were well aware that we would have to return by the way we came, and we knew we needed a drink. We ordered a bottle of Dragon XXX Rhum, and then another. Soon forgot about the road and just about everything else. It was as lethal as any drink could be. With hangovers the next day, none of us cared if our vehicle made it back over the pass or not. Two days later, when we were back in Thimpu, the capital, we still suffered with hangovers.

The Chinese of Singapore are the world's largest consumers, per capita, of cognac. If you go there and are invited to a Chinese wedding, you'll know what I mean. The Chinese drink not for taste, but to get others drunk.

The Japanese are great drinkers, but if you are a tourist without a company credit card, forget it. It could cost you US$200 for a bottle of Scotch whisky. Nevertheless, when I am in Japan I like to drink warmed sake. It goes well with the food, especially on cold nights when you are putting up in an inn that has paper doors.

One of the best spots for drinking in Asia is the Philippines. The San Miguel beer they serve there is hard to beat. It's much different from San Miguel export. The rum is also excellent, and cheap. In the Philippines, you become a drunkard and are unaware of it.

I like vodka made from potatoes, the kind you can only find in Russia. But I am uneasy when it comes to drinking with the Russians. They can be laughing one minute and violent the next. But not all of them. In the Caucasus Mountains I spent an afternoon with peasants during a village wedding feast. I was served huge round loaves of wheat bread with cheese in the middle, cut in fat slices by husky women in babushkas. The men in high boots danced with their hands clasped behind their back holding open bottles of vodka in their teeth. When they wanted to drink, they threw back their heads. I tried, messed it up, and ended up being tossed into the air in a blanket held by a dozen men. I'd go back tomorrow if I could find the village again.

A while back I was in New York and was invited to a party at a posh apartment owned by a man who was a world traveller. He had in his living room a bar that has no equals. He had a collection of spirits from nearly every country in the world.

And what a collection. There were wines, cognacs and brandies, Bavarian beers and South Pacific beers, ales, Spanish Amaretto and French Grand Marnier, liqueurs, Russian vodkas, Greek retsina wine, and other beverages you never even heard of. The bottles were everywhere, and took up shelves and cabinets that lined most of his living room. I envied his collection.

Then one day I read about a wine dealer who paid something like two thousand dollars for a bottle of rare French wine. The big question, of course, was a matter of taste. How would the wine taste after years in a bottle? The only way to find out was to drink the wine. That got me thinking. A collection of wine, or any alcohol beverage, is only good if you drink it.

It's true. What good is it to put bottles on a shelf and never sample the contents? It's not like collecting paintings or sculptures which you can look at and admire. Nor is it like collecting recordings that you can listen to, and still keep. No, with liquor, that's something else. To enjoy it, you have to drink it. Spirits, unless it's whisky ageing in a barrel, are not intended to be kept.

And there's a lot out there to sample, so drink up. Good travelling, and above all, good drinking!

Bali's famous expatriate artists in 1951. From the left Mario Blanco, Arie Smit, two unknown tourists, Han Snel and Theo Meier.

Chapter 10
LOOKING FOR LOST ART IN BALI

One fact no one can deny, Bali is an island of art and artists. Over the years I met some interesting painters on Bali, both local and foreign. This article, which appeared on February 25, 1991, centres around the foreign painters who lived on the lovely island. They led extraordinary lives. A few are still there.

Shortly after World War I, novelist Somerset Maugham went to Tahiti looking for lost Gauguins. At the time, the French Impressionist artist was not yet well known. He had died in the islands a dozen years before Maugham arrived, and the rumour had it that he had left some 130 paintings behind.

Maugham never found any of Paul Gauguin's paintings, except for a small painted window pane in the house where the artist once lived in Punaauia on Tahiti, which he bartered for a plug of tobacco. But Maugham did return with something far more valuable. He had enough background material on the artist's life to write what would become one of his finest novels, *The Moon and Sixpence*, a work based on Gauguin's life.

The novel made Maugham rich and Gauguin famous, and when Maugham died in the late 1960s at his villa on the French Riviera, the window pane went on auction along with his other valuables. The pane fetched a fortune almost equal to the sum for the sale of the villa.

Scores of art dealers today follow in much the same way

Maugham had done; they scour the world looking for lost art. But it isn't Tahiti so much that they search as it is the island of Bali. And for good reason. Since the mid–1920s Bali has attracted some very fine foreign painters. While most of them have passed away, their works have endured and have become valuable art treasures.

The names of these painters are words in the annals of Balinese art—Walter Spies, Rudolf Bonnet, Le Mayeur, Theo Meier, Han Snel, Donal Friend, Mario Blanco, Arie Smit.

Only three of these artists are still painting on Bali today—Blanco, Snel and Smit. Of the others, little of their art, to the disappointment of the collectors, is to be found on Bali, except in the galleries. Nevertheless, collectors and buyers continue to look for their work. Occasionally a piece will show up. Only recently when in Switzerland I saw an ad by a dealer looking for early Theo Meier paintings. Paintings that he sold for $10 in Bali 40 years ago are now selling for $25 to $50,000.

The story is one we hear over and over. We see a painting of an artist who has passed away, and the price is in the thousands, and we hear people say, "Why I could have bought his paintings for a pittance." Perhaps, but they didn't, and the artist went hungry. Unfortunately time does something to the artist's art that he himself cannot control, namely its value.

The underlying question here is why Bali and not Tahiti or other tropical paradises of the South Seas. And perhaps even more important, did Bali make these foreign artists or did they make Bali? Are the young artists we find there today tomorrow's great artists?

Let's first consider Balinese art.

Until the first European painters arrived in Bali in the late 1920s, Balinese painting was an art form that was little developed. Mythological scenes were almost the only subject and these were painted to decorate shrines and religious calendars. "Painting was limited and repetitive," art critic Nigel Cameron wrote in his critique on Balinese art. "Then in the late 1920s two remarkable European painters, Walter Spies and Rudolf Bonnet, came to settle in Bali and stayed to turn the island's young artists into new subjects, new forms, new materials and new techniques."

Walter Spies, German by birth had first gone to Java to study Indonesian music. In 1927 he ventured to Bali for a visit and there he remained until World War II.

Two years later Rudolf Bonnet from Holland arrived in Bali. Both Spies and Bonnet were to make their mark on Balinese painting. Bonnet had been a few months on the island when he was shown drawings done by the sons of a priest in a small town in central Bali. The sketches were regarded by local adults as mere childish dabblings. Bonnet and Spies thought differently. The sketches to them showed considerable promise and they decided to experiment.

They gave the boys painting materials and supervised the work they did. They were careful not to influence the ideas or subjects foreign to the boys or to Bali. The results were unlike anything created heretofore on Bali.

Spies and Bonnet then found a market for the paintings in Denpasar, the town where most Westerners visiting the island stayed. "In a land where cash is not easy to come by," wrote Cameron, "this gave the complexion of painting as an activity a rather more ardent glow." He also claimed that traditional Balinese art was now doomed.

Balinese painting now took on a complete new meaning. Disregarding the old manner of painting with people only in profile, and to a large extent its religious and mythological subject matter, the young new painters began to paint themes from everyday life. The new style was highly decorative. Despite the inherent weaknesses of composition, the simplicity and decorative naivete of the paintings carried them off.

At first, the new painters were not influenced by Western ideas of colour, perspective or effects of light. Their paintings remained basically flat patterns but they retained the lush vegetation of the island that seems almost to engulf the soft figures of boys and girls by streams or on jungle paths. They reflect Balinese reality. Nature is deeply familiar to every Balinese. There is a closeness between people and animal and plant life. It is a natural environment however exotic it may seem to the outsider.

Not all painters at the time agreed with Spies and Bonnet. One man who objected violently was Theo Meier. Theo firmly believed a true artist should not teach; he should be the student, the one who learns from foreign painters as well as from foreign art. Spies and Bonnet, in his opinion, were corrupting young Balinese artists.

Theo was a Swiss artist who had achieved a degree of success before he ever went to Bali in the mid 1930s. He is undoubtedly one of Bali's more colourful foreign artists, and certainly the last of his kind.

In 1930, Theo left Switzerland and went to the South Seas, to Tahiti and the Marquesas to paint, in the close footsteps of Paul Gauguin. He was an adventurer as well as a fine artist. After leaving Tahiti, he journeyed by trading schooner to the remote New Hebrides and sketched savage cannibals, and later with an easel strapped to his back he marched across China crafting portraits of Chinese warlords.

After-several years of wandering he returned to Switzerland where he staged a successful exhibition in his home town of Basel. But he was not destined to remain in Switzerland long. Tahiti was now his love. He fully intended to return to the South Seas.

During a stopover in Singapore on his return voyage, Theo heard about a magical island called Bali, and he decided to visit the island for two weeks before going on to Tahiti. He went to Bali and remained 22 years, and then left only for a visit to

Switzerland.

Theo, however, eventually did leave Bali—some claim after a bad love affair—and with an invitation from Prince Sandith Rangsit he came to Thailand. He lived for a while in Hua Hin and finally found the peace and quiet he seeked, and subjects to paint, in Chiang Mai. Theo lived for more than 20 years in northern Thailand until his death in 1953.

A few other European painters made their mark in Bali before the war. Belgian painter Le Mayeur was one. He moved to Bali in 1932 and lived there for 26 years. He married a Balinese girl, Ni Polok, a renowned Legong dancer and famed beauty. She was the subject of many of his paintings. His art is little remembered today.

In those years before World War II, the paradise of Bali began to be discovered by the world and the fame of Balinese painting spread. European artists found Bali ideal for a number of reasons. It was cheap to live, important for struggling artists, and the women, according to Theo Meier, were more than willing to strip and pose in the nude. Another factor, of course, is the natural beauty of Bali.

Then came World War II and the Japanese invasion.

The war took Bonnet into the armed services and Spies to an internment camp and later to his death at sea. Being Swiss, Theo Meier was able to remain on Bali during the Japanese occupation. He moved into Walter Spies' house in Iseh where he remained throughout the war years.

After the war a new generation of artists came to the island. One was Han Snel, a Dutch soldier who came with the occupation force, but when his time was up decided he'd rather stay. He befriended artists like Le Mayeur and Theo Meier. Theo Meier became his close friend. When Han fell in love with a lovely Balinese girl, Theo helped him to elope with her and gave them his home in Iseh where they could hide out.

Australian artist Donald Friend made an appearance about this same time. He remained for many years on the island and had a great influence on Balinese artists, teaching them individualism.

Another post war newcomer was Jim Pandy, partly Dutch, partly Chinese. He settled in Bali in 1950. Pandy and others like him started Balinese schools of art at Ubud and Mas.

From Manila came Filipino painter Antonio Blanco. He found a Balinese wife and became painter, self–acclaimed poet and bon vivant who enjoyed entertaining tourists with his tales of self-achievement as much as he enjoyed painting. His subject matter was, and still is, nude women. He has recently written a book about his life in Bali, designed by him with his sketches and containing many of his poems.

Han Snel and Antonio Blanco both have galleries in their homes where their paintings may be seen. Their works command high prices.

I met both artists 25 years ago when I went to Bali to promote the island for Thai International who was soon to inaugurate the first international flight to the island. Han then was building a magnificent house of carved stone in Ubud. The house is still there, with his gallery across a lotus pond. His latest addition is a small intimate restaurant where many in the art circles gather for lunch and drinks. I have written in detail about Han in my book about expatriates called *At Home in Asia.*

Blanco built for himself a spiralling villa on a hillside south of Ubud. It's open to the puiblic.

The third foreign artist from the past who still lives and paints in Bali is Arie Smit. Arie, unlike Blanco and Snel, has no permanent residence in Bali. When I last saw him a few months ago, he was living in a rented house in the Neka Gallery compound.

(Suteja Neka is a leading Balinese patron of the arts and curator of his museum near Ubud that houses one of the country's finest collection of paintings.)

This was my first meeting with Arie, having somehow missed him over the years. He was cordial and answered questions with sincerity, careful not to talk down other artists or his contemporaries. I was most interested in what he had to say about Theo Meier, as I am in the last stages of writing Theo's biography.

Arie Smit's own story is no less interesting than Theo's. He arrived in Bali in 1956, 18 years after he ventured from the Netherlands to Indonesia, then the Dutch Indies, as a young soldier. In Batavia, now Jakarta, he partly fulfilled an artistic yearning by training as a chromo-lithographer in the topographical service of the colony.

"I used to etch Balinese mountains onto maps of Indonesia," he said. "And I always promised myself that one day I would go to Bali."

By the time he did arrive in Bali, he had become a full–time painter.

Like Theo Meier and so many others, he intended to stay only a short time in Bali, but like them too he became bewitched by the island and decided to make it his home. "I had always lived in big Indonesian towns, for the first time in Bali, I was confronted with nature."

Smit became an Indonesian citizen in 1950, the year after the country won its hard-earned independence from the Dutch. Now, in his 70s, but still an avid explorer of Bali on foot, he paints mainly landscapes and temples in oil or acrylic. His fame as a Bali artist has spread to all parts of the world.

Arie's work, like Theo's, is certain to long endure. He explained his modus operandi. He constructs his painting slowly working on several at a time and layering colour upon colour. "It is good for a canvas to have several layers of colour," he said. "The more layers you put on it, the richer the colour on top will become."

He admits that he "fractures" his colours because he finds that colours in Bali are fractured. "Sunshine hits a palm tree bounces onto a temple and then reflects unto the shoulder of a man who is passing by."

As one art critic points out, Smit's vision is different from other artists, partly influenced by the unity of Balinese culture and partly by his experience as a prisoner of the Japanese in World War II.

The brutality and deprivation of those years helped to mould his philosophy. "No more war!" he adamantly insists. "My art is realism, but I avoid the harshness of actuality, the explicit, the edge, details that are sharp and merciless. My colours do not clash, they blend. Lines do not divide but unite."

And when I asked him what were his thoughts about Bali's other foreign artists, past and present, he said, "They were great. All of them were great."

With that I had to agree.

Chapter 11
WHEN THEY CALLED JAKARTA BATAVIA

One of my favourite destinations in Asia is Jakarta, but as I explained in this article, it is not the new glass and concrete structures that are the fascination. It's old Jakarta. The article appeared on May 11, 1982.

There's a small open air cafe on the corner of Taman Fatahillah in old Jakarta. It's a neat little cafe, with comfortable cane chairs and tables with checkered cloths. The cafe inside has high ceilings and revolving ceiling fans, and on the walls are old faded photographs of past days.

The square now called Taman Fatahillah was once the centre of old Jakarta, except they didn't call it Jakarta then. It was known as Batavia, and it was the most important Dutch possession in the Far East.

The cafe is a great place to sit and relax in the afternoon, when the downpour of heat is most intense and the town is half asleep. As you sit there and look out over the square, and providing you have spent the morning in the museums flanking the square, you can almost imagine Batavia when it came to life in the 1620s.

Only the year before, the Dutch, under the leadership of Jan Pieterszoon Coen, stormed the town and reduced it to ashes. Coen saw the potential of Jakarta as a suitable headquarters and subsequently attacked and razed the town. He ordered the construction of a new town, to be walled and fortified, and modelled after

Amsterdam. He called the new town Batavia.

Batavia was not the first settlement of importance at the mouth of the Ciliwung River. A port had been founded here in ancient, perhaps by the early Hindu, and later had during the 15th and 16th centuries Jayakarta, the name it went by, had developed into a major pepper port.

Under the Dutch East India Company, Batavia flourished and many of the buildings we see today in Taman Fatahillah square were built by them. Batavia grew rich throughout the 17th Century on an entrepot trade in spices that were found only in the East Indies—pepper, cloves and nutmegs. But Dutch prosperity was not to last forever.

After 1700, a series of dreadful disasters befell Batavia. Declining market prices, epidemics of malaria, cholera and typhoid, and an unfortunate massacre of the Batavia Chinese in 1740, combined with the frequent wars, cast a shadow of gloom over the city that had once fancied herself "Queen of the East."

At the beginning of the l9th Century, under the direction of Governor-General Willem Daendels, a follower of Napoleon, Batavia received a facelift that would completely alter her forever. Most of the original settlement—Old Batavia—was demolished, not for ascetic reasons but mostly to provide building materials for a new town to the south, around what is now modern Jakarta.

Only the town square area survived. It has been restored and renamed Taman Fatahillah, and three of the surrounding colonial edifices have been converted into museums: the Jakarta History Museum, the Fine Arts Museum and the Wayang Museum.

Any tour of Old Batavia should begin at the Jakarta History Museum on the south side of the square. This was formerly the City Hall of Batavia, a solid structure completed in 1710 and used by successive governments right up through the 1960s. It now houses fascinating memorabilia from the colonial period, notably 18th–century furnishings and portraits of Dutch governors, along with many prehistoric, classical and Portuguese period artifacts.

As you walk through the high-ceiling rooms with shuttered windows, across thick plank floors, you can get a feeling how the Dutch lived in opulence and splendour. There are great dining halls and reception rooms, and on one wall hangs a 16th century map of the Dutch East Indies. Batavia is the hub; Sumatra is named, and Borneo; the Celebes is unknown and Singapore is called Aurea and indicates it's uninhabited.

Dungeons beneath the building were used as holding cells where prisoners were made to stand waist-deep in sewage for weeks awaiting their trials. Executions and public tortures were once commonplace, performed daily in the main square as judges watched from the balcony above the main entrance. An execution axe hangs on a wall in of the museum rooms.

For those interested in the arts, the Wayang Museum on the western side of the square is most interesting. It contains many puppets and masks, some of them quite old. Every Sunday a puppet performance is staged at 10 a.m. and 11 a.m. It's well worth seeing.

The third building on the square is the Fine Arts Museum on the east side of Fatahillah. It is housed in the former Court Building which was completed in 1879. The museum has collections of painted sculptures by modern Indonesian artists, and an important exhibition porcelains. Some items date back to the 14th century.

There a cannon on the north side of Taman Fatahillah that faces down a street of busy shoppers. It has a most interesting story to tell. Si Jago, as it is called, is regarded by many as a fertility symbol, perhaps because of the fist cast into the butt end of the cannon, whose thumb protrudes between its index and middle fingers (an obscene gesture in Indonesia).

You can see couples shyly approach the cannon with offerings. The wife then straddles the cannon's barrel, in the hope of thereby conceiving a child.

If you are interested in old Dutch architecture, walk behind the Wayang Museum to view two Dutch houses dating from the 18th Century.

A short walk from Taman Fatahillah Square is the old port of Sunda Kelapa. It is still very much in use today. For the photographer it can be the highlight of a visit to old Batavia. The earlier in the morning you can get there the better.

Sunda Kelapa is the name of the original Hindu spice-trading post which was conquered and then converted to Islam more than four and a half centuries ago. The romance of the days of sailing ships is seen here in the form of traditional wooden Macassar schooners, some of which are fifty metres long and continue to play a vital role in the commerce of modern-day Indonesia. Each day dozens of these schooners with their high jutting bowsprits arrive laden with sawn timber from Kalimantan (Borneo) and is off-loaded along the two–km–long wharf, a wharf that has been in continuous use since 1817. A visit to the port can be an unforgettable experience.

The area around Sunda Kelapa is rich in history. Directly across the river stands a l9th-Century Dutch lookout tower constructed upon the site of the original customs house of Jayakarta. This is where traders once gave gifts and tribute to the native ruler in return for the privilege of trading here. For a little extra change you can get an attendant to open the tower which offers a panoramic view of the city and the coast. Nearby is an old wooden drawbridge that straddles an unused canal, but which recalls the days when Batavia was a Dutch town laced with waterways as was common in Amsterdam.

Across the canal with the drawbridge and to the left stands a solid redbrick townhouse (Jalan Kali Besar Barat No. ll) that was built around 1730 by the then soon-to-be Governor General Van Imhoff. The design and particularly the fine Chinese-style woodwork are typical of old Batavian residences.

Three doors to the left stands the only other house from the same period, now the offices of the Chartered Bank.

Behind the tower stands a long, two-storey structure dating back to the Dutch East Indian Company times. It is now the Museum Bahari. Originally a warehouse, it was erected by the Dutch in 1652 and used for many years to store coffee, tea and Indian cloth. Inside on display are traditional sailing craft from all corners of the Indonesian archipelago, as well as some old maps of Batavia. Down a narrow lane and around a corner behind the museum lies the fish market (Pasar Ikan), beyond numerous stalls selling nautical gear.

For something different, take a walk through these back alleys. Some call it Chinatown but there are no signs with Chinese characters.

The alleys are narrow and dark; the stone walkways are damp and congested. Here, where you will hardly see a foreigner, you will find fortune tellers and casket makers, and you can buy candles, skinned frogs on sticks ready to cook, watches that not only tell time but the phases of the moon, herbs and Chinese medicine and sun glasses. If you want kids' toys, leather belts or glassware, along with piles of coconuts, they are there too. The only thing I advise is not to walk the alleyways after dark.

Those who want to give Jakarta the time will discover it is an amazing city which has much to offer the traveller. It is, certainly, capital to the world's fifth most populous nation and home to 7 million Indonesians. And yet, in spite of its glass and concrete skyscrapers and beautiful monuments in and around the city centre, it is made up almost entirely of small one- and two-storey structures.

Dutch architecture is seen not only in old Batavia but along many of the tree-lined boulevards. Many were splendid residence of the colonial period, styled after their counterparts in Europe. By the turn of the century, Batavia's homes, hotels and clubs were in no way inferior to those of Europe.

The Japanese occupation put an end to old Batavia. The town was renamed Jakarta and dramatically transformed—from a tidy Dutch colonial town of 200,000 to an Indonesian city of more than 1 million. Following independence, hundreds of thousands more Indonesians flooded in from the countryside and the outer islands, and Jakarta quickly outstripped all other Indonesian cities in size and importance to become what scholars term a "primate" city: the unrivalled political, cultural and economic centre of the new nation.

Chapter 12
NOSTALGIC RETURN TO CORREGIDOR

The following article appeared on May 18, 1992, a week and 40 years after the fall of Corregidor. My return visit, with hundreds of returning American G.I.s, was a deep and emotional experience for me as well as for all the servicemen who once fought to keep the rock from falling into Japanese hands.

Shock after shock! The string of light bulbs suspended from the ceiling swing from side to side, grow dim and almost black out. Slowly they come on again, flickering as they do. The concrete floor beneath your feet trembles with such violence you feel you might fall over. And by now the sound is deafening, like a weight, pressing down on you. Dust falls from everywhere and the walls seem as though they might collapse. There is no escape, no place to run; you are as deep as you can get into the bowels of the earth and still you are not safe! God, what must you do to live!

You are in Malinta Tunnel on Corregidor, the volcanic rock that stands as the last defence of Manila, and, in fact, of all the Philippines and Southeast Asia as well. The date is May 6, 1942.

You are made to think it is 1942. Actually this is 1992, some fifty years after the fact. Nevertheless, you are still there, in Malinta Tunnel, and what you are witnessing is "The Malinta Experience" a light-and-sound presentation of the siege of Corregidor, sponsored by the Philippine Tourist Board and the

Corregidor Foundation Inc.

The feeling, the sensation you receive, is about as close as you can get to the real thing. In fact, it's so realistic you may want to break loose from the others and run from the tunnel. You could very easily do that, run for the light at the far end, but for the soldiers who were defending the rock fifty years ago that would have been impossible. They were doomed to die, or else surrender.

The choice was finally made for them.

On May 6, 1942, after defending the island for five long months, General Jonathan Wainwright gave the orders to raise a white flag.

In the coming months, ex-G.I.s, both Americans and Filipinos will be making their way to Corregidor in Manila Bay in remembrance of that fatal day 50 years ago.

For those who want to join in the reminiscence, and take a look at history, at 8:00 a.m. sharp every morning the *M.V. Island Cruiser* leaves from the Convention Centre on Roxas Boulevard in Manila for the ninety–minute run to Corregidor; it returns at 3 p.m. in the afternoon. Or if you wish, you can now remain overnight. There's now a new hotel on the island.

I made several trips to Corregidor over the years, including one in 1967 in which I gathered information on the 25th anniversary of the fall of Corregidor for my travel column in the *Bangkok World*. I was impressed then, but it was nothing like this last trip. And I hadn't even planned to visit the rock this time.

I was in Manila during a quick stopover on my way to Guam, when I read in the local newspapers about the many hundreds of World War II veterans returning to Corregidor in remembrance of the 50th anniversary of its fall. The stories the veterans had to tell about their capture and imprisonment were truly moving.

I then decided to take the time and visit Corregidor once again. So much had changed since I had last been there. In the past, travel to the island was left very much up to the individual. There was no scheduled ferry service and arranging a tour was not too easy. Now the government along with the Historical Society is making Corregidor a destination well worth visiting. I was told I wouldn't recognise the place.

For US$29 that included the ferry trip both ways and a guided tour, I was at the Convention Centre for the 8 o'clock ferry. Among the hundred or so passengers there was a handful of returning veterans, both American and Filipinos. Through one American, Commander Arthur Beale, USN Retired, I was to relive the siege of Corregidor.

Aboard the *Island Cruiser*, a huge relief map of the island hangs on the wall in the main cabin. It's an odd-shaped island, much like a wiggling tadpole, with its head turned westward to the China Sea, and the tail curving east towards Manila. The island is volcanic in origin, an almost solid rock formation four miles long and about half a mile at its widest point. It lies twenty-six miles from Manila and about five miles from Bataan.

The Spanish were first to realise the strategic position of the island in the defence of Manila and took early steps towards its fortification. They set up cannons that had a range of about a mile and could protect the entrance to the bay.

However, the fortifications didn't work as well as they planned. On May 1st, 1898, in the darkness of night, Commodore George Dewy steamed into Manila Bay and with little resistance claimed the Philippine Islands on behalf of the United States of America. Although the islands were considered the "spoils or war," the U.S. did purchase them from the Spanish for US$22 million, a staggering sum at the turn of the century.

In 1902, the U.S. Army further fortified the rock and turned it into a military reservation, reputed to be one of the finest in the Far East.

"It wasn't a bad place to be stationed," agreed Arthur Beale, the ex-commander whom I mentioned meeting on the ferry. He explained what life on the island was like before the war. He had arrived as a young naval lieutenant in the summer of 1941.

The northwestern portion of the island, Beale pointed out, is one massive rock jutting up 500 ft. above the waves, inaccessible from the sea except for two small ravines.

Here on a plateau called the Topside were army headquarters, barracks for enlisted personnel, officer's quarters, underground ordnance shops, the traditional parade grounds, hospitals and schools and the bulk of the batteries which formed the main power of the fortress. The barracks were concrete structures some four storeys high and almost a mile long.

The lowest part of the island was once called Bottomside, a flat stretch of land a few feet above sea level. Here were the docks and the civilian town of San Jose. Once a Spanish town, it had evolved into a small American community, with its paved streets lined with houses and private residences.

The Island *Cruiser* docked at Bottomside where an open bus, built to resemble a San Francisco cable car, awaited us. Our guide was Filipino, a man well versed in the history of his country.

The first stop was Malinta Tunnel, an introduction to Corregidor that is certain to leave anyone awed. The "Malinta Experience" is a light-and-sound show written by National Artist Lamberto V. Avellana. Actual sound recordings have been reproduced, and you hear the voices of President Roosevelt, General MacArthur, Philippine President Manuel L. Quezon and that of General Wainwright when he surrendered Corregidor to the Japanese.

And there are the sounds of the bombs and shells exploding. You heard air raid sirens and warnings and the cries of soldiers in agony. You are told the history of the rock from the Spanish to its recapture at the end of World War II by Filipino and U.S. troops.

The construction of the Malinta Tunnel began in 1922 and was designed as storage rooms for the strategic materials stockpiled on the island. The principal tunnel is 925 feet long and 25 feet wide. Extending out from the sides of the main tunnel are 24 smaller tunnels, each averaging 160 feet long and 15 feet wide.

As the tour takes you down the main tunnel, the guide stops at these side tunnels, many which have been converted into wax museums. Over the public address system you hear the commentary. You can see General Douglas MacArthur and his staff officers sitting at the conference tables, and you hear the first shells hit and see the lights grow dim. The attack is on.

The voice tells you that at the outbreak of World War II, there were twenty-three batteries on Corregidor and the adjoining islands. These consisted of 58 coastal guns and mortars. You hear them open fire.

Simultaneously with their attack on Pearl Harbour, the Japanese bombed Baguio City in Northern Luzon and Davao in Mindanao. Before long Manila was under siege.

General MacArthur had to convince President Quezon that he could better serve the Philippines outside the country as its leader rather than as a prisoner of the Japanese.

President Quezon left Manila at two o'clock on the afternoon of 24 December, 1941, and arrived at Corregidor that evening. With the President were Mrs. Quezon, his two daughters, Maria Aurora and Zenaida, and his only son Manuel, Jr.

Before midnight, General MacArthur, his wife and their son arrived aboard SS *Don Esteban* along with several staff officers.

Corregidor underwent its baptism of fire in an air bombardment a few days later on 29 December. This was considered the heaviest attack by bombing and strafing that the island, now referred to as The Rock, ever sustained during the war.

Beginning just before noon at 11:54 a.m., the first attack lasted a full thirty minutes. Eighteen twin-engine bombers covered by a protective wing of 19 army fighters swooped down for the attack from a height of 15,000 feet and dropped an estimated 50 tonnes of bombs of the 220-and 550-pound variety.

At 12:30 p.m. the second wave of twenty-two light bombers came in from the same altitude and pulverized Topside and Bottomside with their load of sixty-six 225-pound bombs. The dive bombers flew in as the light bombers winged away, to unload a torrent of 35-pound bombs from an altitude of 3,000 feet. At 1:00 p.m. the dive bombers were through, but it did not mean respite, for sixty navy planes came in and continued the attack.

When all-clear sounded practically every wooden structure on Corregidor was in flames. No important installation was destroyed, however, but USAFFE Headquarters had to move into Malinta Tunnel. The cost to the Japanese: thirteen medium bombers and four dive bombers. They found it a costly deal, and never again until the end of April, when all anti-aircraft guns on the Rock had been silenced, would the Japanese dare attack from the air at altitudes of 15,000 and 3,000 feet.

MacArthur realised Corregidor was doomed but with little choice he made the rock his command headquarters and here he planned to make his last stand. But even before Bataan fell, MacArthur was ordered by the president of the U.S. to leave the Philippines and plan for the defence of Australia. Along with his wife and their young son, he made his daring exit on a black night aboard a fast moving PT boat. How they managed to sneak through the Japanese naval blockade was nothing short of a miracle. President Quezon made his escape shortly before this.

The command of Corregidor and the Filipino-American forces went to General Jonathan Wainwright. The odds were against him.

There's no question the fortress could have been bypassed and thousands of lives spared but Corregidor had become a symbol of Filipino-American resistance and had to be crushed.

The Japanese began their all-out offensive against Corregidor after the fall of Bataan. During the 27-day period from 9 April to the date of its capture on 6 May, Corregidor was subjected to bombardment from land and air such as no other area its size ever received. Those on the island had the feeling of standing on jelly, so intense and so continuous were the explosions.

The men began to drop from sheer fatigue, those who were not hit by shrapnel or knocked off balance by the explosions. Even patients in the hospital tunnels were thrown from their beds. One shell hit a company mess, killing or wounding seventy-five men.

Morale had ebbed to the lowest. Decimated by the artillery fire, the beach defence troops grimly held on. Commander Beale relived his experiences for me. “Not everyone was holed up in Malinta Tunnel,” he said. “Many of us were dug in, with shells exploding overhead. We lived on field rations.”

It wasn’t much better in the tunnel. The two meals dished out a day didn’t give real nourishment. The hospital wards were filled beyond capacity. The situation was at its most critical point.

Starting on the night of 15 April and every night thereafter, landing craft, armoured barges and gunboats had been sneaked by the Japanese into Manila Bay through the narrow North Channel. A total of 110 boats of various types equipped with heavy machine guns, and eleven gunboat sections were gathered to transport the assault force.

Against constant shelling, combined lack of food and medical supplies and the ravages of tropical diseases, Wainwright continued to hold on as long as he could. In the final thrust, in one day alone, the Japanese fired 16,000 shells at the American fortress. The surface of the island was reduced to rubble and debris.

Finally, after holding out for five months and with no water and with little food and supplies left, General Wainwright sat down and wrote his final message to President Roosevelt: “With broken heart and head bowed in sadness but not in shame I report that today I must arrange terms for the surrender of the fortified islands of Manila Bay....” He then gave the orders to surrender.

It took three years before American troops would once again

recapture the fortress of big guns and rock tunnels. When the final invasion of Corregidor came it was nothing short of complete and total carnage. Once again Corregidor had become a symbol of resistance, this time from the Japanese.

MacArthur sent everything he had to retake the island. Rockets landed on the shores, troops fell from the sky and commandos swarmed the beaches.

At first the Japanese shot the paratroopers before they even landed. They waited in ambush for the landings on the beaches. But in the end there were just too many invaders. The Japanese then moved deep into the caves carved into the island. Not wishing to surrender, the Americans had to burn and blast them out.

Corregidor today stands as a gallant war monument. The huge caverns are empty and the big guns rust in their positions, forever silent. In retrospect, the battles for Corregidor, both the surrender and the retaking of the island, were gallant fights but in themselves military failures.

MacArthur knew that Corregidor could not be defended. As a young second lieutenant, even before World War I, he had helped with the design of the early fortifications which were primarily aimed for protection against naval attack. He was well aware with the introduction of aircraft for military purposes, Corregidor was obsolete for defence purposes. Big guns mean nothing when artillery positions can be bombed from high flying aircraft.

But the U.S. also had their hands tied when they abided by the rules of the Washington Naval Treaty of 1922. The treaty limited the size and number of weapons the U.S. could place on their Pacific bases. Since they couldn't fortify against air attacks, the military decided to "dig in" on the rock. In the years to follow, the miles of Malinta tunnels were dug.

The rock is there for anyone to see today. But it's more than just a place. It's an emotional experience.

Chapter 13
TAKE ME BACK TO OLD SHANGHAI

Having been to Shanghai when it was one of the most wicked, and most exciting, ports in the world, a few years after World War II, I wasn't too keen on returning. The city would no longer have the excitement of old, I reasoned. But I did eventually go back, and was glad I did. I wrote the following article after that visit, and it appeared on March 8, 1994. I have returned twice since. It's still one of the great cities of Asia.

Over the years I wondered how much of the old Shanghai I once knew, the Shanghai before the 1949 revolution, still existed. I have to admit, I was there only a very short time, but so vivid are my memories of Shanghai that I don't think I could ever forget them. And no small wonder. Imagine, a young man not yet twenty years old, arriving by boat from Tsingtao in the north, and seeing this unbelievable, wicked, vile, and wonderfully entertaining city for the first time.

What absolute excitement when I stepped on to the quay. I didn't know which way to look, nor where to turn. Everything seemed to be happening at once. Out in the river, pulling at their anchors, were naval gunboats flying the ensigns of half a dozen nations. There were great river steamers, rusted freighters and huge sea-going junks. There were lighters with painted eyes, white–hulled government launches with shiny brass rails and so many more vessels of unknown origin. And sculling back and forth, from

Stephens in a rickshaw in Shanghai after the war.

ship to shore, was a sea of tiny sampans.

Along the quay, cargo vessels of every description loaded and unloaded their wares, whizzing cranes swung their booms back and forth overhead, and sweating coolies tottered up and down narrow gangplanks with heavy loads upon their backs.

Trishaw drivers peddled cargo as well as passengers, clanging their noisy bells as they pushed through milling crowds. Stern-faced Sikh policemen, complete with beards, turbans and truncheons, stood guard, not hesitating to use the sticks upon anyone who didn't pay them heed.

And beyond all this, as far as one could see up and down river, rose a wall of magnificent colonial buildings: banking institutions, a custom house, hotels, private clubs, government offices, foreign consulates—buildings with clock towers, columns and domes, powerful and elegant, and so un-Chinese.

They called it the Bund, part quay, part thoroughfare and part promenade. It was the most famous street in Asia.

This was the Shanghai I came to know, a city that was beyond any law; a city that defied human dignity and lived up to the many names people gave it—"Paris of the East," "Whore of Asia," "Capital of the Tycoon," "Paradise of Adventurers," and a score of other such names.

Whatever name one cared to use, one thing no one could deny: Shanghai was the most exciting city in the East. And now, after more than forty years, I was going back.

Since last November Thai International has had direct service from Bangkok to Shanghai, making the temptation to go there hard to resist.

Of course, all the old questions arose. How much of old Shanghai would still be there? Would I be disappointed at what I found, and perhaps was it not better to let old dogs lie. Earlier this year I thought the same thing about Beijing. I resisted going back, but when I did I was not disappointed. Hopefully Shanghai would be the same. I teamed up with Photographer Robert Stedman and in two days we had our Chinese visas, and the next day we were aboard TG-664.

I can't remember ever being so excited as I was when our THAI flight came in for a landing at the new Shanghai International Airport. Robert was no less enthusiastic. It was also his fist visit to China.

We expected Chinese customs and immigration to be harsh on foreign travellers. Not so. Within minutes we were through.

And instantly we could see that Shanghai, where money means everything, has joined the capitalistic world. Even at the airport commercialism is everywhere you look. In the very centre of the carousels where baggage is unloaded there is on display shiny new Zingfu motorcycles and China–made automobiles.

Once through customs we checked the long line of hotel booths—Westin, Sheraton, Mandarin, Shangri-La, Garden Hotel, the Shanghai. We were trying to make a decision when a Thai gentleman approached with an extended hand. "Welcome to Shanghai," he said. I recognised him at once, Passakorn Koopitakachorn. I had met him earlier this year in Beijing. He was the THAI station manager there, and knew Beijing as well as anyone. He had been very helpful. Now, he said, he was sent to Shanghai to set up the THAI office.

Passakorn had the first words of encouragement I heard about Shanghai, which I needed. On the plane that afternoon I opened up a book on Shanghai and read in the introduction: "On seeing the city again, those who knew it in its heyday are inescapably saddened." I asked Passakorn what he thought about the city. "I like it even better than Beijing," he said. And then he recommended we stay at the J.C. Mandarin. The location, he explained, is close to the heart of town.

Robert and I were like two excited kids on the drive into town. Nothing failed to catch our attention. A sign: Hail the Shanghai

Far Eastern Games. Trucks, cars, some buses, driving on the right-hand side of the road. Bicycles with separate lanes. But not as crowded as one might expect the world's most populous city to be, with some 13 million inhabitants, in an area that covers 145 sq. miles (375 sq. km). Trees without foliage neatly trimmed. Rows of hand–painted billboards advertising Chinese products along both sides of the road, side by side, forming an almost solid fence. Low rise buildings, mostly of brick, and as we came to the outskirts of the city, high rises began to appear. These are the new international hotels. We entered the city and came to a magnificent hotel that rose up before us—the Shanghai J.C. Mandarin.

Before we unpacked we went back out into the streets. I had one direction in mind, the Bund, the area that I remembered most about Shanghai. We followed Nanjing Road, past endless garment shops and department stores, and magnificent hotels like the Park Hotel, until the street came to a dead end—at the Bund.

It was a short walk, perhaps five miles, and little more than an hour, but it was my Shanghai reawakening. I quickly discovered that in Shanghai time has stopped. We stood at the Bund, now called Zhongshan Road, and before darkness fell, we returned to our hotel by another meandering route though the city's back streets. At no place did we see massive reclamation projects, no destruction of old buildings by wreckers hammers, no signs that said 'condemned.' Old Victorian buildings have not been razed to make parking lots nor to provide space for new high rises. Bits of Paris and London appear at ever corner. Pealing plaster and crumbling stonework are commonplace but through the neglect we find the authentic, the real Shanghai. Shanghai, thus, has been preserved, wholly.

Standing there at the Bund you can't help wondering why. Why did Shanghai become so utterly Western?

As far back as the 14th century Shanghai had been a major port, trading goods between the coast and inland provinces. The port prospered and as a result drew the attention of Japanese pirates. After repeated attacks, six in one two-month period, in the mid-16th century the Chinese defenders constructed at 27-foot-high wall with a surrounding moat. The pirate raids stopped.

While the wall kept the pirates out, it failed to prevent the attack of colonial greed. Europe wanted in; the Chinese wanted to keep the "foreign devils" out. Only limited trading rights were granted to Western powers, until the British introduced opium. For the first time in her long history, China's balance of trade was disrupted. Opium flooded in; her silver drained out.

The Opium Wars (1840-1842) erupted and China lost. The British imposed the Treaty of Nanking in 1842 which paved the way for the opening of Shanghai. A British gunboat sailed up the Huangpu River and hoisted the British flag over Shanghai—where all foreigners now could enjoyed "free" access and extraterritorial rights. Chinese justice did not apply in Shanghai.

From the latter part of the 19th century, much of Shanghai was transformed into an European city. On west of the bank of the Huangpu, they built the Bund and gave names to streets like Edward VII and Park Lane. Next to the walled city, the French built their "Concession" and added names like Quai de L'Ouest and Avenue Joffre.

American and Russian concessions were developed along Suzhou Creek, to be absorbed later by the British in to the International Concession.

The official languages of Shanghai became English, French, German and Russia, but not Chinese?

Finding old Shanghai is both physically and emotionally possible. Lacking are good guide books and maps, but this didn't deter us from getting around, nor should it for any traveller. All one needs is a good pair of walking shoes, and no fear of getting lost. Discovery waits at every turn, at every corner.

The streets are clean, and in spite of the traffic there seems to be little pollution. For one thing, there are few motorbikes giving out nauseating fumes, and public trams are driven by electrical wires overhead. Street signs appear on all the corners with Chinese script in bold letters and the names in English below.

One street I wanted to find was Blood Alley. I remember it well. When my three–year tour of China duty was up, I came to Shanghai for further transportation back to America. The marines I met wanted to show me "their" Shanghai, and they took me to Blood Alley. The street got its name from the bloody bar–room brawls that were nightly affairs. Sailors from the Seventh Fleet and marines from the local garrison swilled down Huba Huba vodka and Tsingtao beer in smoky bars like the ABC Bar and the Prime Club. White Russian hustlers in frayed linen suits had deals to make and taxi dancers in long silk dresses slit up the sides slithered along the walls waiting for customers. Those who had rich boyfriends wore Western dresses.

Today Blood Alley is Xikou Road, and it's not even a shadow of its former self. The alley is in a state of total dereliction.

In the early morning, the Chinese, young and old, do exercises in the streets, and in all the alleys elderly people sit outside on stools, chatting, knitting, playing cards or just guarding the bedding which has been spread out in the street to give it an airing. There are no animals to be seen anywhere, not a single dog nor cat.

Apart from the Bund, there are many buildings that have survived, to varying degree, from the 1920s and 1930s. These are particularly apparent in the former French Concession, which was once wedged in between the International Settlement and the old Chinese city.

Today in the old French Concession new hotel skyscrapers look down upon tree-lined streets of two-storey houses with red brick roofs and backyards. Here and there are old estates with extensive gardens, now used for schools and government offices.

Walk down any street and through wrought-iron gates Victorian mansions are still visible.

One place I wanted to see in the old French Concession was the home of Dr. Sun Yat-Sen, the leader of the 1911 revolution that overthrew the Manchu Dynasty. Dr. Sun served briefly as provisional president of the new republic before devoting the rest of his life to encouraging people to follow his economic and social reform programmes. Between 1918 and 1924, he lived at No. 7 Xiangshan Lu with his wife Soong Quingling.

After his death in 1925, his widow converted his house into a museum. It includes Sun's library of 2,700 books, the popular uniform he designed, his medical instruments, writing brushes and ink stone, various maps and a display of photographs, among them one of him and Soong Quingling in Guangzhou, the first ever to be assembled in China.

Sun's books are shelved behind locked glass doors; the titles depict the man that he was—*The Monroe Doctrine, Problems in the Pacific, Democracy and the Empire, The history of Old Japan, The Imperialist, The Problems of Local Government.*

Also a landmark in Shanghai is Soong Quingling's house at 1843 Huahai Zhong where she lived after the death of her husband Sun Yat-Sen. It's now a museum and open to the public.

Today, Shanghai Harbour has moved from the Bund farther down river. It's the third biggest harbour in the world and an important factor in the city's industrial prowess. Harbour cruises start at Huangpu Park and carry on to the confluence with the Yangzi. The tour shows visitors the international character of the harbour.

Huangpu Park facing the river was once the pride and joy of the British community. But for Chinese it meant humiliation. There was a sign at the entrance: Dogs and Chinese not allowed.

Faded colonial splendour can also be found on the other side of the Suzhou River: Waibaidu Bridge leads directly from Huangpu

Park to the Seaman's Club and the Shanghai Dasha Hotel. The bridge is usually crowded with pedestrians, cyclists and labourers pushing bicycle carts heavily loaded with wares.

Before leaving Shanghai, I had to go back to the Bund for a final visit. I couldn't help wondering how a way of life that dominated Shanghai since the middle of last century could vanish so completely. The capitalists fled and the street names changed. The glitter faded and both foreigners and glory were gone. The bubble had burst.

But as we must so often do in life, we have to face the truth. Old Shanghai could not possibly have endured. But the memory will always be there.

Broadway and music star Mary Martin and Stephens aboard a river boat on the Chao Phraya.

Chapter 14
LOVE, AND THE HAPPY BACHELOR

I lost many friends and had nasty letters in the mail at the Post *when this article appeared in December 1985. I don't mind having it reprinted here, for perhaps I can make amends. A few months after it appeared I got married.*

"The trouble with you is you have to settle down. You know, get married, have kids!"

I go through it all the time, from friends, even from friends of friends whom I hardly know, but mostly the advice comes from wives. They are constantly telling I me that I should get married. They insist that I am not happy.

As readers might gather, I am a bachelor, and even if I must whisper, I'm a happy, contented bachelor.

But, the truth be known, people don't like to see a happy bachelor. If he is, there's something wrong. He's either perverted, homosexual, mentally ill, or terribly self-centred—in which case no one wants him. I've been accused of them all.

How do I, as a bachelor, convince people I don't want to settle down, and that there really isn't any "trouble with me" because I'm not married; and that by not being in love doesn't mean I am living alone. I happen to like living with women, for short periods.

And I do not agree—"Man wasn't intended to live alone."

I really get annoyed when friends throw prosaic quotations at me, like "Behind every successful man is a good woman." Do they mean I haven't done a thing with my life? That sailing oceans, climbing mountains and searching for lost cities isn't important. It's almost as bad as saying, "God wouldn't have created Eve if Adam was happy by himself."

But then the really touching arguments why I should marry are "Nothing is more beautiful than man and woman in love" and "Love makes the world go around." Let me say, nothing is more ridiculous.

Just by saying I can do without love, I find myself doomed in society, like the teacher who tried to preach Darwin's "Origin of the Species" in his classroom a few generations ago. He went to trial and lost. But never mind. Here's a bachelor's view on love, a very misunderstood and misused word.

Society, that world we chose to live in, emphasises the necessity for love to precede sex. You have to be in love, they say, to enjoy sex. Although in recent years, through women's lib, many disregard this restriction, but others remain frightened or disturbed by the idea of a purely sexual relationship. And how do these morally conscious people get around it? The only way for many sexually aroused individuals to avoid frustration or anxiety is to fall in love —as quickly as possible. Then they can make love.

Why do people fall in love? Security, for both men and women. It's the need to possess. When we love we want to hold on to that person, and not share her, or him. Another reason for falling in love is social conformity, because everyone else falls in love we must do the same, or something is wrong. And finally there is the need for sexual satisfaction and it's much easier making love when we say we are in love.

Ernest Hemingway in one of his novels said falling in love is like riding a Ferris wheel. When one gets on he never knows when to get off. I think love is more like a seesaw; you must depend upon the other for balance. You are not the one in control. It means dependency.

The idea of dependency is difficult for non-bachelors to understand. They don't want to admit that when we are in love, our dependency upon the other increases, and soon we develop the fear of losing the other one. It isn't the thought of losing the other through death that is so disturbing for we are all aware we all have to die, but it is the thought that the loved one will find somebody else, and here is our grief, being dumped. The most important factor to breaking off any such relationship is the thought of what others will think. We are deeply concerned with losing our self-respect.

We are products of the society in which we live, of our growing up. This business of love is what we are taught to believe, as children. LOVE. LOVE. LOVE. We see the name LOVE plastered all over the place. The name appears in love poems, on bathroom walls, on doilies, on car bumpers, in comic strips. We have come to say I Love You but it no longer has meaning. How can one possibly believe in indiscriminate love when a panhandler, a bum, in shaggy clothes, and smelling awful, comes up to you on the street, as one did to me in San Francisco, pins a paper flower on you while he mutters, "Love Brother, Love," and then asks for a dollar. My advice—get a job.

Nevertheless, there is something wrong, we are taught, if we say we don't believe in love. But for us to state that love is a superior emotion is to express a current cultural axiom. What it really means is that nothing is good or bad except what our culture makes it. The panhandler on the street with paper flowers is harmless if he preaches love, but not war.

But let's examine the meaning of the word love. We talk about love, the act of being in love, as something beautiful. But is it really? Think about it. Isn't being in love being out of control? For it one can steal, murder, or commit suicide. When one falls in love he no longer cares about others, except for the one he is in love with. Values then become distorted. When in love one can squander fortunes, lose one's reputation even self—respect. Love follows no rules, disregards logic, and is self—devouring. And we call this beautiful?

Are we not brainwashed about our concept of love? Have we not come to pity or scorn the person who is not in love. Our society really scorns the bachelor when it comes to love, and now with an added complication—sex. We are taught one must follow the other, or else they are both wrong. To many it does matter what others will think. We are deeply concerned with losing our self-respect.

When you have love, jealousy is always lurking somewhere around the corner. Those people who say they are not jealous, they are not in love. And certainly our most destructive emotion is jealousy; yet it's the inevitable component of love, and certainly an unhealthy one.

Then how many times have we heard it said that nothing is greater than "mature" love. Mature love, these philosophers of the heart insist, is a broadening, deepening experience. I never did quite understand what this means. The claim that love promotes maturity just doesn't make sense. Does it mean that the individual would not have matured just as readily had there been an absence of love. Since love fosters dependency, then it may be considered that love is a deterrent to maturity and not the other way around.

Contrary to what most people believe, the individual who does not need dependency, in other words who is secure, and who has a satisfying sex relationship, will not need to love. He then is a contented person who does not find his own company boring—a person whose inner resources are such that other persons, although they may provide pleasure and stimulation, are not absolutely necessary.

When we achieve this independency in life, we are thought to be self-centred. Perhaps we are, but is that so wrong? We seek love relationships with others only when we do not love ourselves sufficiently. Yet to be self-centred does not mean to disregard the worth of other people. I just don't have to love them.

So, I am told, as a bachelor I am selfish, conceited, self-centred and I am not happy. I guess, really, I am unhappy then—unhappy being happy.

A Thai farmer, drawing deeply on his cheroot, hasn't heard the Surgeon General's message that smoking is bad for your health.

Chapter 15
Kipling's Last Cheroot

One day our children, or our children's children, will ask, "What do they mean when they say he smoked?" Smoking will be something of the past, and the lines written by Kipling will no longer have meaning. Bad or good, I gave my views in an article on June 2, 1987.

I went to Kanchanaburi the other day, and visited the museum at the Death Railway. It's an incredible museum building, a replica of the bamboo huts with straw roofs where the Japanese kept their POWs. I don't think anyone can go through the place without feeling the horrors of war.

The photographs in the museum are the most touching. Many were taken when the prisoners were being released, and there was one in particular that caught my attention. It shows three GIs, all Brits, puffing on their first cigarettes. You could see the gleam in their eyes, the ecstasy of being freed, and having that first cigarette.

Then suddenly, the thought came to mind, what if this had happened today, and a Red Cross nurse was there to greet the boys, and one of them asked her for a cigarette. I could imagine her response. "Cigarettes, you know they are bad for you." And probably the guard who had just come to take over from the Japanese would say, "Sorry, bud, but there's no smoking allowed in here."

Yes, indeed, the world has really changed. When I was a young

U.S. Marine they issued us K and C rations, and inside the cartons were neat little packets with four cigarettes enclosed. The sergeant used to call out, "Okay, you bums, the smoking lamp is lit," at which everyone would sit down, take out their cigarettes and light up. Five minutes of every hour was allotted for smoking and resting. I felt sorry for the guys who didn't smoke. They usually had to do some situps or run around the field a couple of times. To be a rough and tough Marine, you were expected to smoke. But even back then people were aware that cigarettes were bad, but who cared? If you wanted to kill yourself, that was up to you. The marines used to joke when passing around a cigarette butt, "Here, another nail in your coffin."

But there's no denying, smoking was in vogue. Hardly a Hollywood movie star who appeared on the screen in the '40s and '50s didn't have a cigarette in his or her hand. They set the standards, and, of course, we all envied the stars.

Even before then, back in the Roaring Twenties when a Ford 5-passenger sedan sold for $1,258, it was fashionable to smoke store-bought, rolled cigarettes. In fact, the ads proclaimed smoking was good for you: "Smoke in the morning; it's the beginning of a perfect day." State Express, the world's most popular brand of cigarettes, went for six US cents a pack.

In the '20s the first studies on the effects of smoking revealed that it could be harmful. According to the research, the combination of alcohol and cigarette smoke could cause tobacco blindness. No one ever mentioned cancer.

Now the world of authority is emphatically proclaiming that smoking is deadly. It's beginning to take effect. I remember reading Truman Capote's *In Cold Blood.* The two young protagonists, the main characters in the book, had already been condemned to death for their crimes, and the author went to visit them on "death row" in prison. He describes in detail the meeting. During their conversation, Truman offered one of the killers a cigarette.

"No thanks," he said.

"But I thought you smoked," Truman said.

"I did, but I quit. Heard it's bad for your health." Two weeks later he was executed, and probably at the last minute turned down a cigarette. That's what being influenced means.

I wonder if the world is unjustly tough on smokers nowadays. Smokers are losing all their rights. Hotelier Barry Cross, a long-time resident of Bangkok and former GM of the Oriental, told me on one flight he couldn't find a seat where he was allowed to smoke. Not even standing in the hallway. "Didn't I have any rights?" he asked.

Whatever happened to that good cigar, or cigarette, after a fine meal? I still remember when I was growing up, the women got up from the dinner table and left the room while the men lit up. Why is it now the men have to leave, or maybe even go to jail. (In Singapore, with the rigid laws they are passing, that may happen. It's going to be a smokeless society, the government says.)

Maybe the men of yesteryear were different. I have heard tell of one wife who, after dinner one evening, announced to those gathered that she could no longer stand her husband's cigar smoking. Boldly she said to her husband, for all to hear, "You must choose between me or your cigar."

The man calmly took out a cigar, lighted a match, and, holding it for a minute, said, "This is the easiest decision I ever had to make." He then lit his cigar.

Let's not forget, smoking can be an art. The American Indians perfected it. Nor did they abuse smoking by running around puffing smoke all day. They sat down in their tepees, or wherever they sat, and passed the pipe around. How could they possibly have made peace without tobacco? On second thought, they weren't too successful. The white man still got what he wanted.

Sir Walter Raleigh was the first person to take tobacco back to England from America, and Queen Elizabeth threw a bucket of water on him, thinking he was on fire. But he did start a fad that hasn't ended.

As a kid I admired Ernest Hemingway. He never smoked, not that he considered it bad for his health; the reason, he said, was that he wanted to keep his sense of smell acute, so he could better hunt big game. Hemingway was the epitome of health—could drink a few tumblers of brandy and a couple of litres of red wine every day. However, in the end it did him in.

I often wonder how Hemingway's writings would have read had he smoked, especially since he wanted to capture "truth" in his writing. "It was good to kill and kill clean and come back to camp and light up a cigarette and watch the smoke circle in thin shafts to the sky above and know that one day these little sticks will kill you too. But you know you have to fight it, like the matador fights the bull, and then you can beat it—the cancer that is."

A couple of years back I was in New York, walking down Fifth Avenue with a friend, and he complained bitterly about the heavy pollution in the city. He quoted a study that claimed that those who lived and worked in New York smoked the equivalent of two pack of cigarettes a day by breathing the unhealthy city air. He swore that one day he would move out of New York. He complained, but he never considered giving up the two packs of cigarettes he smoked every day.

Smoke shops are rapidly disappearing. They used to be everywhere, and even if you didn't smoke, they were nice to step into. The Oriental Hotel has such a shop right off the main lobby, with a sign on the door THANK YOU FOR SMOKING. Step inside and the fragrant odour of tobacco greets you. In a smaller second room, behind a see-through glass door, there are on display endless wooden boxes, some collectors' items themselves, all with the lids laid back, displaying their contents—every make of cigar one could possibly want. The room has a dehumidifier to control the moisture in the air. The odour that comes from that room when you open the door is sensational.

Not many people, national leaders included, smoke in public any more. It gives them a bad image. Castro gave up cigars a while back, and I heard the cigar industry in Cuba went into a slump. But on the other hand, Winston Churchill created an image with his fat, foot-long stogie and inspired a nation to fight a war. He was the symbol of Britain with his cigar in one hand and the "V" for victory sign in the other.

And there was Rudyard Kipling, the champion of smoking and good cigars. Remember his poem, "The Betrothed" and how he tells his followers how a devoted cigar smoker fell out with his wife.

"Open the old cigar-box, get me a Cuba stout,
For things are running crossways, and Maggie and I are out.
We quarrelled about Havanas—we fought o'er a good cheroot,
And I know she is exacting, and she says I am a brute.
Which is the better portion— bondage bought by ring,
Or a harem of dusky beauties, fifty tied in a string?
A million surplus Maggies are willing to bear the yoke;
And a woman is only a woman, but a good Cigar is a Smoke."

So why don't we let the smokers be! Smoking is a privilege. And I almost forgot. Kipling didn't smoke.

Pornsri Luphaiboon and Ankana stand in the Author's Wing at The Oriental Hotel, beside the former General Manager, and once their boss, Barrie Cross.

Chapter 16
A TALENT FOR HOSPITALITY

We give credit to hotel general managers for making a hotel what is. What we often forget is the office behind the general manager, an office usually run by women—the publication relations department. The Oriental Hotel in Bangkok was voted best hotel of the year by businessmen for ten consecutive years. This is a story about an unsung PR lady at The Oriental Hotel. It appeared on December 28, 1991.

In the cramped, hectic public relations office on the second floor of the Oriental Hotel there stands on a shelf a photograph of Elizabeth Taylor mounted in a heavy silver frame. Engraved across the top of the frame is the name Pornsri Luphaiboon, and below the heart-shaped photograph of the famous movie star are the words, "with best wishes and thanks, Elizabeth Taylor."

And if you look closely, there's a letter attached to the back of the photograph. It's dated January 27, 1990 and is addressed to Pornsri. It reads: "The Oriental Hotel is well known as being the very best hotel in the world. What's not as well known is that people like you make it that way.

"Thank you for taking such wonderful care of us during our recent stay. You were so terrific in assuring that all went smoothly and making our trip such a memorable one. I've always loved your beautiful country, and you managed to make it even more special for me. Best wishes to you."

The letter is signed, Elizabeth Taylor.

On the bookshelf behind the desk, a desk stacked with papers, letters and promotion material, are rows of books by famous authors, with inscriptions inside the covers. James Michener and Gore Vidal, Morris West and William Golding, to name only a few, they all give their "best wishes" and "thanks."

If you want to pry deeper, the desk drawers are filled with cardboard boxes and over-stuffed manila envelopes with more photographs—a young Pornsri standing with John Steinbeck, and another, again a youthful Pornsri, walking along side-by-side with comedian Danny Kaye.

And as the years progress, with an older and wiser Pornsri, you see her standing, dining, greeting, talking with the world's leading political figures, from Israel's Moshe Dayan to Canada's Pierre Trudeau; with royalty from Queen Rambhai Bharni to HRH Prince Charles of England.

And there are endless photographs of her with actors and actresses, authors and journalists, photographers and painters, dancers, singers, composers, and musicians. In fact, anyone who is somebody, or who was, and many thousands who aspire to be, are there on record with Pornsri Luphaiboon.

But there's more than just photographs. There are also stories to go with them.

"William Holden here, this was taken when he was on his way to Tiger Tops in Nepal. He used to come stay every Christmas." She fumbles for a photograph of Gore Vidal and another of Peter Ustinov. "They come and spend Christmas and New Year every year... they are our family."

Then she finds Tennessee Williams. "He always wore a white shirt and white trousers." And so it goes, story after story of the rich and famous. There isn't enough time in a day, or month, to go through all the pictures.

But soon all the memorabilia will be removed from the tiny

office to make room for another public relations woman, whoever that might be.

Someone else will sit in the chair. Pornsri Luphaiboon, after 26 years with the Oriental, is leaving.

"I never thought I would ever be here this long," a smiling Pornsri says as we sit in the Sala Rim Nam across the river from the hotel. From time to time I have to look up from our table and glance over at the Oriental across the river. It was nothing like that when a young and inexperienced 19-year-old girl, fresh out of commercial school, walked into the office to apply for the position of secretary to the manager.

"I went home and told my mother I would never get the job," she says. "Two women also applied. They were older and had experience. I felt so bad."

Her two older brothers worked as receptionists for the hotel, and Pornsri often went there to visit them. She looked around the hotel and dreamed. How wonderful it would be to work here, she thought. Today, though, she has to admit, thirty years ago the Oriental wasn't anything like it is now, and certainly not a world class hotel.

But dreams are what Pornsri is made of, and the job was hers. The year was 1965. The war in Vietnam had started and tourists by the score began to arrive in Thailand. From a sleepy hotel, Pornsri was soon to find herself faced with one of the greatest challenges a young girl could ever have. She was to witness miracles. "We only had a 110 rooms then," she recalled, and we went through a succession of hotel managers, from Robert Sessions to Mr. Ursheler, until Kurt Wachtveitl arrived a few years later in 1968.

Robert Session was the 72-year-old manager who hired Pornsri, and with Mr. Ursheler taking the reins, Pornsri was promoted to Public Relations Manager. Ursheler, she recalls, was promotion minded. He began promoting food and invited the press. The old

Bamboo Bar became the most popular meeting place in Bangkok, and the unofficial Foreign Correspondents' Club. Live entertainment, usually singers from Australia and jazz musicians from America, were part of the menu. Pornsri came to know them all.

This also was about the time when I first met Pornsri, and our meeting, I must say, was most unusual. Pornsri gets embarrassed when I tell it, but maybe she won't mind this time. It happened that she had just been given a new office on the ground floor and was determined to prove that she could do the job as public relations boss. That morning I had signed with the *Bangkok World* to write a weekly column on travel, and was standing, still in my suit and tie (to impress my editor), talking to Pornsri by the poolside.

A European lady with three young children walked past on their way to the railing along the river. Suddenly we heard screaming — "He's drowning, he's drowning."

Pornsri and I rushed up to the lady's side, and from the river we could see bubbles coming to the surface. It was Pornsri's turn to shout. "Save him, save him," she cried. She had to mean me: there was no one else around.

With no choice, I kicked off my shoes, tore off my coat and dove into the river. It was impossible to see, only to feel my way, when finally I felt arms encircle me. Relief, until I felt teeth sink into my neck. I hastily kicked my way to the surface, and found myself looking directly into the face of a very wet gibbon. It was not one of the lady's children that I saved but the hotel's gibbon. They kept two of them, on chains in the garden, and evidently one had got away, still clinging to his chain, but when he reached the branches that hung over the river, the weight was too much and he fell into the river.

Poor, worried Pornsri. The prized hotel gibbon had almost drowned. I passed the beast up to those waiting on the dock, and

I could hear them sighing over the animal—"you poor thing"—as they walked away, leaving me to scramble the best I could up the pilings, which were barnacle encrusted and cut into my legs.

I made my way to Pornsri's new office, where she had gone with my shoes and coat. I looked a mess, and I expected sympathy from her. "Careful," she says, "careful. You're bleeding all over my floor."

That was Pornsri, even then she was concerned about the hotel image. I never did find out if she knew it wasn't the lady's child in the river.

It was also about this time that Pornsri fell in love and married a young and promising civil engineer recently graduated. Eager to further his career, he applied to do his Masters in the U.S., at Fargo, North Dakota, and was accepted. Pornsri wanted to join him but since her husband was a student, she could not get a visa. Pornsri remained behind, with an infant son.

U.S. Senator Goldwater and his wife were vacationing in Thailand and staying at the Oriental. They befriended Pornsri, who went out of her way to make them comfortable, and when the Goldwaters left, they arranged for Pornsri to join her husband, and also to work at the Gardner Hotel in Fargo. Kurt Wachtveitl, who was by then the general manager, assured her she would have her job back when she returned.

Eighteen months later they were back, and after giving birth to her second son, Pornsri returned to the Oriental. And to make her life a little easier, Senator Goldwater had arranged for five years' free diaper service. Pornsri keeps up an active correspondence with the Goldwaters and over the years they have sent many of their friends to visit her at the Oriental.

Big things were happening at the Oriental in these years. In 1972 the hotel merged with ItalThai and in 1977 the company built the now famous River Wing.

But tragedy struck in 1983. The doctors informed Pornsri that her husband had incurable stomach cancer. They couldn't tell how long he had to live, which could be months, or years. Pornsri resigned from the Oriental to be with her husband during his last days. He died five months later.

Pornsri now had four children, three sons and a daughter. Her husband had founded with two partners a successful engineering company, and the partners assured her she would not have to worry about her children's well being nor their education. Her immediate family and her in–laws were supportive. Pornsri went back to the hotel and put all her energy into her work.

"I couldn't have done it without my family's support," she says. "They made it possible."

Pornsri has her little secrets which she doesn't mind sharing now. Although only seldom did her children come to the hotel they were always very much a part of it. They had great pride in their mother's work.

"It's very often difficult meeting all these varied people," Pornsri says, "and to keep up conversations with them, I had to do my homework. This is where my children helped out." She went on to explain that her eldest son, Tanhapol, who is now studying at USC in Los Angeles, thanks to her husband's partners, was keen on sports.

When the boxing promoter Don King was coming to town, he briefed her on all the boxing champs. Her second son, Amate, now studying architecture at Chulalongkorn, is a movie buff. He could tell her what movies Michael J. Fox had starred in and which were Harrison Ford's most noteworthy films. Chaicharn, the youngest and now in his second year of architecture, knew all the singers, and told his mother what she should know about Elton John and Dionne Warwick. Her daughter Dolrudee filled in her mother on all the general gossip that accompanied the new arrivals.

"I was worried when Larry Hagman was coming," she says. "I

had never watched Dallas on TV." What did Pornsri do? She invited all her friends who had watched the programme to her house, and after a couple of hours she knew who Sue Ellen was flirting with and what J.R. was up to.

Those close friends who know Pornsri best will tell you that she is a giver. She is always on the giving side, never the taking side. Her philosophy, developed in part under the leadership of Kurt rules that one should never take advantage of guests. "I never take hotel guests shopping, nor do I make recommendations to them," she explained. "I leave that to someone else. This way, you don't get involved with commissions and things like that."

Pornsri does, however, take an interest in everyone. "Sometimes important people come and they are very lonely, and I become their only contact. They have to know that they can trust me." Friendship with Pornsri becomes everlasting.

Often, tasks must go beyond her normal duties. This happens when a movie company comes to Bangkok. Her credits include working with such productions as *Man with the Golden Gun* and *Deer Hunter.* "It takes a great deal of red tape and long hours to get a movie started," she says. "But somebody has to do it, and I don't mind. Maybe I enjoy doing it because it's a good investment for Thailand. They could very well choose another country." Another one she enjoyed helping with was Hal Bartlet's story of John Everingham and his courageous swim under the Mekong to save his Laotian wife. The late Michael Landon starred in the film.

When I question Pornsri about the overwhelming success of the Oriental, she responds with the standard reply: the generous kindness of the Thais. "Service with the Thais is an art," she says. "As Thais we don't look down on service as you do in the West. When you have that attitude, you put forth your very best."

Two other ingredients, she says, that make a hotel are location and history. The Oriental could not be better located, right on the banks of the Chao Phraya. The scene is forever changing from hour to hour, minute to minute.

And, of course, the Oriental is bathed in history, and that you cannot give to any hotel. "But," she says, "you must let the international writers promote it. If journalists find they are happy with the hotel, the service you provide, then they will say nice things about you."

But what Pornsri doesn't tell you is that she has the talent for making everyone who comes to the hotel feel great, and important.

However, public relations at the Oriental is a joint effort, she insists, not wanting to take all the credit for herself. "We all have to work at it, and it starts from the top, with Mr. Kurt at our morning meetings."

One of the topics at the morning briefings concerns arriving guests. Who is coming? What do they require? Sylvester Stallone is coming. Alert security he will be arriving with half a dozen bodyguards. Barbara Cartland... tell housekeeping to fill her suite with pink pillows and cushions. Detail is important.

As detail is important, so is the personal touch that Pornsri extends to hotel guests. John Steinbeck wanted complete privacy while he wrote in his room. Pornsri assured him he would get it. She personally screened all his calls, whenever they came, day or night.

When a guest wants his arrival to be incognito, Pornsri meets him at the airport, sometimes in the wee hours of the morning. Harrison Ford and his wife were arriving at 3 a.m. Pornsri met them with flowers and arranged to have a Thai dancer waiting in the lobby until they arrived. Mrs. Ford was thrilled. "What better welcome could we have?" she said.

Pornsri, after 26 years at The Oriental, feels that it's time to make a change, to move to something new, and, she said, to broaden her outlook. "I'm not looking for a challenge. The Oriental was a challenge every day."

Pornsri Luphailboon leaves her mark at the Oriental. For me, and for so many others, it will never be quite the same without her.

Frederico Alcuaz grimaces behind bars, not in jail but behind his crutches.

Chapter 17
THE INGENUOUS CREATIONS OF FREDERICO ALCUAZ

Writers, musicians, singers, artists, they all make interesting story material, for they are the ones who keep us in some way or another entertained. One man who has done this far above all others is the subject of this article which appeared June 18, 1992.

Filipino artist Frederico Alcuaz doesn't like to waste time, not even a minute. At eight sharp every morning he is at work in his studio, even if he had been up late the night before. He takes an hour for lunch, sometimes two, and goes back to work in the afternoons and stays until at least 6 pm, and often longer. That's his schedule, a full seven days a week, holidays included.

But that's not all. Even during the evenings, when he's entertaining friends, he's still working.

Alcuaz enjoys the company of others and reserves his evenings to be with them. At 10:00 p.m. he catches a taxi to the President Hotel in Makiti and takes his usual seat in the lobby. It's his nightly meeting place.

But then, when he is relaxing, he isn't idle, not Frederico Alcuaz. Anyone who sees him there might think he has a nervous habit, or that he can't simply keep still. He fidgets with small pieces of paper which he takes from his shirt pocket and rolls into small sticks, almost as thin as match sticks. While he keeps the conversation going, sometimes without even looking to see what he is doing, he bends the paper sticks into shapes resembling miniature boomerangs. He seemingly does it with no conscious effort. If you ask him what he is doing, he might tell you that he's making "paper wads" to sting waiters who are inattentive.

But the imaginative artist is not doodling. When he finishes half dozen pieces, he drops them carefully into his coat pockets and takes them back to his studio. The next morning he lays them out on a board, like a draftsman lays out his tools on a drafting table. There may be a hundred or more. The night before, while no one suspected it, he saw a pattern taking shape. Now he works on it, moving this piece here, that one there. The colours begin to blend; a form takes shape. It's a bird, he says to himself. It's a bird that's free. That's what I'll called it—"Bird of Freedom." He begins pasting the sticks into position. He'll need another thousand, maybe two thousand pieces.

Bird of Freedom could be an abstract painting, except it's not a painting. It's a mosaic. It is, what its creator calls, an Alcuasaic.

Artists have been known to apply different medium to create a given effect. There are those who paint on leaves and some who stand high on ladders and dump paint onto their canvases below. Others have pasted soup can labels on boards while still others have been known to coat the naked bodies of their models with paint and have them roll over on their canvases.

Most of the methods are simply gimmicks to attract attention.

But Frederico Alcuaz needs no such gimmicks to attract attention. The 52-year-old artist has been in the limelight most of his adult life, for he is, unquestionably, the Philippine's best known artist, the "El Gran Pintor Filipino" they call him. He has gathered some 13 awards—five from Manila, three from Spain and four from the French, who also gave him the 1962 Genius Award in Paris. He has had more than 50 one-man shows. His paintings hang in galleries around the world and he is noted not only for his oils but equally as well for his deftness in figurative expression, his sculptures, his abstracts, and his foray into tapestry making. And soon it will be for his Alcuasaic.

So what is an Alcuasaic?

In the true sense of the word they are mosaics, mosaics which are alive and vibrant. They are mosaics with movement, like fire burning out of control. Alcuaz achieves the effect with the use of colours, patterns of colours which he finds in pieces of printed paper. When rolled and placed sided by side, a painstaking task, they create a unique art form that is wholly different.

"No one has ever attempted this before," Alcuaz said when he showed me his collection in his 18th–floor studio in the Manila Pavilion Hotel. The studio is one of two he maintains in Manila. He has another in Barcelona where he goes to paint a few months every year. Until recently he had still another studio in Manila, on the top floor of the famous Manila Hotel. When he gave it up (the old Manila was becoming the headquarters of too many coups, he said) it was so crammed full with oil paintings, including several wall-size murals, it took a crane to lower them from his window to the ground floor.

But it's now the Manila Pavilion where he spends most of his working hours. When I visited him there a few months ago, he had created 104 Alcuasaics. And no two were the same. Each and every one was different. And they seem to change form as you move about the room. They are very much alive, in colours that glow.

It takes infinite patience to create one mosaic. Alcuaz came upon the idea five years ago when he was seated in the hotel lobby and did actually make several wads of paper to shoot at the waitresses. But when he laid the wads on the table in front him, he was bemused by the colour scheme that they created. He slipped the wads into his pocket.

Back in his studio the next morning he studied the wads again. Indeed, he knew then he was on to something. He reached for an old magazine on a shelf and began tearing out pages. The ads he found the most colourful. He cut the pages into small squares. When he rolled them and bent them in two, he saw strange and fascinating colour patterns begin to form. It was almost like a revelation. With a bit of practice he was able to create a new art form.

Does he intend to have an art exhibition, to sell his Alcuataics? For the moment they are not or sale. Alcuaz is creating them because the urge is there. What happens later is another thing. This, certainly, is the meaning of a true artist.

Chapter 18
A YOUNG GIRL'S ORDEAL ON THE CROSS

As a journalist I try not to analyse but only to report life as I find it in Asia. I don't wish to tell readers why things happen the way they do, only that they do happen. I form no conlusions about the young girl on the cross. Her tale appeared as I witnessed it on April 7, 1985.

It's not always easy to come to terms with Asia. Social structure is often far more complicated than most foreigners will ever understand. I realised this when I met a young Filipina. "I come from a poor family and I am doing it for them."

Eighteen-year old Precila Almario from the Philippines was going to let herself be crucified for her family, and she and her father invited me to witness the drama.

Ever since I saw my first photographs of flagellations and crucifixions in the Philippines, I wanted to go to Manila during Holy Week and see if they were real, or if they were fake. How could anyone survive being nailed to a cross? Last year I finally went, and it was only after I arrived in Manila that I learned that a young girl was going to go through the ordeal. It's not unusual for men to be nailed to a cross, but for a young girl, it was unheard of. Why was she doing it? What was her motive? Could she be a religious fanatic? I wanted to meet her.

A hired a taxi for the day and the driver drove me to her village. It took two hours to get there, and another hour to find her

Eighteen-year-old Precila Almario is crucified, by being nailed to a cross, in the Philippines.

house, located in a slum area with unmarked streets. When we knocked at the door of one of the shacks, a young girl appeared, and when she said she was Precila, I was taken back by her youth. She couldn't have been more than 13 or 14. She later assured me she was 18.

Although shy and a bit nervous, she seemed fairly composed for a person who was going to be crucified in two days. Her father, an out-of-work labourer, appeared at her side. He picked up the conversation. His daughter, he insisted, was not a crazy masochist. By letting herself be crucified, she could find fulfillment by making a *panata,* a sacred vow. The *panata* in this case was not for past sins or wrong-doings on her part but for a promise of something better in the future.

The crucifixion was to take place in an open field at Bulacan, some 48 kilometres from Manila. Precila was not only going to be crucified but she also had to carry her heavy cross through the streets while thousands of spectators watched. When Precila's family asked if I would like to come to the chapel with them on Good Friday morning, I confirmed that I would be there.

I was still in doubt. I had been living in Asia most of my adult life, and I have been witness to other strange and bizarre religious gatherings in Asia over the years, but now I was uncertain what course this one might take. Only a week before I arrived in Manila I had attended a Hindu gathering at Batu Caves north of Kuala Lumpur. It was the noted Thaipusan festival. Hindu devotees there submit themselves to incredible self–torture by driving long spikes through their flesh and carrying *kadavi,* a large fan-shaped religious altar of sorts, above their heads supported by skewers. I watched half–crazed Hindu fanatics carry their heavy burdens up 276 steps to deep caves above where priests removed the *kadavis* and withdrew the spikes and skewers—and there was no blood and no wounds to show. Their secret, I concluded, was self-hypnosis, a trance they put themselves into.

Also in Malaysia, I met *bomohs,* witch doctors, and I was present when a rain-stopper was called to a football match—and it didn't rain. In the Philippines, I witnessed faith-healers in Dumaguete, and left still not convinced. Now I was going to witness crucifixions, people who were going to let themselves be crucified and hung on crosses. As I stood there talking to Precila, this young innocent girl, I was still finding it hard to believe. Were she and other Filipino Christians, like the Hindus at Thaipusan in Malaysia, putting themselves into some kind of a trance?

In a sense, the Philippine nation as a whole puts itself in a trance during Holy Week. Each and every Filipino is deeply embedded in his own interpretation of Christianity mixed with pagan beliefs. On Good Friday every town and barrio in this country numbering some 7,152 islands plunges into their own meditations on death.

For example, the *cenaculo,* the Philippine version of the European passion play, is acted out in every plaza. Christ's seven last words are mumbled on everyone's lips. Flagellants who wear white cotton hoods to mask their identity, over which are placed crowns of thorns, take to the streets and lash their back with glass-spiked leather thongs.

All along the streets in the provinces from Cavite in the south to Pampaga in the north, both young and old alike stumble along carrying heavy wooden crosses in emulation of Christ's march to Calvary. But in the village of Bulacan real crucifixions take place.

I arrived in Bulacan in the early morning of Good Friday. The heat of day had already begun. People by the masses were arriving in taxis, buses, jeepneys and private cars. At the edge of the field, where the crucifixions were to take place, police had road barriers set up and here everybody disembarked.

In the distance, across open rice fields now turned brown stood a church with two high bell towers, and nearby was a man-made hill with a wooden platform on top. Here was their Calvary.

After half an hour of walking across the field, I reached the site. Stone steps led to the top of the hill. A kilometre away stood the church; I had to push through the crowds to reach it. Suddenly the crowd parted: a troop of Roman soldiers, wearing togas, and waving spears and sabres, appeared. Behind them came a young man, bearded, a crown of thorns on his head. He carried a cross. He would be the first to be crucified.

I finally made it to the church, just as Precila and her family were coming out. They were pleased to see me. Precila was now ready for her march to Calvary. I felt a sudden pang of pity for her. She looked tired and worn.

She wore a brown, loose fitting sack-like skirt and a white blouse. She was barefooted. As she stepped into the churchyard, two soldiers stepped up and seized her by the arms. A look of bewilderment and fear came to her eyes. Her mother began wailing; her father stepped aside. They stood in a kind of disbelief that this was happening to their daughter. It was now beyond their control.

The soldiers placed a crown of thorns on her head: blood trickled down her forehead. The soldiers lifted the cross on her shoulder. The weight almost toppled her over. She began struggling forward. The crowd stepped aside to let her pass.

It was agony, every step she made. She slipped once, twice. Her knees were bleeding. Blood ran down her shins and dried in the dust she kicked up with her bare feet as she struggled along. She perspired profusely. Her blouse was wrung with sweat and dust. Her mother, who had been following in her footsteps, turned away and slumped on the wayside. Her father remained behind with her.

I pushed ahead of Precila and was lucky to find room to stand on top the platform. A woman martyr, an old lady in her late 60s, was already there. The lines on her face were drawn tight. She had lowered her cross to the floor and now faced the crowd. She had a look of terror in her eyes.

A soldier held two huge nails in one hand stepped forth; in the other hand he clutched a heavy hammer.

That poor old lady, she looked at the solder, then the nails. She hunched her shoulders, slouched back and withdrew. The crowd gave a cheer, and two soldiers led her back down the stone steps. Precila was next. Would she too change her mind? I could see her below coming through the dust.

She approached the steps. The cross was too heavy for her to carry up the steps. Soldiers nudged her, helping her lift the heavy burden. Once she reached the top, like the old lady before her, she lowered the cross to the floor. I worked to a position directly behind her. A sea of bewildered faces looked up and stared at us. It was awesome.

I could feel her agony now. She stretched out her arms, as though she was pleading, asking forgiveness from all those gathered before her. Thick dust was gathered on her arms and legs. She began to tremble slightly.

The soldier, her executioner, stepped forth with nails and hammer in his hands. He stood before her, saying nothing, waiting. She slowly lowered her eyes. She accepted the crucifixion.

The soldier turned to the crowd. Like a magician who shows his audience that his tools of trade are real, he held up the nails and hammer for all to see. Two other soldiers then tied Precila to the cross, a band around her waist and two others around her forearms. With the trembling girl securely tied, the cross was then lifted into place.

Precila's moment of truth had arrived.

She turned her head slightly. The expression on her face did not change. The soldier placed the point of a nail against the palm of her right hand—she lifted her eyes to the sky—and with one blow of the hammer he drove the nail into her open hand. Three times the hammer struck, driving the nail deeper into the wood with each blow. He then nailed her left hand to the cross. Blood ran down her arms and dropped to the rocks at the base of the cross. She remained there, for all to see, for twenty minutes.

I watched when Precila was lowered from the cross and the nails removed. The pain while pulling out the nails was more agonizing than when they were driven in. She passed out and was carried from the platform through the crowd to the church. I followed her and then lost her, and later found her again kneeling in church. Her hands were cupped together swathed in white bandages. Her smiling happy family stood at the back of the church and greeted friends. They shook my hand when I arrived. They posed for pictures with Precila in front of the church. She had her reward— the two nails used in the crucifixion.

Twenty-five martyrs were crucified in Bulacan that Good Friday. One crucifixion took place outside of Bulacan, at the maximum security compound of the National Prison, when convict Gerardo Cecubag, who was awaiting the death penalty, was crucified.

I watched Precila and her family disappear down a dusty lane as I walked back across the empty field to where my taxi waited. I looked back and Calvary hill was deathly still. The crucifixions were over.

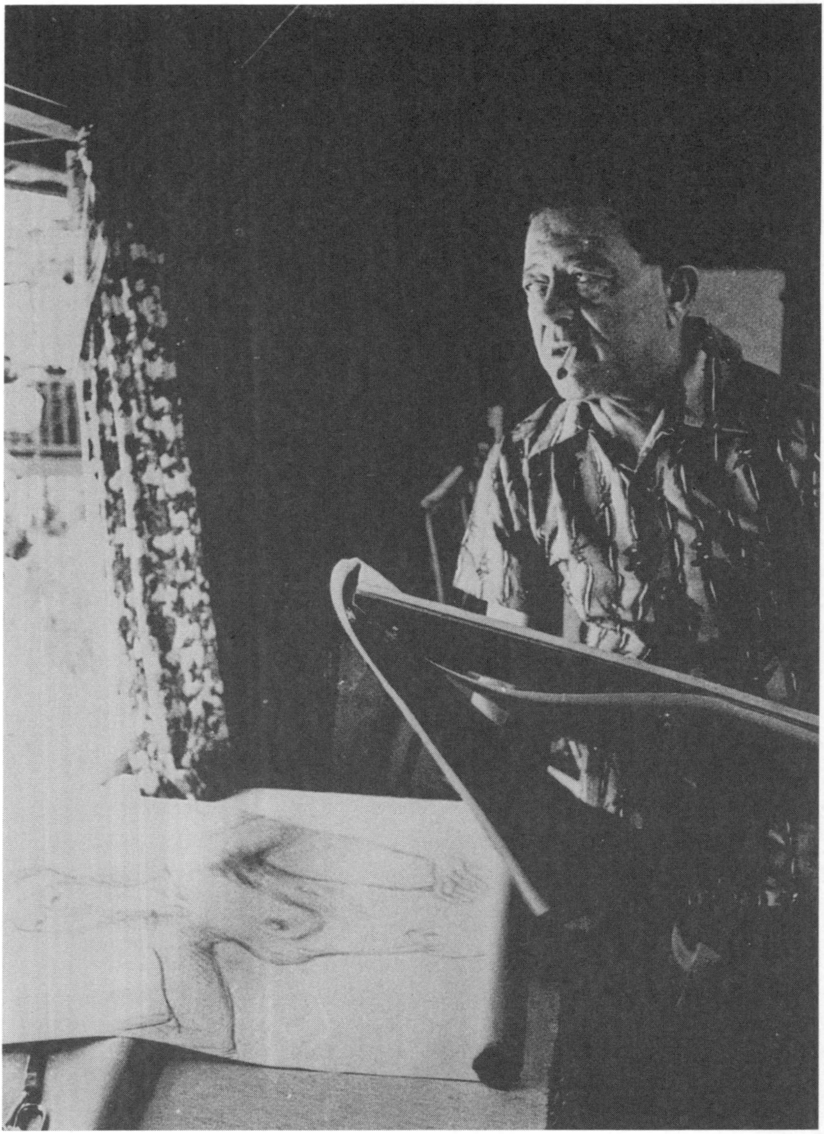

Theo Meier, who had spent 22 years living on Bali, stands at his easel in his studio in Chiang Mai, where he spent the last years of his life. His paintings today are listed with Christie's in London.

Chapter 19
THE LEGEND OF THEO MEIER

When I first began writing my travel column in 1966, I heard about a Swiss artist, Theo Meier, living in Chieng Mai in north Thailand. I went to visit him and soon we developed a close friendship. I wrote dozens of newspaper and magazine articles about him, and included his life story in a chapter of my book Asian Portraits. *After a dozen years of research and interviews, I managed to complete his biography,* Painted in the Tropics. *Theo was one of the most remarkable men I have ever met, and truly the last of his kind. He was never moved by money or riches, and his life was a struggle even though he was well known. Today his paintings are listed with Christie's in London and command top prices. I wrote the following article about Theo a year after his death. It appeared on July 1, 1984.*

Theo Meier was 23 years old when he left Switzerland and in the footsteps of Paul Gauguin went to Tahiti to paint. After two years in Tahiti and the Marquesas islands, he returned to Switzerland with a bundle of paintings. He had a successful one-man show, sold all his canvases and set out for Tahiti once again.

This time Theo travelled by ship via the Suez to the East and intended to travel eastward across the Pacific to reach Polynesia. When he arrived in Singapore he altered his schedule to enable him to visit the Dutch East Indies, specifically an island called Bali which everyone was claiming to be so beautiful. He reached

Bali on a tramp steamer, allowed himself two weeks and stayed 22 years. Bali was the Marquesas and more. Bali was Theo Meier's advantage over Gauguin.

But why Bali? What made Bali so special? Was the Bali Theo Meier came to know 50 years ago so much different than the Bali we find today?

Theo's photographs taken at that time tell the story. I was deeply moved by these remarkable black-and-white prints when Theo first showed them to me years ago in Chieng Mai.

I had gone up to Chieng Mai to meet Theo. He had moved there from Bali a few years before and was living with his young Thai wife, La-iad, in a small Thai house near Wat Dorn. It was only later, after he sold a few paintings, that he built from a collection of old Thai farm houses his grand house on the Ping River.

From our first introduction we found we had something in common. I too had spent a number of years in Tahiti and the Marquesas. Although Theo had been there some years before me, there were places and still a few people left whom we both knew.

"No, don't tell me they are still there," Theo would say when I mentioned people like McCullens from Moorea and Bob McKitteridge from Nuka Hiva. He would then pull out his photographs.

He kept the photos in his studio, stuffed in envelopes and in cardboard boxes tucked away in drawers and on shelves in closets. Sometimes when we were on the verandah having a Mekong and soda, he'd remember a name or a face from the past, and without another word he'd rush to the studio with me in close pursuit and would start pulling down boxes and dumping the contents on the floor. When he found what he wanted, he'd hold it high. "See, I told you," he'd shout. "This is the captain on the trading boat." Then he'd go into a long spiel about a trading boat captain who carried him back from the Marquesas to Tahiti.

The photographs weren't the snap-shot type people generally keep, the slightly out-of-focus family album prints of birthday parties and Christmas gatherings, and of weddings and pets. Theo's photos were taken by him, an artist with an eye on composition. Many were scenic shots of Tahiti; they captured the island as it appeared half a century ago. Others were portraits of people, people most likely long since dead. There's Theo on a horse riding along a beach, and another of him with his easel on his back climbing in the hills. They all tell of Theo's extraordinary story of a reckless, happy youth in the islands, of wild and savage dancing and drums in the night, of cane chairs pulled out on verandahs and Theo's working on a painting in the cool shade, of shining mountain pools and tumbling waterfalls and beautiful women.

And there were his photographs of Bali. Seeing them one can easily understand why Theo settled on Bali rather than return to the South Seas.

"Bali did not have the loneliness of the South Seas," Theo explained in his studio as we studied the photos. "And the Balinese are not ones to idle away their time like the Polynesians. They are active. They will do things. And the women," he sighed, waving his arms, "it was frustrating in Polynesia. You could not get a girl to pose in the nude. She would not even take her sarong off. The Balinese were only too willing to undress. Painting in Bali was natural. The painter is understood."

Theo's photographs, like his paintings, reveal the natural beauty of Bali, as it was then, and as it remains very much today. Bali rises like a myth out of a blue, blue sea. Her smoking cone-shaped volcanoes give the island an air of mystery. Her hills and valleys are perpetually carpeted in velvet green, her forests are deep and dark, her land is always bathed in bright sunlight, important for an artist working in oils.

And there was the man-made beauty that Theo captured. "I could not imagine anything so beautiful," he recalled 50 years later. "Trimmed hills and terraced rice fields give the island a manicured look, as if by design they were planted there for their beauty alone." Theo marvelled at the island's 10,000 temples, on deserted hill tops, on beaches, among tangled roots of banyan trees, among barren rocks along the coast, in market squares, in rice fields, in cemeteries. He found some hidden from sight in thick forests, while others with as many as 11 superimposed pagoda-like roofs could be seen from one hillside to the next.

But what fascinated Theo mostly about Bali was the people. Theo's paintings and photographs reflect their moods, their inner souls, their lifestyles, both in work and at play. Much like the Polynesians, Theo found that the Balinese lived in primitive simplicity, in thatched huts close to the soil. They went half nude and bathed naked in streams and rivers. They were children of nature. But here the difference stopped. Unlike the Polynesians, these same simple people of Bali had highly refined tastes. Come nightfall they gathered in elaborately carved stone buildings to worship their gods. They clad their bodies in garments of magnificent designs and colours, spun of fine silks and laced in gold. Their music and dances were highly developed and showed great technical skill. They were serious people steeped in a mystic religion, and unlike the unfortunate Marquesians who had lost their culture a century ago, the Balinese could not be swayed by seaman's tales or tempted by nails pulled from yard-arms to make fishhooks. Theo had found his island paradise and his subject matter—the island of Bali and the Balinese.

Theo began painting the moment he arrived on Bali, fast and furiously, without regard where and how he would live, as though it was all a mirage, or a dream, and if he didn't hurry he would awake and it would all be gone. And when he wasn't painting, he was taking pictures. Most of Theo's paintings, except those his wife still manages to keep, have long since been sold; they hang in galleries and museums and in private collections around the world. I guess that's the tragedy of being an artist, you put your heart and soul into your work and then sell it in order to live, to survive, and most likely never see your work again. Theo often lamented on this. I think he could remember every canvas he ever painted.

Bali certainly has changed since Theo's time. During the years that he lived in Chieng Mai he often returned to the island, but he was never saddened with what he saw. Theo never let the changes affect him. He didn't stopped at Kuta or Sanur, today's tourist hangouts; instead he went directly to East Bali where he lived for so many years and continued to maintain a house. No, Theo Meier never stopped loving Bali in spite of the changes.

Any time that I found the need to get away for a while, I took the night train and travelled up to Chieng Mai to spend some time with Theo. I spent some happy hours in his house, dining on great meals that he enjoyed preparing, and listening to his tales, about walking across China with an easel on his back and living among the savages of the New Hebrides, painting Chinese warlords and busy-haired cannibals. But all that is gone, forever. Theo died a painful death two years ago in a hospital in Switzerland.

No person was more shaken by Theo's death than Prince Sanidh Rangsit. Prince Sanidh knew Theo on Bali and it was Prince Sanidh who invited Theo to come to Thailand to live. "Something went out of my life when Theo died," Prince Sanidh said when I saw him. In truth, something went out of all of our lives.

Recently I returned to visit Theo's wife La-iad at their house in Chieng Mai, to begin research on a book I intend to write about this extraordinary man. La-iad greeted me and led me to Theo's studio. She took down his letters and private papers and photographs. As I picked up each photograph and studied it carefully, I could hear Theo's voice, talking excitedly about the picture, recalling the very day, the very instant in time he snapped the shutter, half a century before. It was like he never left. But then maybe he hasn't, for his legacy will always be with us—his paintings and his photographs.

Climbing Mount Kinabalu, Southeast Asia's highest mountain.

Chapter 20
CLIMBING SOUTHEAST ASIA'S HIGHEST MOUNTAIN

I saw Mount Kinabalu when I first came to Asia, and I wanted to climb it then. Thirty years passed before I was able to realise that dream. My story about my assault on Southeast Asia's highest mountain appeared in the Post *on August 17, 1992.*

One of the great adventures in Southeast Asia, and a very rewarding one at that, is to climb Mount Kinabalu, the highest mountain in this part of the world. It is, without doubt, the most popular trek in the whole region. Rangers in Sabah's Kinabalu Park report that some 20,000 people walk up to Low's Peak, the highest point along this route, every year.

All types of trekkers —from young children to geriatrics—have followed the trail up the top of the mountain. No particular skill or experience is required; the route is suitable for anyone who is reasonably fit. But there are warnings as not everyone, even those who think they are fit, can adjust to the high altitude.

The air on the summit is only two-thirds the density of air at sea level, and you can quickly become breathless. Still, you won't know unless you try.

To climb Mount Kinabalu was a thing I wanted to do since I first heard the name. But there was always some obstacle. For one thing, tourist brochures said you couldn't simply go to Sabah and begin climbing but had to put in your name weeks and perhaps months in advance. (Which is not true.)

I was fortunate. I wrote to the Malaysian Tourist office and asked if they could assist with an itinerary. Wan Zawawi Mohammed, the director, went ahead and booked me for the climb. There was no turning back now; the staff at TDC in Kota Kinabalu was awaiting us.

The only essential equipment that I needed, the tourist office in Kota Kinabalu informed me, was a good pair of walking shoes or boots and a raincoat, plus some warm clothes as the temperature at mountain huts can fall to two degrees Celsius at night.

Two others were joining me: Joe Shaffer from Philadelphia, an avid mountain climber who has done most of the toughest peaks in America and some in the Himalayas, and photographer Don Bianco. Don had not climbed before but he keeps a home in the mountainous redwood country of northern California and is one of those people who is in great shape and doesn't know it.

In spite of 20,000 people making the climb each year, you can't help wondering if you can do it yourself. The trek to the summit and back takes two days from Park Headquarters, with the trail starting at the Power Station at 1,830 metres and rising all the way for about eight kilometres to the summit at 4,101 metres. That's like taking the tallest building in Bangkok and walking up to the top some 350 times in two days.

Furthermore there's the weather. It can get cold, and when you live in the tropics a 10-degree drop in temperature can be torture. To make matters worse, I met a lady in Bangkok who informed me that her son, a young boy who was fit and on the swimming team, had to abandon his attempt because of altitude sickness.

All this went through my mind when I was tucked into my comfortable bed at Park Headquarters, waiting to begin the assault next morning.

Mount Kinabalu is an impressive-looking mountain. You can't take your eyes from it when you drive through the countryside. Lacking foothills, it appears to shoot straight up into the sky, its jagged granite peaks like a broken bottle, floating above the clouds.

The mountain summit is the prominent landmark for seafarers approaching northern Borneo by sea. The first written account of the mountain was the impression it made on a British naval officer, Captain Dalrymple, when he saw its outline in the distance in 1769: "Though perhaps not the highest mountain in the world, it is of immense height."

There is no evidence that Kinabalu had been climbed in the distant past. Up to about 3,000 years ago much of northern Borneo was still in the ice age and the summit was barricaded by glaciers. This would have prevented anyone not equipped with proper boots and crampons from reaching the peak which, according to geologists, was jutting above the ice cap.

In more recent times, local people were deterred by taboos. Kinabalu was believed to be inhabited by the spirits of the dead.

The first recorded ascent of Kinabalu was made in 1851 by Hugh Low, a British colonial officer in Labuan. Borneo was all dense jungle then and there were no roads or tracks from the coast to the base of the mountain. Low had to walk from village to village taking on fresh guides and porters for each stage. Local chiefs made outrageous demands and it was necessary that Low and his party went armed.

It took Low 15 days to reach the base of Kinabalu. Local guides then took him and his party of more than 40 porters up to the highest known point on the mountain, Paka Cave, a big overhanging rock at 3,200 metres.

After a day's rest, Low pushed on, arriving at the bare rock face near today's Sayat-Sayat huts, above which soar the jagged rock peaks. Presumably thinking the peaks formed the mountain top, Low climbed up a gap only to find there was a higher peak beyond.

Rising clouds and bad weather forced Low to turn back to Paka Cave. It took him another two further attempts before he finally reached the summit.

Times have changed, which is fortunate for Kinabalu climbers. You don't need 15 days to reach the base and another week to make the summit, and the route up the mountain is nothing like it was in Low's time. Now it's a kind of celestial highway, with steps carved out of stone and fortified with planks, and in many places hand rails. This description may make it all sound a little too easy but believe me it isn't. When you begin climbing, you need all the help you can get.

After a night at Park Headquarters we began. The trail is marked with signboards every 100-metre interval, with notices telling climbers YOUR ARE HERE. In addition to the signboards there are six shelters along the route to Panar Laban, and a hut at Carson's Camp halfway up the mountain.

The trail starts in an oak forest. After a few minutes it drops down to a small waterfall, where we filled our bottles. This was the only dip in the entire trail; from there on it was uphill all the way.

It was still early morning and mist hung in the valleys below. Tress were dressed in ferns and on the sides of the trail appeared pale pink flowers, the Kinabalu Balsam. Along the way we also saw a number of the famous pitcher plants, those red and green bowl-shaped plants that capture insects and devour them. Further up, flowering rhododendrons grew in great masses and hung in loose folds from the branches of trees. Small ferns and tiny orchids also grew on many trees.

In half an hour of steady climbing we reached the first shelter, Pondok Kandis, at 1,981 metres, and already we were panting. In another half-hour we made it to the second shelter, Pondok Ubah, at 2,095 metres.

At Pondok Lowii, the third shelter, muscles were beginning to ache. Markers told us we were at 2,286 metres, only slightly more than half way. The trail above the shelter now steepens. Thick mist began to blow in, with an occasional light drizzle and nil visibility.

Finally we reached Carson's Camp at 2,621 metres and broke for lunch. It took every effort for me to begin again, but once on the trail the beauty of the climb made me forget protesting muscles. There were more pitcher plants, but now of a rare variety found only on Kinabalu.

From Carson's Camp we had two more shelters to go, Pondok Villosa, at 2,942 metres and Pondok Paka, at 3,052 metres. Each step was agony. At Pondok Paka there is a turn-off that leads down to Paka Cave, a large overhanging rock on the bank of a quick-flowing stream. The cave is the furthest point down the mountain that the glaciers reached. This was the normal camping spot in the old days, before the huts were built.

After we passed the last shelter, the vegetation quickly thinned. It took another hour to reach Panar Laban where we spent the night at the modern Laban Rata Resthouse. Panar Laban marks the edge of the tree line at 3,300 metres.

The view here at sunset was breathtaking. A massive layer of clouds were below us and the red glow of the setting sun gave the appearance that the world beyond was afire. But our thoughts were not on the rest of the world; we could only think of what was above. We were aware that the trekking part was mostly over and now the climbing would begin. In the half-light we could not see the rock face above us, but we knew well that not far above we would have to rely on ropes to reach the summit.

It was indeed a restless night, at a time when rest was so important. Our thoughts were on the mountain. Maybe the natives are right when they believe Kinabalu is inhabited by the spirits.

The wake-up call at 2:30 a.m. comes all too quickly. We were told it was necessary that we begin at that early hour if we wanted to reach the summit for sunrise.

Later, after the climb, I was convinced there might well be another reason. If climbers were to see out when it was light, they might change their minds once they saw the threatening rock face above them. I'm afraid few people would venture beyond the resthouse.

But when we fell in line, one after the other, it was dark and all each of us could see was the light of the torch before us. Each climber has a light and follows close in the heels of the person before him. The climb is almost sheer now and each step is exhausting. We have to stop every ten paces to catch our wind. Even breathing is difficult. Don went on ahead with his guide, to be certain to have his cameras set up on the summit for sunrise. Joe and I tagged behind.

The guides say it takes only three hours to reach the summit from the rest house, which may well be if one has Sherpa blood. It took Joe and me the better part of an hour just to reach Syat Syat hut at 3,800 metres. The hut marked the end of the vegetation, and from here on it was bare rock.

Above and behind the hut the rock face rises almost straight up into jagged pinnacles. The route heads west, running parallel to the pinnacles. Climbers now have the aid of rope line to help them along. Suddenly I look up and there above is the South Peak—the first big peak we must scale. We must not linger for dawn is rapidly approaching.

South Peak is at the lower, southern edge of the summit plateau. As we came up to the plateau, the face of the mountain turned to smooth worn rock, almost as slick as glass. We could see the chatter marks made deep in the granite millions of years ago by the glacier flow. It was like a forlorn African desert without sand.

Joe and I feared the sun would break before we reached the summit. Already its rays were beginning to creep up over the distant clouds below us. It was a 500–metre walk across the plateau marked with cairns of sorts. At last Low's Peak came into view. I remembered now our guide telling us how two climbers got lost on this section and were never seen again, despite a team of professional mountaineers from America who spent several weeks looking for them. Their bodies are still there, somewhere.

Each step was now an effort; our lungs ached and we could only drag our feet. Don and his guide were nowhere in sight. Finally, almost in desperation, we reached the last pinnacle, Low's Peak, and there, another 100 metres higher, were Don and his guide, sitting on the very summit. The sun broke on the horizon.

A short scramble and Joe and I were at Don's side on Low's Peak; we'd made it to the top of Southeast Asia's highest mountain.

What everyone told us was true: the view from the summit at dawn is spectacular. Our guides pointed out the sights and named the ranges. Ahead of us was the Trusmadi Range, and to the west the coastline and the South China Sea. North of us loomed two magnificent peaks—St. Andrew's Peak and Victoria Peak. To east of where we stood, the summit plunges almost vertically into Low's Gully.

Our guides informed us that we had to leave the summit before 10:30 a.m. Any later and we would be trapped by clouds as they raced up the mountain and immersed the summit by early afternoon.

We signed the log book kept in a nook in the rocks and began our descent. By evening we were back at Park Headquarters, so weary we had a difficult time getting up from the dinner table once we sat down. But we made it. We had reached the summit of Southeast Asia's highest mountain!

Stephens sits in the Author's Wing at The Oriental with his solar topee on his lap.

Chapter 21
THE CASE OF THE MISSING SOLAR TOPEE

One of my favorite cities in Southeast Asia is Kuala Lumpur, the capital of Malaysia. It's an Arabian nights city with its dazzling Moorish architecture and onion dome mosques. Sit in the Selangor Club facing the Padang and you are transported back to the days of the British Raj. Some of the old charm still lingers on, especially in places like the Coliseum Cafe. My article about that delightful place appeared on December 28, 1992.

The Coliseum Cafe and Hotel on Batu Road in Kuala Lumpur might not sound like an old English pub from the bygone days of the British Raj, but it definitely is. If you happen to go into the place and can find a seat at the bar, there's certain to be an old timer there who will bend your ear. They like to brag that the place hasn't changed in over 50 years, and then sooner or later they will tell you about the low-down thief who stole a solar topee from the hat rack in the corner. For those who may not know the East, a solar topee is a pith helmet and at one time everyone wore them outdoors. In fact, it's said the British military would court marshal any soldier who went out into the sun without his solar topee on.

About the Coliseum not changing, the old timers are right. Enter the swinging doors any afternoon of the week and you will find sitting at the bar old rubber planters, tin miners, and a retired government district officer or two. And most likely you'll find one of the more prominent local figures there too: Humphrey Brooke, Third Cousin Removed from the last White Raja of Sarawak, whatever that means. Like the others, he finds the place an escape from the noise and humdrum of the fast growing city outside the doors. For a few hours every afternoon he sits and drinks here with his cronies.

Around the bar are stools and a brass foot rail. Above the bar on the second level are a half dozen hotel rooms, the kind you see in the Old West, with keys hanging on wooden pegs and next to them an old fashioned "in and out" board that tells if guests are in their rooms or not. The rooms have ceiling fans and shanghai jars in the bathrooms.

The bar is filled with nostalgia, and as it has always been, it is one of the last gathering places in town for those who served in the Colonial Service. Unlike the Selangor Club which is closed to non-members, the Coliseum is open to everyone.

Conversation is much the same as I imagine it was when the British were here: problems with servants, rising prices and the influx of tourists. You hear stories how planters came in from up-country during the Emergency and hung their rifles and handguns on the hat rack in the corner. Sometimes their drinking and carousing lasted all night.

One late night after the place had emptied out, the bartenders were cleaning up when they noticed that a customer, a planter no doubt, had left his solar topee hanging on the rack. They looked it over. It had no name or identification. Never mind. The owner was certain to be back that night, or the next, or maybe in a few weeks when he returned from up-country.

The days came and went. A few weeks passed by, then months, and still no one came to claim the helmet. The months passed into a year and there were no takers. Now the old solar topee hanging on the hat rack in the corner became the topic of discussion, and an object of veneration. Customers saluted it when they came in, but no one dared touch it. It became dust-covered and faded with time, which only added to its mystique.

Twenty years passed, and a thousand guesses were made about its owner. He died in an accident. His wife found out he had a mistress and he couldn't go out again with the boys. He was called into battle, never to return. He skipped out on his bar bill. He stole the topee himself. And so it went, but the truth never became known.

Then, as mysteriously as it appeared, it disappeared. No one saw it being removed. The bar opened one morning and it was gone when the bar closed. The old timers flew up in arms, even offered a reward. They call it "the case of the missing solar topee" and some still mourn its passing.

Incidentally, to the right of the bar is the restaurant, with a high panelled ceiling and elderly Chinese waiters with frayed white coats, who have been around for half a century. The menu is one you hardly see outside of England: ox liver and bacon. English pudding and Irish coffee. It's just the fare you'd expect for men who could be upset by the absence of a faded solar topee.

In Asia it could be anything, measured in katis or picu.

Chapter 22
WHAT IT IS, A KATI OR A PICUL?

Travelling in Southeast Asia can be confusing at times, as this article, which appeared in July 1986, will testify.

Asia has long gone over to the metric system. Milestones along the highways have vanished; now there are kilometre markers.

Today when we buy fuel at petrol stations, it's by the litre, and there are roughly four litres to a gallon. But what gallon? US or imperial?

For the answer, read on. But first, how about trying to answer some other questions that often puzzle travellers in Southeast Asia.

We are in Singapore or Malaysia and turn on the radio; we get the stock market report. We learn that rubber is selling at so much a picul. You ask someone how much does a picul weigh, and they tell you a picul is 100 katis. What then does a kati represent?

We drink a San Miguel beer in Hong Kong but find it tastes different from the San Miguel we drank in Manila, and the barman tells us it's because it's 3.5 San Miguel export. Then he compares it with Mekhong whiskey which he says is 35 per cent proof. What is he talking about?

We want to buy a ruby and ask the salesman the price. He must weigh it. Not in grammes. In carats. What is a carat?

You go to buy a camera. It doesn't have a guarantee, but a warranty. Which is better, a guarantee or a warranty?

Two men are talking, one English, the other an American. The conversation is about over-eating and gaining weight. The American says he has gained 10 pounds; the Englishman says he has put on more than a stone. Who gained more?

At the duty-free shop you want to buy a gift for your boss, perhaps a bottle of fine cognac. He likes Spanish wine–why not a Spanish cognac? At check-out they tell you there is no Spanish cognac. Don't the Spanish make cognac?

An assistant in the duty-free shop tries to help, and makes matters worse. "Do you want to buy a VSOP or an XO?" What's the difference? You're too proud to ask.

On your flight you look in the back of the inflight magazine and it lists distances to various cities, given in nautical miles. Is a nautical mile more or less than a land mile? What, then, is a sea mile, and what did that rug salesman mean when he asked how many knots did you want?

You look around Asia and you see a Dynasty Hotel and a Dynasty Restaurant. And when you flip on the television in your hotel room, you watch the American soap opera Dynasty on the screen. What actually is a dynasty?

We all know what a rickshaw is, but what about a trishaw, and how does it differ from a pedicab? A becak? And where does the samlor come in?

And when it comes to the names for Asian boats, we really become baffled. We can take a sampan or a wallawalla, dine on a junk, and cross a river in a prau. Or is it a prao? And then there are the dhow, banka, pumpboat, Macassar schooner and Rhio trader. From which countries do they come? And here's another one for you. How many riggers does an outrigger canoe have?

We begin to fill out our landing cards, and on the customs declaration we read that it is unlawful to carry more than US$2,000 in cash without declaring it. What's the difference between unlawful and illegal?

We use terms in our everyday life without really knowing what they mean. We talk about wine having vintage, putting our children in kindergarten, that a gun is 12-gauge or 22-calibre, that we prefer pilsner to lager—yet what do all these things mean?

When we travel it's even more confusing; we are suddenly confronted with more terms, weights and measures we don't understand and with strange names that baffle us. But don't let it turn you off. It's all the fun of travelling.

To answer the questions above, first, which is larger, an imperial or a US gallon? Before the metric system was adopted throughout Asia, all fuel—petrol, gasoline, benzine or whatever you want to call it—was sold not in litres but in gallons, imperial gallons, which are slightly larger than the US gallons. The US gallon is a liquid measure equal to four quarts or 231 cubic inches. The imperial gallon equals 277.42 cubic inches. Thus the imperial gallon is larger.

Piculs and katis are still widely used as measurements in Southeast Asia. A kati is 1.33 pounds, and a picul is 100 katis, or 133 pounds.

When it comes to alcohol, the relative strength of an alcoholic liquor with reference to the arbitrary standard for proof spirit is taken as 100 proof. Pure alcohol is 100 per cent — but not 100 proof which is approximately half alcohol, half water by volume. Most whiskeys are 86 proof—42 per cent alcohol. Wine is about 12 per cent; beer averages less than six per cent. Mekhong whiskey, surprisingly, is 35 proof, and it is not aged. The date of bottling Mekhong is printed inside the label. San Miguel beer sold in the Philippines is a strong six percent, but by law that which is exported to Asian countries is 3.5, a rather weak content.

While on the subject of beer there are also pilsner and lager. What's the difference? Lager is beer stored for six months before it is used. Pilsner is merely a light lager.

What do the experts (or those who want to impress others) mean when they say wine has either a good or a bad vintage? The wine of a particular region in a specified year is called its vintage. In Europe there can be good and bad years for grape-growing in different regions.

That gem you are thinking about buying, it's value is determined, in part, by its size. A "carat" is a unit of weight for precious stones and pearls, equal to about 3.086 grains troy, or 0.2 of a gramme. When weighing gold, 24 carat is pure gold; 20 carat gold is 20 parts pure gold and four parts alloy. In Thailand we use the baht weight for gold. Also confusing are jewels in watches. The jewels are part of the inside workings of a watch. They are precious stones — even diamonds—which act like ball bearings.

For that camera you buy which is better, a warranty or a guarantee? A warranty is an official authorisation or sanction, in law, stating that the product purchased is real. A warranty specifies that a Canon, for example, is a Canon and not another brand sold under that name. On the other hand, a guarantee is a pledge by the manufacturer that something is as represented and will be replaced if it does not meet the specifications; it offers positive assurance that something will be done in the manner specified.

The American and his English friend who were arguing about weight: the Englishman would have gained more. The American put on 10 pounds (4.5 kilos) while the Englishman put on one stone or 14 pounds (6.3 kilos).

When it comes to buying cognac in a duty-free shop, the sales girl is right. The Spanish do not make cognac. Only the French do. It's a trade name, and the French are very fussy about it. Cognac is nothing more than French brandy distilled from wine in the area of Cognac, France; loosely any French brandy. Brandy is any alcoholic liquor distilled from wine. Thus, cognac is brandy.

The assistant wanted to know if you preferred a VSOP or XO. VSOP means "very special old pale" while XO means an "extra old" brand. Generally, the XO is more expensive.

Which is longer, the nautical mile or the land mile? The nautical mile is 6,080 feet while the land mile is 5,280 feet. Nautical miles and sea miles are the same. And the more knots in a rug, the better the quality.

We usually associate Dynasty with age, but what it really means is a span of time. Thus, a dynasty is the period during which a certain family rules; or it can be the succession of rulers who are members of the same family.

Naming the different modes of transport in Asia is not difficult. We know that nowadays the rickshaw is only seen in Calcutta and some remote towns in Bangladesh. The modern version of the rickshaw is the trishaw. It's any pedalled vehicle with three wheels, regardless of where the passenger may sit—out front (Penang), on the side (Singapore), behind (Honolulu). The name trishaw is interchangeable with pedicab, and in Indonesia it's called a *becak* (pronounced "betjuh"). Motorise a trishaw and in Bangkok it becomes a *samlor,* or tuktuk, and in Indonesia a helicak.

Now for boats. Everyone knows what a junk is. In dictionary terms a junk is a seagoing ship used in Chinese and other waters, having square sails spread by battens, a high stern, and usually a flat bottom. Next is a sampan which means three boards in Chinese. It can be any of the various small boats seen in Asian ports. They are propelled by single sculls over their sterns, and many have mat roofing. In Hong Kong sampan taxis are called wallawallas.

Next comes the prau. It can also be spelled proa, prao and prahu. Basically it's a swift sailing boat which is balanced by a single outrigger. They may vary in shape and size and are seen throughout Southeast Asia and among the pacific islands.

In many Asian ports to this day you may see sailing craft from a dozen nations: dhows (also dau and dow) from the Arabian Sea and Indian coast, Macassar schooners from the Celebes and Rhio and Bugis traders from the Sulu Sea. There may even be a banka ferry from the Philippines, and these ships that anchor out in the roads must transport their cargoes and passengers ashore by bumboats, sometimes called pumpboats, by launches and by painted-eyed scows towed by tugs.

And how many riggers does an outrigger have? In the South Pacific, one. In most Asian countries, Philippines included, two.

I almost forgot. In weapons the gauge is the size of the bore of a firearm, especially of a shotgun, while the calibre is the size of a rifle determined by the bullet or shell as measured by its diameter. And finally, unlawful and illegal. Give up? Unlawful is anything done against the law, while illegal is a sick bird. Sorry. I couldn't resist.

Chapter 23
WILL THE REAL MISS UNIVERSE RISE?

Beauty depends upon who's doing the looking, as this article which appeared on July 18, 1976 reveals.

Someone once remarked that a beautiful girl is one who when you first look at her, takes your breath away. If this is true, any one who has attended any of the beauty contests around Southeast Asia, like the Miss Singapore, the Miss Philippines or the Miss Thailand contest, has certainly ended up short of breath. And as we know, every year these countries not only select their own national beauties, but they send their winners to compete in the real breath-taking-away event—the Miss Universe Contest.

Over the years I have attended a few of these contests, and each time I do find myself wondering, between gasps for air, how these lovely damsels can develop into such shapely, beautiful women in a short span of 18 or 19 years.

Then another question that comes to mind concerns the judging. How objective can a judge really be? Is he truly making a wise unbiased choice? We can only be subjective when we say we either like something or we don't. When judging the Miss Universe contest we might take it a step further. How "universal" is the contest really? I started thinking about this when I saw a recent Miss Singapore contest and remembered an incident that happened to me some 15 years ago. The place was South America.

I had an assignment with a big American magazine to cover the efforts of the US Geogedic Survey team who were mapping the Choco Jungles. The jungles and coastal islands are the home of the primitive Cuna Indians. It was on one of these islands in the San Blas that I had to wait two weeks for a small bush plane to pick me up.

After a few days I came to know the Cunas rather well. Once you break down the initial barriers they can be quite friendly and quite curious. They were interested in everything I had with me, including several old magazines.

I didn't think much about it. I was stretched out in a hammock one afternoon, half dozing, and somewhere behind me I could hear a couple of women talking and turning over the pages in the magazines. Suddenly they stopped turning and their voices became excited. Other women came over to have a look. Something had their full attention. Curiosity seized me. I got up to look. It was a page of advertisement with a photograph of a very sleek New York fashion model doing her thing. The model was stunning. She wore her hair back, with her eyes made up with blue shadow. She held a cigarette in a slender holder, and her fingers were finely manicured. She was leaning over the fender of a shiny sports car. I can't remember what she was advertising, but I do remember the model.

The San Blas Indian women were actually stunned by the photo. They kept staring and studying the model in great detail, and they discussed their observations among themselves. In many ways, I felt rather proud that they were admiring a woman of my world but then, slowly, I discovered it was not admiration they had for the lady; it was more on the border of ridicule.

The model was to them everything that a woman should not be. Foremost what decent lady would paint her lips and eyes? In the San Blas culture the women draw a thin line down the bridge of their nose, which makes their already long noses appear even longer. And rings are not to be worn solely on fingers or in ears;

they are to be worn in one's nose. The Indian women wear golden rings in their noses, much like an angry bull in a pasture has a ring through his nose.

The girl in the advertisement, as I recall, was rather shapely. Disgusting! From the age of three or four, young San Blas girls bind their forearms and calves to keep them from growing. Beauty to them is when a lady's arms and legs resemble matchsticks. Nor do they believe in over-weight. To assure that they do not become plump, the girls in the tribe eat only every other day. They are even forbidden to drink water in between. Considering that they live in the tropical jungle, it cannot be an easy task to adhere to. As I mentioned, my stay on the island was 15 years ago, but I'm sure conditions haven't changed. The question is, however, how would a Cuna Indian girl from the San Blas be placed in a Miss Universe contest.

I'm afraid that the saying 'beauty is in the eye of the beholder' is true. Are not the San Blas men justified in judging beauty with their own society? Unfortunately Miss San Blas 1982 would not receive many votes in Hong Kong and Singapore, unless the judges were also from her homeland, which is not likely.

Also, our concept of beauty changes from day to day. What we consider beautiful at present may not apply a few years hence. Think about it! I remember growing up in China after the war. A Chinese beauty then wore only silk gowns and had bangs, a white-washed face and gold teeth. When she smiled all you saw was gold. I understand that today in China a lady in vogue goes totally without make-up, and her dress is the blue uniform of the Red Guards. I don't know which is better; the latter perhaps.

Nor was it long ago that a Malay girl who was about to marry had to have her teeth ground down and then stained black. (Young girls on Bali still go through the teeth-filing ceremony.) Also, staining women's teeth was not confined to Southeast Asia. If we are to believe the Japanese prints, geisha girls a hundred years ago followed a similar custom.

But one doesn't have to delve into the past to discover the meaning of beauty. I can imagine the Dyaks in their longhouses in Borneo selecting one of their women to represent them in a Miss Universe contest. Dyak women there continue to elongate their ears until their earlobes reach down to their shoulders. They also shave their eyebrows and practise walking tippy-toed.

In places like New Guinea and the Solomon Islands, women who want to be fashionable have their torsos tattooed with intricate designs. Fortunately the Maori women on New Zealand have given up the custom of tattooing their lips and chins, although in some Maori settlements a few older women can still be seen with these unbecoming beauty marks. And now I'm being prejudiced by saying 'unbecoming'. To Maori men they must certainly have been marks of beauty.

Who could ever imagine a Miss Universe with the physique of a sumo wrestler? There are many societies who grade their women on a poundage scale. The Arabs are one. I once went to a belly dance in Istanbul. The audience was mainly of Turkish sailors who became quite boisterous when a dancer appeared. The bigger and fatter they were, the better they liked them. One young and rather lithe girl was shooed off the stage.

Nor are the Polynesians of the Pacific much different. There are some people who will argue that the contrary is true. They are certain to mention those lithe Tahitian girls doing a fiery tamure dance to the rhythm of shark-skin drums. The truth is, those dancers are merely export models. Among the real Polynesians, the huge, blubbery woman who leaps up and does a wild dance is the one who captures the hearts of the locals. It is not so surprising however when one remembers that at one time all Polynesian royalty were forbidden to exert themselves at all. Not only were they carried about from place to place, but they were handfed by their subjects. In fact, for anyone of royal blood to touch the food they ate was taboo. And the more weight they gained, the more pride the people had in their reigning aristocracy. In Samoa today there is hardly a woman who walks down a street in Pago Pago or Apia who doesn't weigh 200 pounds or more. It would cost the Miss Universe Committee double to bring them to a contest. They couldn't fit into one seat on an aircraft.

One mistake we make, I believe, in judging a woman's beauty is to try to put her into a light where she doesn't belong. I've seen it happen so often. I had a Swiss friend who was engaged to a Balinese girl. He invited me to attend their wedding on Bali. I went a week before the ceremony, and first saw the girl in her village surroundings. She was coming up a steep hill carrying a water cask on her head, along with a dozen other young maidens. I could see why my friend had fallen in love with her. She was absolutely lovely.

Their wedding was traditionally Balinese. I had never seen a young bride look so radiant. She was, of course, dressed in her Balinese wedding costume. My friend too was dressed in native costume, and they both had to go through a tooth-filing ceremony, although it was more symbolic than anything.

A few years passed before I saw them again. They were living in a flat in Singapore. My Swiss friend had made every attempt possible to transform his lovely wife into a Westerner. He spared no cost on her clothes, but somehow they didn't suit her. She was trying to be someone she wasn't, and at great loss to her charming beauty.

It also happens the other way round, mind you. I've known Western women married to Indians. Nothing can be worse than an Indian gentleman wanting his European wife to 'fit in' by putting her in a sari. Few Western women can ever wear a sari as elegantly as an Indian woman; nor should they try.

Maybe what the world needs is a revised Miss Universe contest judged by ethnic rules. Should not the contestants be from all the diverse groups the world over? The problem, of course, would be setting up standard rules for the judges to follow. But then what would the judges do with a Malaysian beauty who refused to pose in a bathing suit, or a Muslim girl from the Middle East who wouldn't remove her veil? It could present some rather peculiar difficulties.

Chapter 24
IT ALL STARTED AT TRANQUEBAR

Discovery can be many things, a new restaurant, or a lost tribe; an antique shop, or a vanished city. In Asia all these are possible. Rather than tell my readers about restaurants and antique shops, I preferred to tell them about lost tribes and vanished cities. In the following article I tell about searching for a lone Danish fort on the southeast coast of India. How many other hidden treasures in Southeast Asia remain to be discovered? The article appeared on July 17, 1983.

It's a long way to travel from Bangkok to a small unknown town in southeast India just to find an old Danish fortress. And what's so important about an old Danish fortress anyway?

Historically, an old seaport called Tranquebar played an important role in establishing Siam's first contact with Europe. But the records are sketchy. We set off not knowing if the old fortress still existed. And when we stopped at a village 20 kilometres from the coast, it didn't look too good. The locals not only didn't know where it was, but they had never heard of the place.

Had we come all the way from Bangkok to reach a dead end? For two people in our group, it would be a great disappointment. Niels Lumboldt and Robin Dannhorn, both long-time residents of Thailand, wanted to verify information they had gathered and published in a book called *Scandinavians in Siam.* Tranquebar was the focal point. They formed an expedition of sorts and in-

The Danish fortress at Tranquebar on the southeast coast of India. The fortress was one of the first European settlements in the Far East.

vited me and several interested Bangkok residents to join them—Roy Howard, Bob Papazian, Dan Thygesen and Paul Weber. We flew to Madras, armed with reference material and notes, and engaged two motorcars from SITA Travel to carry us south.

Southeast India is far off the tourist trail with only pockets of interest for the traveller, but that doesn't mean the countryside is without interest. On the contrary, if you were to make a comparison by taking a stretch of road two kilometres long anywhere else in Asia, you would not find as much diversity, or call it activity, as you would in southern India. The reason is people. Given a one-word description of India, it would be people. And if you had a choice of colour, that would be brown.

The people of southern India, the dark-skinned Tamils, are everywhere. Stop your car on a seemingly empty stretch of road, and in minutes they appear by the hundreds, no, thousands. But you don't even have to stop your car. The roads for the people of India are their gathering place. They come to the roads to meet, hold prayers, demonstrate, sleep and in some cases even to die. Religious celebrations appear to be the main events, with everything from weddings to funerals taking place along the roads. Processions move along, swinging incense and beating on drums and cymbals. You might be driving forward in kilometres, but at times you feel you are going backwards into the pages of Kipling. Here are the hot, sweating, friendly faces he so well described, with their naked bodies, their bandy legs, forever toiling in the hot Indian sun.

And the country is brown. The fields are brown, the houses are brown, the people are brown. Even the green foliage on the trees is brown from dust. The many cattle, mostly cows and goats, help contribute to the brownness of the land. They eat everything living, and some things that aren't, like the posters on the mud walls and on the tree trunks. No sooner are posters put up than cows come and eat them off. And following the cows are Tamil children, picking up the dung which, our driver explained, is used for cooking fires. He also explained the reason for all the numbers on the trees. It appears they are government owned, and if they weren't, they would have long ago been chopped down.

Europeans gave the southeast coast of India a romantic name, calling it the Coromandel Coast. The name, known only to Europeans, came from a village 35 miles north of Madras, formerly held by the Dutch. Charo was the Hindu name for race, one of the three dynasties controlling the Tamils to the south. The coast became known as Chola-Manaoloor, and was the scene of some significant events during the 17th and 18th centuries. Both France and England fought over Madras and some of the key seaports to the south.

Fifty-three miles to the south of Madras on the sea coast is Mahabalipuram. What more romantic sounding name can there be? The port was once the main harbour and naval base of the great Pallava Empire more than 1,200 years ago. It was known as the "City of the Seven Pogodas." Both shore and cave temples contain monolithic figures and bas-relief carvings, many out of solid rock.

Seeing the shore temples as we did was encouraging. If these temples have withstood the ravages of the sea for some 12 centuries, then the fortress at Tranquebar might still be there. We explored other ruins and temples on the way south, at Pondicherry, Chiambaram and Tanjore. Finally we left the trunk road and turned towards the town of Tranquebar on the coast, or rather where we thought it should be.

We were certain about the Tranquebar connection between Denmark and Siam. We knew the Danes had made contact with Siam as early as 1621, when Captain Roland Crappe sailed from Tranquebar up the Chao Phaya to Ayutthaya in an attempt to capitalise on the overland "spice and silk" route between the Gulf of

Siam and the Bay of Bengal. This was during the reign of King Song Tham. It seems much of early Siam's wealth came from controlling the transshipment of goods between China and India. A royal decree, written in pencil on handmade Siamese paper, was found in the National Museum in Copenhagen. The decree granted Denmark trading rights with Siam.

Such trade concessions were what every maritime nation in Europe—Spain, Portugal, Holland, England and Denmark — desperately wanted. The opening of sea routes to the rich ports of the Far East ended the 800-year-old overland caravan trade between East and West. It was now more profitable to ship by sea, and considering that a bag of peppercorn was worth its weight in gold, nations would go to any extreme to capture that trade.

Today it seems incomprehensible that nations would go to war for something so minor as spices, a commodity we can pick up at any corner market or in the local supermarket. But 200 years ago it was quite another thing. It was for this reason that Denmark found Tranquebar.

Denmark was governed in the beginning of the 17th century by King Christian IV, an energetic and well-informed monarch who like so many of his contemporaries saw overseas trade as a means to enrich his country and himself. In 1616, Holland formed the Dutch East India Company to open up trade routes with the East. King Christian knew he had to act fast. In 1618 he dispatched four ships to the Far East, to try to establish trade with Ceylon.

The command was given to a young sea captain named Ove Gjedde. He was only 24 years old but he proved himself to be very capable. The perilous and incredibly difficult voyage to Ceylon took two long years. Gjedde lost two ships at Cape Verde to French pirates and by the time they reached Ceylon, more than half his crew had died on the voyage.

But Admiral Gjedde's troubles were only beginning. When his tiny, crippled fleet arrived in Ceylon, the Portuguese had won favour with the King of Kandy. Other European nations were no longer welcome. While stalling for time Gjedde sent Captain Crappe to explore the Coromandel Coast in hope of finding another suitable port they could use. It was a clever move. Captain Crappe singled out the Rajah of Tanjore and negotiated for a Danish concession at a small port called Tranquebar.

In September 1620, Gjedde arrived at Tranquebar and signed an agreement with the Rajah. He then immediately set his men to work building a walled brick fortress which he called Dansborg. He appointed Captain Crappe the first Danish governor of Tranquebar after which he returned to Denmark where he received a hero's welcome. It was the following year that Denmark made more gains when Captain Crappe found his way up the Chao Phaya and secured a trade agreement with the King of Siam at Ayutthaya.

Things went rather well for the Danes at Tranquebar during the next two decades. The treaty with the Rajah of Tanjore was extended to include farmlands beyond the town, and Tranquebar now traded with Malacca on the coast of the Malay peninsula. An average of two ships a year arrived from Denmark and filled their holds with ivory and pepper. In return, Danish manufactured goods, including cannon and muskets, reached Siam through Tranquebar. Some of the big Danish guns imported at that time can still be seen at Samut Sakhon and in Songkhla.

Then came the year 1643, and war between Denmark and Sweden. Denmark could no longer send ships to the Far East and Tranquebar was all but forgotten. It wasn't until 1669, 26 years later, that the next Danish ship arrived. They found only one man alive, a corporal of the guards who had taken command and refused to surrender the fort.

Denmark quickly re-established her old trade routes and Tranquebar prospered. The town was further fortified and by 1690 had grown to more than 3,000 inhabitants, with 100 to 200 Danes at any one time. By 1790, the population reached 20,000 and soon the Danes had rich farmlands along the coast. They grew rice for paying salaries, and since Denmark was able to avoid war on the continent with France and Britain, their ships were free to come and go.

But Britain's increasing influence on the Indian subcontinent became a threat. Trade at Tranquebar began to decline due to a number of unforeseeable circumstances. The British merchant fleet was growing in strength and merchant ships were now able to make the long passage from ports in China and Siam without making intermediate stops. Furthermore there was a recession in Europe. By 1840, Denmark was bankrupt. Three years later, in 1843, she sold to the British East India Company the port of Tranquebar and all the surrounding territories for the sum of 1,125,000 krones, or 125,000 pounds sterling.

Under the British, the importance of Tranquebar declined. The last available photographs the authors of *Scandinavians in Siam* could locate for publication were taken in 1936. One photograph shows King's Street, the main street through the town, and the Land Gate, all in semi-ruin.

We drove the last few miles to Tranquebar, not knowing what to expect. We were astonished at what we found. A few miles before we arrived at the partially-walled town, the air turned cool as it blew in from the sea, a refreshing treat after the hot drive down the trunk road from Madras. We passed through Land Gate, beneath an embossed Danish emblem, and entered not a town in ruins, as we thought it must be, but a very pleasant community. Tranquebar was laid out in neat streets, well planned, with an eye for order. The architecture was European influence, thick stucco walls, massive pillars supporting classical pediments, carriage porches and verandahs on second storeys above the street.

We studied the map we had dated 1671. It showed the walled city with "Dansborg Castle" on the sea front. There were pagodas, a Portuguese church, the admiral's house, a mosque and numerous godowns. Three hundred and twelve years later most of the structures still stood, with the exceptions of the godowns. At each intersection we stopped and looked down the side streets. Each street had something different to see.

There were, obviously, things that weren't on our plan, like Land Gate. We learned later that it wasn't built until 1792, after a French pattern. Also in 1845, two years after Denmark sold the colony, an impressive Collector's Residence was constructed above the beach. Although it has been neglected, it's still a showpiece of India's past glories.

On a large open field facing the Collector's House, schoolboys played volleyball, and beyond the field facing the sea rose the fortress of Tranquebar, or as it was once called, Dansborg Castle.

It was late afternoon when we first saw the fortress. The sun was low in the sky and cast a reddish glow across its facade, giving it a kind of strange animation. We almost expected Danish soldiers with tall muskets and pointed helmets to be standing on the ramparts behind the gun embrasures. And indeed, it was a great satisfaction to sit on the verandah of our resthouse that night and look out at the fort. The next morning we were up at dawn and began exploring the fort.

It's a marvel that Dansborg Castle, with the Indian Ocean lapping at its very foundations, has withstood the passage of time. We walked along the ramparts, climbed up to the towers and edged our way into dark passages deep below, and we had the feeling that the Danes had left only the day before. Everything is that well preserved.

A caretaker showed us the museum, a few old rusted cutlasses and clumps of musket ball. Souvenir-hunters had taken everything else of value over the years.

From the ramparts we looked out at the sea. Tranquebar has no port. Ships had to anchor offshore while loading and unloading their cargoes. The old square-rigged ships are gone, but the Tamil fishermen still pull their slender fishing craft up on the beach as they did when Admiral Gjedde and Captain Crappe first arrived. We could only imagine what the lone corporal must have felt when he waited 26 years for a Danish ship to arrive. But it was due to his efforts and to those who preceded him that Dansborg fortress was built and ties with Siam and Europe began. And Niels Lumboldt and Robin Dannhorn had proved their point. We weren't disappointed.

Time has not changed the traditions and customs in Malay weddings.

Chapter 25
NOT ALL WEDDINGS ARE ENJOYABLE

Weddings, births, burials and creamations, they all call for special celebrations in Asia and the South Pacific. However, in each society customs and traditions differ, as I pointed out in my column on July 16, 1978.

Every society from the very primitive to the most advanced, regards the marriage of two young people as one of the most important events within their social structure. And in almost any case, it is performed with a high degree of pomp and ceremony.

We who live here in Southeast Asia are generally familiar with the multi–racial weddings of our area, namely Buddhist, Christian, Muslim and Hindu.

If we are invited to a wedding, we know, more or less, what to expect and what to do. We may not always understand the reasons for doing something, but nevertheless we have come to accept them.

But imagine being invited to a wedding that is totally alien, perhaps even involved in some pagan rites of sorts. How do we act on such occasions?

What do we do? In my travels in the jungles of Asia and more recently aboard my own schooner through the islands of the South Pacific, I witnessed some strange wedding ceremonies, indeed. Anything can happen, like the time we sailed into Apia in Western Samoa.

A longboat paddled by twenty or more sturdy oarsmen came out to lead through the narrow passage. They waved excitedly and were most anxious for us to drop anchor.

Arriving in these far-flung ports aboard a schooner has many advantages, which we had quickly learned. Doors are opened to us that would otherwise be closed. Everywhere we go, it seems, we are invited to some function or other. And if there isn't one scheduled, the islanders create one. But when we arrived in Samoa things were happening. The longboat crew invited us to a wedding, native style. It sounded great. "When?" we asked.

"In three weeks," they said.

Our hosts could see the disappointment on our faces.

"But never mind, never mind," they quickly explained. "The wedding is in three weeks but tomorrow the young men who are to marry start their preparations. You must come!"

We couldn't have refused if we wanted to. Early the following morning a dozen islanders, all wearing colourful "lavalavas", or sarongs, and flowered wreaths for head-dress came to escort us to their village.

Before we reached the village we could hear the drums. The ceremony had begun. We rounded the last bend in the path and came to a compound of thatched houses. We were led to one which seemed to serve as the community centre.

It was a huge building, with a thatched, high ceiling, and a raised earthen floor upon which everyone under the roof sat on layers of soft mats. But something strange was going on.

Two young men, with their faces drawn in agony were being held fast by village elders, while two other men clutching crude, evil-looking instruments in their hands, bent over them. They stopped whatever they were doing when we entered. Kava, the local drink, was passed around in half coconut shells, and shortly the ceremony continued. It was too awesome to watch for long.

The two men with the evil looking instruments were performing the ancient island art of body carving. It was the young men's preparation for adulthood, a pain they have to endure before they were eligible for marriage.

The men doing the tattooing used jagged pig bones dipped into lampblack to do the work. Crude but the results were no ordinary tattoos. They are almost solid designs which extend from the waist down to a few inches below the knees.

The ordeal which everyone came to witness and to drink kava lasted three days. Each young groom submitted to the tattooists "tapping" for half an hour and then rested for two. The tattooist would then move on to someone else. We saw about dozen boys under the roof, most of them awaiting their turn, unsmiling. Assisting the tattooist was an elder whose job it was to inspect the wounds and wipe away the blood and excess ink with a dirty, soiled cloth.

I don't know how long the custom will prevail in Western Samoa but most of the young men we met had their lower bodies elaborately carved. It was the mark that distinguished the men from the boys.

By the day of the wedding, the young men's scars were well healed. Like in all Polynesia, the wedding feast was a real banquet, and the grooms, with their tattoos oiled until they glistened, sat cross-legged on the ground in front of the "pepas," with their lavalavas pull up higher than usual, displaying, of course, their tattoos to their fullest. They were now men, with the right to marry. The girls were very proud of them. I sat next to one young lady who was beaming at the young man across from her. She seemed very pleased with him. But I was curious. The design of his tattoo, really, was no different than those of the other young men, at least as far as I could determine.

"Tell me," I said to her, "what makes him so different?"

"He has a jeep," she said proudly, without taking her eyes from him.

It was explained to me that the art of body carving came to Samoa by the way of Fiji. Legend tells us that two goddesses swam the distance with instructions to "tattoo the women but not the men." We can be thankful they became confused. They arrived singing "tattoo the men and not the women. "

In several Polynesian societies I've visited, I found it the custom where a man could not marry unless he went through certain rituals in which he had to earn his manhood. Some of these rites were enough to make any man think twice about getting married.

In the Taumotuas, for example, a man must dive into a pool in the lagoon and wrestle with man-eating sharks, while, in the Gambiers young married men must paddle their young brides to distant islands through open seas to prove their worth.

A rite which I recently witnessed was on the island of Pendercost in the remote New Hebrides. A young man here who wants to win the hand of any village maiden is expected to dive from a 90-foot tower, head first, to the ground below. Tied to his legs are vines that stop him in flight a mere six inches from the ground. It's one of the most frightening spectacles I've ever seen, including the cliff divers at Acapulco. The flimsy tower the natives dive from is constructed from short sticks that seem to disintegrate when the divers make their leap. I was a nervous wreck from climbing half way up the tower for photographs, let alone diving from the top.

This strange custom started when a young man threatened to dive from the highest tree in the jungle when a girl he was pursuing refused to marry him. She didn't believe he would. He had to jump. What he did was tie vines to his legs, and when he climbed the tallest tree, he called out once again to her to change her mind. She still refused to believe he would jump. When he leaped she screamed she would marry him. Imagine her surprise, and everyone else's, when the vines broke his fall. Unfortunately, the young buck set a precedent. All the young ladies thereafter expected their wooers to make the same death-defying leap.

To date only one native on Pendercost has died from the jump, and he did so because he was drunk and used someone else's vines.

One of the most weird weddings I ever attended was in the Gambier Islands south of Tahiti. It began as a typical island festival. Pigs and fowl were slaughtered, and together with breadfruit and tarro they were placed into open pits lined with hot stones. The pit was covered over with moist earth, and while the contents slowly baked, the party began.

It started after dark, when it was cool, to the tune of wood blocks and shark-skin drums. Fires were lighted, and with grass skirts swinging—worn by both men and women everyone did the fiery "tamure" dance.

Finally, just before the ovens were opened, the wedding ceremony began. Since everyone was dressed alike, with grass skirts, flowered "leis" and wreaths for head dress, it was impossible to tell who was the bride and who was the groom. But when things grew quiet a very pretty girl appeared from the darkness. By the sound of the cheers from everyone, I gathered she was the bride. But who was the groom. It became more confusing. All the young men on the island immediately formed a large circle and sat down upon the ground. Drum beats suddenly erupted with such a fury the earth shook. The bride stepped into the circle; and in rhythm to the drums, with everyone clapping, she began to dance. The tempo increased, to a fever pitch. There was apparent tense excitement among all the males sitting in the circle.

But still, where was the groom?

The young lady was now dancing with full body gyrations. She would dance her way up to a young man sitting on the ground, enticing him to rise, but as soon as he made an effort to do so, she quickly darted off to someone else. Whenever she left a young man, a great sigh arose from the audience. Thus she continued, from one man to another.

When the suspense was more than I could bear, I asked the man next to me, "Where is the groom?"

He looked at me with a puzzle stare. Maybe he didn't understand. "You know," I continued, "her husband, the man she is going to marry. Where is he?"

The man now looked at me and chuckled. "How should I know?" he said and the dance continued.

Finally the girl stopped in front of man who had been looking up at her in great anticipation. The drums continued and the clapping grew more intense. But now instead of enticing the man to rise, she continued her hipswinging dance, dropping lower and lower on her bended limbs until she was down on her knees.

The drums stopped as suddenly as they started. With her hands lowered, she stretched out her arms to the man. Immediately the drums picked up the beat, and instantly the couple leaped up. Together they danced savagely and frantically, but only for a few short minutes. Then to the teasing and taunting of everyone present, they made a dash for the darkness of the forest of palms nearby.

It was over. They were married. And I was still confused. I didn't learn the full story until the next day.

It seems that the young lady was very popular with all the men on the island. Now, unlike in most societies around the world, the young maidens in these islands are encouraged to discover life when they are young, and to enjoy themselves. The more experience they have, the better will be their life later on. And, of course, there is no stigma attached to a young daughter who doesn't return home until dawn most mornings. She's a healthy woman, they say.

But finally the time arrives when the girl's family thinks it proper that she finds, or picks, one partner and settles down. In the wedding I attended, the girl had made her choice, but no one knew who the lucky man would be until the last minute.

And so it went. The ovens were opened, the food brought out, wine bottles uncorked and all through the night there was much singing and dancing. I was surprised to see the bride and groom make their reappearance a half hour later, but no one paid much attention to them. They were now only guests at their own wedding.

In Bali young lovers often elope. It's an accepted custom, called "ngorod." On a specific night, declared auspicious by a Hindu priest the bride is forcibly taken by her suitor to the house of his friend, generally a long distance away from her village.

The parents are then informed of the event, and they feign horror. The matter, of course, has been pre-arranged. The marriage ceremony takes place in a gay atmosphere in the friend's village. My friend Han Snel, a Dutch artist who has lived on Bali for more than 25 years, did it that way. He jokes about it now, but at the time he thought the girl's father and brothers would track him down in the night.

I had another friend, Willy Mettler, who eloped with a lovely Balinese dancer named Rubic. He took her all the way to Bangkok where they were officially married through the Swiss Embassy. Willy was quite happy, but not Rubic. In fact, she was very unhappy. The civil ceremony they had in Bangkok was not like the Balinese weddings of her people. Furthermore, her family had lost face in their village. No feast! No celebrations! Willy realised if he wanted his wife to be happy, they would have to return to Bali and marry there—Balinese style. He was rather nervous about it and asked if I'd accompany him. It seemed like a novel idea, so I packed and flew with them to Bali.

Willy had no idea what he was getting into. The weddings was traditional, in every respect, from the clothing their wore—fine sarongs and head-dresses—to a "kris", a curved Indonesian sword that Willy had to carry. There was one last item which was held back from Willy, and when he learned what was happening, it was too late.

Immediately before the wedding, in full view of the village, he was laid back on a table, along with his wife, their heads hanging back over the side. He looked ridiculous, and he knew it, but he could not protest when the priest came and stuck a hand in his mouth and began filing his teeth. In Balinese tradition, both Willy and Rubic had to have their teeth filed. Which they did.

The wedding, incidentally, was a success. Rubic's family regained their loss of face and Willy gave me his kris which to this day hangs on the wall in my stateroom aboard my schooner.

Not so long ago teeth filing in Malaysia was in vogue. It was part of the wedding ceremony. The bride-to-be's teeth were filed down to a quarter of an inch of their natural length by means of a hard Sumataran sword stone. The operation lasted about an hour, and the girls' gums continued to be swollen and painful for days to come.

Afterwards, girls blackened their teeth by chewing betel nut, accelerated by applying a black liquid obtained by burning coconut shells on iron.

Fortunately some customs do pass, like the one on Borneo where a young man had to go out and take the head of his enemy in battle before any girl would marry him.

The only place I have found where there is no wedding ceremony as such, is with the primitive Negritos of the deep jungles of central Malaysia.

In the spring last year I made a lengthy expedition with Chief Game Warden Mohammed Khan into the unexplored northern reaches of the National Park. We encountered families of Negritos moving on bamboo rafts down stream. These mysterious people of the dark jungles have no permanent shelters. They live by fishing, hunting with blowpipes and gathering fruit from the forest.

In one group we counted 22 members, all more or less from the same family. Marriage within this close circle would, of course, lead to incest. Finding a mate in the jungles is mostly by chance. If the wandering tribe meets another tribe, and there are unmarried youths in each, then they are paired off. There is no ceremony. The couple merely wander off into the jungle and generally return only when the girl is pregnant. We did find a number of Negrito couples alone in the jungles.

A poet once said that beauty is held in the eye of the beholder. Marriage is the same. But regardless what the custom might be, the purpose and results are the same. It's a natural institution which will be around for a long time. And in every clime the early spring seems to be the months to tie the knot. It's also the time for the dedicated bachelor to beware. But then we all weaken at times, and jump from the tower, get that tattoo, and fight that shark—and say nice things we don't mean to a lady who becomes our mother-in-law. That's marriage!

Stephens drinking from a vine in the Malay jungle.

Chapter 26
ENJOYING ASIA OUTDOORS

Since the following article was published on September 14, 1975, the world has drastically changed with regard to the outdoors. People have become aware of protecting our environment and names like "ecotourism" have entered our vocabulary. Visitors have become aware of Asia outdoors and have turned to scuba diving and island exploring. Contrary to what I reported there are now travel and tour agencies that specialise in jungle, river and diving trips. But still a lot remains for the adventurer looking for new thrills.

Mark Twain once remarked "Everyone talks about the weather but no one does anything about it." Asia's outdoors is much the same way. Everyone talks about the jungles and rivers, about the wild animals and native people who inhabit the forests and hills, about all there is out there to see but "no one does anything about it."

It always amazes me how much of Asia people actually miss. Oftentimes those who live here keep putting it off, for some reason or another, until it's too late. With visitors it's something else.

A few years ago a travel agency in Singapore contacted me and asked if I'd help promote safari tours into the Malay Jungles. It seems they had read a report about an expedition I made with the Chief Game Warden in which we explored parts of the Malay jungles never before seen by anyone except the Orang Asli (aborigines) who live there.

The agent had an idea. The jungles are little known to the outside world yet here are some of our greatest riches on earth. Nature that has been untouched and undisturbed by mankind. Jungles over one hundred million years old. Wildlife in its natural environment: elephant and tiger, rhino and buffalo, gibbons and siamang. Primeval forests and flora found nowhere else.

"Tourists would love it," the agent explained. "They'd eat it up. What we need is a campaign to sell the jungles. Let people know what it's all about."

The plan was for me to take half a dozen tourist-types into the jungle on a bonafide safari. The agency would do a movie short about the trip, which they would take to Europe and America to help sell the idea to their clients. They engaged one of Asia's top cinema photographers, Kurt Rolfes of Singapore.

We did the safari, through the help of the game department. There were eight of us, aside from the photographer and assistants. A businessman and his son, a salesman, a lady art dealer and others with various occupations. It was a fun trip, and everyone loved it.

When I saw the movie prints several weeks later I was impressed. It had all the thrills: riding rapids, hiking through dense jungle, spending a night in a tree hide, fishing for giant carp and glissading down waterfalls.

It was a happy agent who tucked the film and stacks of brochures under his arms and set off for Europe and America. "It's certain to be a success," he assured me. His last instructions were to set up some kind of safari itinerary.

Would you believe, with all the promotion—a movie, talks, brochures—not one person showed up for a jungle tour, ever. In fact, no one even enquired. The jungle safari plan was a complete failure.

The reason became obvious. We concluded that those who come

to Asia come for one or two reasons, and it isn't to go looking for the great outdoors. It's quite the opposite. They come to see the cities and take in the sights, and certainly to take advantage of the good shopping.

Those who live here seldom have the time, and usually when they do have time, they go off to Europe. They say they can always go on safari or raft down a River or visit a hill tribe. But do they? Very seldom.

On the other hand, there are some who would like to see more of the outdoors but they lack the know how of arranging it. I can think of only one tour agency in Bangkok (and none in Singapore or Kuala Lumpur) which provides such excursions, and that is Tour Royale with raft trips on the River Kwai. Generally speaking then, you have to get out and hustle your own trip, by making all the arrangements. It is possible.

One place I always enjoy visiting, as a kind of retreat, is the National Park in central Malaysia, deep in to the green heart. A trip to the park can be relaxing, with wife and kids, or it can be turned into a real jungle safari. And it's surprising how few people know about this, about the possibilities of exploring the jungle.

What makes it attractive is that there are no roads into the park, nor any landing strips for aircraft. The only access is by river. By prior arrangement only, government longboats pick up clients and take them on a Disneyland-type of trip upriver that lasts three or four hours, depending upon the condition of the river.

Headquarters is remote but comfortable, with a resthouse, private chalets and a restaurant. Or you can hire a lodge deeper in the jungle, travelling there by river, and do your own cooking. Then there are tree hides where you can watch wild game at the salt licks. Some are within walking distance of the resthouse.

For the adventuresome, the National Park can be the starting place. Through the Park Headquarters you can hire guides and porters and go trekking into the deep forest. As I mentioned, there are areas there that are virtually unexplored.

In these same jungles I have run across primitive Negritos who had never seen a stranger. We had come face to face with wild elephants and heard tigers growling in the night.

The Malay jungles can be interesting from another standpoint. It was here that the dawn of man began. The anthropologist could have a field day. The entire peninsula abounds in limestone caves, where early man first found refuge.

Some of the more famous caves have been explored, but not to their fullest. Batu Caves seven miles north of Kuala Lumpur is one example. There are regular tours to the major cave, as large as a cathedral. But there are countless lesser caves that wend their way deep into the bowels of the earth. A few years ago one expedition set out to explore one of these passages and after the second day came across the remains of a previous expedition, members who obviously became lost and perished. There is no record of them having been missing.

There is another area of caves that truly fascinates me, and one day I hope to explore them. They are in the northern reaches of the park. Aerial photographs show the region is covered with mist, due to the many waterfalls. The game warden referred to the area as "the land of the waterfalls." What is there is anyone's guess.

On the East Coast of Malaysia there is another cave worth visiting. It rises up from the flat alluvial plane like a skyscraper in a large city. Half way up the cliff a Thai Buddhist monk constructed a giant reclining Buddha. It was only a rumour that led me there years ago. Since then I have written about it often, and as a result the government tourist bureau placed the cave on their list of tourist attractions. The point is, this was only one discovery. What else does the jungle hold?

Hunting is discouraged in Malaysia, and wisely so. But for the sportsman there is some incredible fishing, freshwater fishing for giant carp. One of the best rivers for this is the Endau in the State of Pahang. The difficulty is getting there.

I've been on the Endau several times, and once made it to the source. It took five days of rough going, by edging up some 50 rapids. We had elephants blocking our way and once had a tiger chase us out of the jungle. But the fishing was worth it. In two days there we caught 400 pounds of carp, including Indian marshee, sebrau and barrmundi. A few marsee weighed close to 40 pounds. The barrmundi, which top the scales of 20 pounds, give a fight like the American tarpon. We hadn't caught any giant catfish but our Orang Asli guides said they weigh as much as 300 pounds. On my next trip I may find out whether or not it's only a "fish story."

What do you do with 400 pounds of fish? We smoked them and our guides took them to their village down river.

Closer to home are the rivers of Thailand. One man who has spent years rafting and canoeing down most of them is Bob Stevens who runs Colorado Eastern Boat Yard south of Bangkok. Bob doesn't advise any trips on the Mekong River, but, he says, there are several smaller rivers worth exploring. One is a 75-kilometre trip from Banthadon to Chiang Rai in the north. Another is on the Keck River. To do the Keck he suggests you put in at Ban Pak Yang, near the Phitsanulok and Lomsak Highways. You can follow the river all the way to Wang Thong, with four waterfalls to portage around.

All you need is a boat. But according to Bob this is no crisis. Anyplace along the rivers you can hire local boats, along with the boatman. Or you can take your own kayak and do your own navigation.

The latter can be the most enjoyable, and it's not as difficult as it might appear. At the small town of Rangsit north of Don Muang Airport there are several kayak builders. The price is reasonable, ranging from 250 baht to 1,000 baht and you have your own boat.

"There's good truck freight service throughout Thailand," Bob says. "Express Transport Organisation will ship your boat to even the smallest village."

For kayak travel don't over burden yourself. Travel light, with perhaps no more than a mosquito net, shelter and ground cloth. According to Bob, pup tents are too hot. Also, it may not be everyone's diet, but Bob takes sticky rice in bamboo tubes and dried food found on the local market. The rice will keep for weeks, if you intend to stay that long.

An adventure that might intrigue the hearty is going out on a Thai fishing boat for several days. Here again, you'd have to make your own arrangements. One of Thailand's biggest fishing ports is at Samut Prakan at the mouth of the Chao Phaya. For a few extra baht most skippers would be willing to take you on. It would be an adventure worth remembering.

A sport that is becoming more and more popular in Southeast Asia is scuba diving. Scuba diving has taken on a new impetus since the discovery of several Chinese wrecks in the Gulf of Thailand. But it has also led to tragedies. Jeff Farrell, a leading authority on the underwater world in the Gulf, strongly suggests that diving for treasure not be the objective for taking up the sport.

"Wrecks belong to the government," he says, "and it's one way of getting yourself into difficulties. Besides, there are other aspects that make it attractive. Exploring coral reefs, even spear fishing." I'd follow Jeff's advice.

At one time or another we all dream of the perfect escape to a tropical isle with a quiet lagoon, palms nipping at the blue sky and empty white sand beaches. In a man's lifetime he could not visit all the islands in the area. From Pattaya down the coast of the Malay Peninsula to Singapore there are hundreds worth visiting. Some are inhabited, mostly with small fishing settlements, while others seldom see trespassers. Last June I sailed my schooner up from Singapore and made 16 island stops. Each island was different, with it own beauty and charm. In some lagoons we dropped anchor and watched it settle into the sand thirty feet below.

Tioman is one of the largest, and now boasts of a first-class hotel. The island is so beautiful that MGM decided to shoot "South Pacific" there, and it became the legendary "Bali H'ai" on the silver screen.

One of my favorites is Redang. You enter a still lagoon through a narrow reef, and a Malay fishing village as old as time is nestled at one end of the coves. At sunset when the fishing boats come in, the fishermen give you choice fish for your evening meal.

In Thailand it's Ko Samui. If MGM is ever looking for other shots for a romantic isle, then Ko Samui is the place. A large island, it is indented with coves. It would take several days to walk around it.

It's helpful having your own boat, of course, but it's not necessary. If islands don't have ferry services from the mainland, you can always hire a fishing boat to take you back and forth. You can arrange to have the boat pick you up in a few days, or keep it and sleep aboard. I know people who have done both. For accommodations, islands like Tioman and Ko Samui have hotels. The other alternative is to camp. Where else can you have an island to yourself, and yet be so close.

A sport in Asia that one hardly ever considers is mountain climbing. We all hear about climbing Mount Fuji, and perhaps Mount Kinabalu in Sabah. These certainly are two mountains worth attempting. But there are others that you seldom, if ever, hear about.

One is Mount Ophir, a mountain with a legend. It lies a dozen or so miles inland from Malacca. It's said that a fairy goddess makes her abode on the mountain. Her beauty is striking, and she has a way of luring men into her charms. Once a man rests his eyes upon her he never wants to leave.

To reach the summit takes two days. Once you begin climbing, what may have sounded like fantasy, suddenly takes on new meaning. You being to wonder. The trail of sorts leads through an almost forbidden forest. The twisted and gnarled trunks of trees are green with damp moss and everywhere hanging in deep folds are vines and creepers. So thick is the vegetation that even at midday the sun cannot penetrate to the trail below. It becomes eerie. Is it night or day? Water in rivulets makes gushing sounds and everywhere is mist and fog rising upwards.

You may not believe in the myth but you find yourself looking. Just in case. You might even imagine you've seen her. A warm fire and a brandy at the summit puts you at peace with the world.

Another mountain that only a few have tackled is Mount Tahan in central Malaysia. It's the highest on the peninsula. Just to reach it takes a week, by dugout up the Tembling for two or three days, and then hacking through the jungles for another four. The Park Headquarters can arrange for guides.

Wild rivers, jungle safaris, the undersea world, cave exploring, mountain climbing, trekking, island hopping, game fishing—it's all there, and more.

Fortunately we don't have to be wealthy or friendly with a rich maharaja to enjoy Asia's great outdoors. Cost for guides and porters are only a few dollars per day. We can buy bedding and clothing from surplus stores—but don't be too military looking. And there is good transportation to about every place we want to go. People are often asking me, "How do you ever afford all those trips." I find it cheaper going on safari than visiting any of Asia's bigger cities.

Probably what Asia needs is an explorers' or adventurers' club, where ideas can be exchanged and expeditions organised. It would help a lot of people to do the thing they have always wanted to do.

But until then, it's up to the individual. But don't let it all pass.

Chapter 27
THE ORIENTAL JUNGLES, ASIA'S VANISHING FRONTIER

The following article appeared on April 25, 1976. I sadly say that the jungle is not the same as I knew it years ago. The Endau River that I wrote about now has roads running through it and the rhino have disappeared from that area. Logging interests have claimed much of the area.

One of the great authorities on the world's jungles was the late Dr. Ivan Sanderson. I had the pleasure of meeting with him several times. He lived in New York and often when I visited the city I called upon him. Sitting with him in his dusty library was always thrilling. We talked for hours about the jungles.

Dr. Sanderson had spent a lifetime wandering through tropical rain forests from South and Central America to Asia. As a naturalist he wrote widely on the jungles and the people who inhabit them. His essays appeared in hundreds of magazines and his lengthy *Book of Jungles* was used as a university text.

In lecturing and writing about the jungles, Sanderson spent a great deal of time debunking the modern myth most of the public has about jungles. "The existence of these tropical forests had been known for hundreds of years, but hardly anyone had actually entered them. Men had passed around them and boated through them on rivers. Primitive tribes and civilised peoples had lived on the edges but none of them knew what it was like inside."

A negrito couple and their child on a bamboo raft in the Malay jungle.

According to Sanderson, even British hunters "in the jungle" were scarcely learned men, and their name for the forest was never adopted by science as a description as anything. Scientists thought, in fact, the word is as meaningless as "dinosaur," adopted by the French to mean any and all large fossil reptiles thought to be extinct.

Our concept of "jungle" came from noted writers like Rudyard Kipling whose only intent was to give the tropical rain forests a romantic sounding name. In his jungles Kipling placed not only all the animals and plants he had not seen, but others of which he had only heard, whether or not they were typical of jungles or even could live there. Kipling's jungles were a kind of Hans Christian Andersen never-never land which was so vividly described that readers took it for the real thing.

The world's ready acceptance of the Kipling concept of a jungle is quite understandable. Until recently virtually no genuinely scientific studies had been made of the interior of these closed canopy tropical forests.

Perhaps the reason jungles have been ignored for so long was that man supposed the inside must be an extension of what he could see from the outside. If you look at a jungle from a river, for example, all you will see is a solid green wall of dense vegetation cascading down to the ground from the tops of trees. It appears impossible to enter the jungle from that position.

My impressions of the jungles of Southeast Asia came many years ago when I made my first trip into the Pahang jungle of central Malaysia. We never left the river, and had we even tried, I would imagine we could not have penetrated the green wall. Furthermore, no one thought of doing so anyway; it had to be the same tangled mass of vegetation on the interior as we saw along the river. It wasn't until subsequent trips that I learned how far from the truth I had been. Once through the wall, the interior is altogether different.

Then there is the other concept that is misleading—"The law of the Jungle." It is widely held that the law of the jungle is nothing more than a ruthless competition for survival, a kill or be killed situation. People use the term "jungle law" when they refer to a particularly bitter fight without pity or scruple.

Such competition does exist, certainly, but it is not the only rule by which jungle vegetation must grow. There is an interdependence, a mutual aid, and without this the forest could not exist. The jungle plant fights not only for itself alone but for the general welfare of all our jungle vegetation.

Of all the jungles of the world, the jungles of Southeast Asia, called the Oriental Jungles by scientists, are by far the largest, and perhaps the most fascinating. They begin across the Bay of Bengal in Burma and spread out over a vast number of Burmese islands, both large and small. On the mainland they include the forests of Thailand, Laos, Cambodia, Vietnam and the Malay Peninsula. They spread out to the Philippines and Indonesia and reach as far as New Guinea and its islands. And of all these, the jungles of the Malay Peninsula are by far the most interesting and unspoiled.

The Malay jungles are the oldest on this planet, so old they make the tropical rain forests of Africa and South America seem adolescent by comparison. While creeping ice fronts were swelling and shrinking across the northern hemisphere, the Malay jungles had slept through an estimated 100 million years or more of uninterrupted slumber. And while the far–reaching climatic changes were affecting the rest of the globe, and the animal species there were forced into new revolutionary channels, Malaysia's wildlife was left undisturbed and developed into unique species.

As we are aware, the process of evolution is slow and mysterious. Given enough time, under the right conditions, anything can happen. In the upper foliage of the jungle trees, where branches are densely thick and interlaced, there live bizarre specimens. Frogs and lizards— which have grown leathery membranes that pass for wings—fly from tree to tree. Most striking of these is the flying lemur, on earth for about 70 million years; they dwell only in the Oriental Jungles of Southeast Asia. There are also tree snakes that lie solely above ground.

Living in the same matted vegetation 60 feet above ground, these reptiles developed over the centuries of existence without ever climbing down to earth, while their nearest relatives elsewhere in the world are the common burrowing snakes and other such reptiles.

The Oriental Jungle's wide profusion of rare wildlife stimulated trade in luxuries which has thrived for more than a millennium. Even before the days of Kubla Khan, Chinese merchants journeyed to Borneo in quest of exotic medicines like bezoar stones, extracted from the stomach of a monkey, or rhinoceros horn, used to make cups which could detect poison. Powdered rhino horn is still an expensive ingredient to the Chinese apothecary, just as bird's nest, fetched from gigantic caves in East Malaysia and southern Thailand, are to the Chinese chef.

Clouded leopards, tigers, tapirs, elephants, deer, wild pigs and porcupine still roam the isolated hinterland. But big game is most elusive. Due to the denseness of the undergrowth, animals, other than monkeys and gibbons, are frequently heard but seldom seen. Years of callous butchery at the hand of profiteering hunters have depleted the ranks of some beasts. The one-horned rhino, which Marco Polo mistook for the mythical unicorn, has vanished from Malaysia's jungles and is on the verge of extinction. The orangutans, famous Wild Man of Borneo, have been rounded up and placed in a special sanctuary in Sabah.

The Thai, Malaysian and Indonesian governments have set aside vast tracks of land as game reserves, and strict hunting laws are enforced. The Chief Game Warden of Malaysia, Muhammad

Khan, has proposed that instead of shooting wild elephants that tear up garden patches in remote kampongs, Malay villages, the elephants should be captured and relocated in protected park areas. The government is initiating a project to do this now and are training rangers for the task.

As amazing as the jungles are, they are no less so than the primitive people who live there. Take the jungles of southern Thailand and Malaysia as an example. The aborigines who inhabit the forests, or Orang Asli as they are called, are divided into three distinct groups: the Negritos, the Senoi and the Proto-Malays. Sometimes we hear the name Sakai, but it is only another Malay name for Senoi. And oftentimes the Proto-Malays are called "aboriginal Malays." However, together they are called Orang Asli, a name they prefer.

The Negritos live in the north close to the Thai border. Anthropologically they are Malaysia's oldest existing race. They move about in groups, seldom more than a dozen.

Their life is simple. They have no shelter, except during monsoons they throw leaves over poles to ward off the rain. They are basically hunters and collectors of forest produce. Some do plant small patches of ground with crops such as tapioca and bananas.

Negritos are dark chocolate-brown in skin colour, but no darker than this. In the remote forest they wear pieces of black cloth twisted around the waist and the women may weave leaves to make skirts. But where Negritos are living close to advanced communities, shorts and sarongs are common sights.

With blow-pipes and poison darts the men hunt for squirrels, monkeys, rats, lizards and birds. The women and children gather fruit and vegetables from the surrounding forest. The men catch fish in traps or else spear them with sharpened bamboo lances. Sometimes tuba, a strong form of tranquiliser, is used to stun the fish and bring them to the surface.

The Senoi people are sightly taller than the Negritos and are usually somewhat of slimmer build. Their skin colour is medium brown. They have the bone features and characteristics of the Chinese and it may be difficult to tell them apart.

Some Senoi paint their faces and tattoo themselves. Others pierce their noses and insert decorated pieces wood or bone or porcupine quills. Most of the Senoi groups practice shifting cultivation of some kind, often combining it with permanent types of agriculture such as growing rubber trees and harvesting the latex and rice cultivation. There are estimated to be some 60,000 Senoi. They build semi-permanent type dwellings near their fields. There are simple attap covered huts, built above ground on stilts. The walls and floors are split bamboo. Hearths for cooking fires are made from hard-packed earth set in wooden frames.

The Proto-Malays or aboriginal Malays are heavier built than the other two groups. They are by far the most advanced and many have been incorporated into the Malay population and way of life and culture. They often find employment as policemen, labourers, boat builders and fishermen. Their homes and dwellings are similar to the Malays. Many are sea people who live with their families on their boats. They number about 30,000.

Over my years of touring in Malaysia, I came to know the Senoi and Proto-Malays. On an Endau River expedition I lived in Senoi villages and spent weeks in the jungles and on the rivers with Senoi guides and boatmen.

My curiosity naturally led me to the elusive Negritos. In Kuala Lumpur I had been continuously warned, even by the experts, that it was doubtful that I'd ever see them. "They are always on the move," people insisted. "They are shy and always hide, and you'll certainly never get near enough talk to them."

Not long after, I was invited on an expedition to Kelantan jungle with the game department. Our guides were Negritos. One day, as they were poling us on rafts across some shallows on the Liber River, one of them, for no apparent reason, began waving an arm and talking to the jungle. We wondered what he was doing. He spoke out in a loud voice, waited and then spoke again. From out of the foliage a voice came back, speaking the same language. We could not see a soul. It was eerie and even a bit frightening.

We knew now the Negritos were there, unseen in the dense green covering of the forest, watching us. We felt uncomfortable, to say the least.

A few days later we befriended a man and his wife we unexpectedly met on the river. The woman cradled a small child. The man's only clothing was a breechcloth. She was naked. They were travelling up river on a three-log bamboo raft, loaded down with a dozen ripe durians. They had nothing else.

We spent time after that with other Negritos. Here truly were Rousseau's "noble savages." It was Rousseau who wrote in the 18th century that the ills of civilisation could be cured if man returned to his primitive state.

Their secret, I learned, was one of adjustment to their environment. They had fears, certainly, but they knew how to cope with them. There was nothing complicated to their existence. Life was simple. A man when he went into the forest took his wife and child with him. They shared their pleasures as well as their problems. They were Rousseau's children.

The Orang Asli who live in tropical forests aspire to nothing. They have no ambitions, other than to feed themselves, and they have no objectives. Happiness is simply measured by the amount of leisure it brings. The people of these quiet jungles do not crave excitement.

Friendship need not be a display of emotions. A nod is sufficient. On an extended river trip up the Endau I recall spending the evenings talking to our guide Bujong. He spoke longingly about his wife, and his desire to return to her and his people. After a few weeks we did return, and I was astonished to see, when the villagers came down to watch us arrive, there were no warm greetings. A few people nodded.

Bujong's wife stood in the background. There was a smile between them that quickly passed. It was sufficient. Later that day I stopped at their hut. They were sitting on mats, drinking tea, talking as man and wife do.

Hopefully in the coming weeks I will be able to report on wildlife in the Malay jungles. At the time when this article appears in the *Post,* I will be on another expedition with the Chief Game Warden, Mohammed Khan. Joining us for his first jungle trip is Mike Yamashita, one of Asia's foremost photographers. The warden requested that we make no reference to the area where we are going, expect to say that it's an unexplored region of the National Park. His reason is that he believes the game Department has located a herd of Sumatra Rhinoceros, hereto believed to have been extinct. Hopefully Mike will be able to photograph these rare beasts. However, were we to make it known where they are, poachers would be tracking through the jungle in hot pursuit. A rhino on the black market, even a dead one we are told, brings well over US$100,000. It isn't only the horn the Chinese would grind up for their aphrodisiac powder, but the entire rhino as well would go into the grinder. In my next article, I hope we can relate a successful expedition, that the Sumatran rhino are alive and safe in the Malay jungle.

We did find rhino in the wild, and Mike was able to photograph their habitat. Also the chief game warden was successful in transporting threatened wild elephants into other protected areas of the jungle.

Train travel is still the way to go in Southeast Asia. From Thailand to Indonesia and from Myanmar to the Philippines you find trains in operation.

Chapter 28
GREAT TRAIN RIDES OF ASIA

My first train travel in Asia was in China, from Tiensin to Peking, which is Beijing today. That was before the People's Republic took power. It was a memorable trip that I can hardly forget, and it began my love for train travel around the world. I wrote the following article about taking the train in both Russia and Southeast Asia which appeared on May 23, 1976. Since then I made two train trips which I have longed to do for years, one in the Philippines and the other in Borneo. Unfortunately, while many countries of the world are expanding their train services, the Philippines is rapidly disbanding hers. The last remaining line in the country is from Manila down the long, narrow arm of the Luzon Peninsula to Legaspi. I had to make that run before it is lost forever. It was an exhilarating ride. The engineer let me ride with him in the locomotive. The other train journey was in Sabah, Borneo, from Kota Kinablu to Tenon. It was a trip through the jungle, with tattooed Ibans and Punans, once head hunters, as fellow passengers. Hopefully that line will be around for a long time.

The Orient Express! Few names can conjure up more romance than the mention of the "Orient Express." Intriguing plots for spy stories, novels and movies have been built around this legendary train trip from Europe to Asia.

I hate to be the one to debunk old romantic notions, but the name was a misnomer. It's true, there was once a train called the Orient Express, and it did start in Europe, but it terminated where Asia merely begins, at the gates of Istanbul. Although a Europe-Asia line may have been a great dream of rail magnates from time to time, there never had been a through train from Europe to the Far East, say from London to Singapore. The gaps along the route are too many—eastern Iran, Afghanistan and Burma. Nor does such a dream look hopeful in the near future. In fact, 50 years ago it was easier to travel a greater part of the distance by rail than it is today.

But rail buffs travelling in Asia should not fret; there are some great train trips that would be hard to equal in the West. Certainly heading this list, and perhaps what is closer to the true Orient Express, is the Trans-Siberian railway, from Moscow across Siberia to the Sea of Japan, a 5,000-mile journey.

The famed railway was built in 1890 and completed just before the 1917 Revolution. Closed to foreigners down through the years, it was only opened to general travel ten years ago. No sooner had Intourist, the official Soviet Government tourist bureau announced its opening, than I applied. Regretfully, I can't say I made the Trans-Siberian journey. Intourist granted my visa for an overland journey, but it was a motor permit to drive across Russia. I covered my 5,000 miles in Russia in an old army jeep I bought for the occasion. But I am looking forward to the rail trip one day.

Those who have travelled on the Trans-Siberian line call it an experience of a lifetime. By boarding the train in Moscow, passengers cross the entire expanse of Siberia to Khabarovsk in the Soviet Far East. From there it's an overnight train ride to the Port of Nalchodka, near Vladivostok, aboard a special tourist train. Then it's a 48-hour ocean voyage to Yokohama.

The only complaint about the Trans-Sib, as seasoned travellers call it, is that the seven days it takes can become awful boring. Rail buffs suggested taking the Bullet Train in Japan instead. "It does 200 miles per hour," they say. But speed isn't our only quest.

One problem with the Bullet Train is to get good seats you have to book weeks, and sometimes months, in advance. If you don't, you are certain to spend a thousand miles, or five hours, squeezed into a compartment that required several ex-sumo wrestlers at the doors to pack everyone in.

When it comes to recommending train rides in India, I have to think twice about it. It might be easier to get first class tickets than it is in Japan, but then when you locate your compartment, you might find half a dozen other passengers there too, all holding first-class tickets. Even worse, unless you lock your door, when the trains starts to move away from the station, an army of people without any tickets at all will try to rush aboard. Since Indian trains have no passageways connecting compartments, no conductor will come to assist you.

But India is not all Asia. Every Asian country, with the exceptions of Afghanistan and Laos, has at least one railway in operation, some offering exceptional rides. In the island Republic of Indonesia, for example, there's a very popular line—with air-conditioned compartments—which runs on a daily service between Jakarta and Surabaja. Travellers going overland across Java to Bali usually take this train.

If you are in Savannakhet in Laos and see the railway station, don't let it fool you. There's no railway. The French, it seems, built the station but never got around to constructing the rail line. The British did much the same in Kuala Lumpur. They built the train station long before they had a rail line. The engineers also had problems getting the home office in London to approve the design. The roof of the train station, the report stated, wasn't strong enough to withhold three feet of snow, a standard requirement.

There are far more rail journeys in Asia than one might think. In Hong Kong you can take the short two-hour journey from Kowloon to the New Territories, and if you have a pass and proper visas, you can remain aboard the train for its journey into Canton.

Most train travel in Southeast Asia is not international, that is, from one country to the next, except for the service from Bangkok down through Malaysia to Singapore. It's one train journey I would suggest anyone take. It's a two and a half day journey that runs the entire length of the Malay Peninsula. I try to manage a trip once or twice a year. I find it a great way to relax.

The fact that there is a train running the length of the peninsula is intriguing enough to tempt one to try it. The building of the rail line can be compared to the digging of the Panama Canal. Engineers on both sides of the world had to defeat nature and battle a myriad of diseases and fever before they could succeed.

Prior to the railway, towns of Malaya were only pockets of civilisation, each one existing in isolation. Even Kuala Lumpur was little more than a jungle village hidden away amid dense forest. The only means of transportation was by bullock car or elephant back over way of narrow jungle tracks. In most opinions of the time, the building of such a rail line—the cutting of a path through seemingly impenetrable jungle—was an impossible task. But it was more than clearing a jungle; there were vast gorges and rivers to be bridged and swamps to be crossed. Surveyors discovered in some areas they would have to descend through eighty feet of mud before they could reach solid footing.

The jungle provided other obstacles even more formidable. While labour crews battled intense heat and disease, they also had to fight off beasts of prey that continually plagued them. One report states that seldom a day passed without a hungry tiger snatching up a lone worker and dragging him into the jungle for his evening meal. Even after the rail line was completed, the threat of the jungle continued. There's one rather tragic example.

Shortly after the section between Tapah Road and Teluk Anson was opened, a passenger train met with an unprecedented accident. While defending it's herd, a wild bull elephant charged the train head on and derailed it. No one was hurt but the impact did throw the engineer from his cab into the jungle. The track was blocked for five days.

The first rail line in Malaya was opened on June 1, 1885, connecting Port Weld with Taiping, covering a distance of 8 1/2 miles. Eighteen months later another line was opened, connecting Kuala Lumpur to the coast. The line made headlines. It was no less important than our modern day landing on the moon.

The *Straits Times*, dated September 22, 1886, called it a momentous occasion, with brass and royalty aboard, from His Excellency the Governor and Lady Weld to His Highness the Sultan of Selangor and his hundred attendants. "It started at twenty to ten and at quarter past eleven the train steamed into Kuala Lumpur," the reporter wrote. "The run of about twenty miles had been done in ninety minutes."

The article goes on to say that "as the train neared KL the speed was greatly accelerated and we were doing about thirty miles an hour." The article concluded by saying "the motion was very pleasant."

What did the arrival of the Iron Horse mean? One reporter saw it as a tourist promotion scheme and nothing more. In the same article he wrote: "The train will mean an increase in foreigners and strangers who will come, much to the profit of the country."

Singapore island had its own rail system but it wasn't until 1923 that the causeway connecting the island with the Malay mainland was completed and carried the first through train from Singapore to Penang.

A few years ago I was writing a book on Malaysia for Apa Press and thought that some of the anecdotes of building the line might make good reading. In Singapore I called the Superintendent of Railways and explained what I wanted. He was most pleased to help me, and stated that the public should know something about the fine railway. He promised to post the information which I wanted, and it arrived at my hotel the next day.

I opened it. "Dear Mr. Stephens," it began; "The system is of high standard, with maximum gradient of 1 in 100. Rails are of 80 lbs per yard, with some at 60 lbs. Sleepers are of local hardwood, the rails being fastened by dog spikes. The average life of a sleeper is 14 years. More important lines are ballasted with limestone of 2 1/4 inch..." At the conclusion of the report he sincerely hoped I could use the information in my writing. I have.

As I mentioned, anyone travelling in India by train should attempt to go first class. On the Bangkok-Singapore Express I prefer second class, non-aircon. Second class is comfortable and clean, and the price is attractive. (It's only half of first class.) With the windows open you can feel the countryside, and in the stations there are all kinds of goodies you can buy through an open window. But then, travelling first class in a wood panelled compartment, all to yourself, is travelling in real luxury.

Whenever I make the trip I usually take along a good book with the intention of catching up on my reading. Instead of reading I spend hours looking out the window at the unrolling countryside. One minute you might be passing through dense jungle and the next shooting across fields of rice paddy. In the south there are large tin mines and endless rubber estates with trees in neat and orderly lines.

For the rail buff who really likes to see jungle, there's another section of the Malaysian line that runs in a north-south direction. This one is from Singapore through the central peninsula on a wood-burning train to Kota Baharu on the East Coast. There are no roads, only the rail line. If you are motoring, you can drive up the east coast of Malaysia to Kota Baharu, put your vehicle on a flat car and take the same train, through the jungle, back to Singapore.

Anyone who plans to make a train trip through Malaysia and

wants further information, I strongly suggest you don't write to the Superintendent of Railways, unless, of course, you want to build your own railway.

One of the most exciting train trips in Asia is also the shortest. It's the famous "Toy Train" to Darjeeling.

Darjeeling is a mountain retreat in northern India that dates back to the days of early British rule. At more than 7,000 feet above sea level, her northern and eastern frontiers are the Himalayan kingdoms of Nepal and Bhutan on one side and Tibet and Sikkim on the other. The resort is 416 miles north of Calcutta. From Calcutta there is regular train service, or a bi-weekly air service, to the town of Silliguri at the foothills of the Himalayas. From there the traveller has the choice of going by Land Rover, which takes two to three hours, or boarding the Toy Train, which winds and twists through rugged mountain passes and takes five hours. It's amazing how many people will give up the chance of riding this incredible train only to save two hours.

Two miniature coal-burning engines pull four small passenger cars over a track of very narrow gauge. When I first saw the train I thought it wasn't for real, that perhaps it might have been a transplant from Disneyland. But it was real enough, with real steam and real passengers squeezing into real undersized compartments.

We started off across the lowlands at ten to twenty miles an hour, with the engine picking up steam en route. Then came the first hills. The track twisted into sharp S-curves, and the engine chugged and groaned and spat out steam as if it was about to explode. For fifty miles it continued upwards, not even stopping in small villages where passengers have to hop on or off the moving train. Had it stopped, I'm certain the engineer could never have gotten it started again. The steeper the climb the more ear-shattering became the noise as steel ground against steel, slipping and sliding but never giving in.

After five hours we rounded a bend and suddenly there was Darjeeling, built on a hill, with houses and buildings standing on the crests of steep ridges, and in the background loomed the snow caps of the rugged Kanchenjunga Range.

They have porters at the train station in Darjeeling you would find nowhere else. A very tall tanned Sherpa came up and asked for the name of my hotel, and no sooner had I told him when he summoned a little old lady who had to be in her sixties. Before I could protest she immediately scooped up my luggage, adjusting it to a headstrap and set off through the streets at a pace which I had a difficult time following.

Taking the Toy Train to Darjeeling is one thing; taking it back is something else. It's a journey that would make a roller-coaster ride in an amusement park seem mild. When I first boarded the train to come up to Darjeeling, I wondered why there were huge buffers at the end of the line. When I returned I discovered the reason. It's all the brakeman can do it bring the train to a screeching halt at the terminal. The buffer, I assume, is what hopefully will stop the train if the brakes fail.

There's one other train trip in Asia that has something of the same down-hill thrill as the Toy Train. This one is at Wulai in Taiwan. The line here is only three miles long, and it takes you to an aboriginal village in the hills.

The railway is unique in that the locomotives are not electric or even steam-powered. They are muscle-powered, driven by humans. The compartments are actually push-cars with two seats, which run on narrow gauge tracks. The operator walks behind and pushes the occupants up the three-mile twisting track to the settlement. For the return ride, the operator jumps on the back of the cart, takes hold of the brake and it's a race non-stop to the finish. What makes it so harrowing is that the line is also used by people who prefer to hike to the settlement rather than pay the fare. There follows screaming and shouting as only the Chinese can do. I was assured that few people ever get hurt.

Train travel in Europe is still a great way to travel, and in America it's making a comeback. In Asia it never left, and it will be around for a long time. It's efficient, inexpensive, and it can be fun. And one thing for certain—if you found it became boring after a long journey, you could always return by jet. They couldn't do that 50 years ago.

I did make the Trans-Siberan rail journey a few years after I wrote this article. There are no more coal-burning locomotives in Malaysia, and Hong Kong has regular train service into China. Also, the Eastern & Oriental Express has a luxury train from Bangkok to Singapore.

The E&O Hotel in Penang, Malaysia, was built by the Starkies brothers in the latter part of the last century, along with Raffles in Singapore and the Strand in Rangoon.

Chapter 29
WALKING THROUGH HISTORY AT PENANG'S E&O HOTEL

The following article appeared on November 6, 1989. It's about one of my favourite hotels in Asia.

Three grand Old Ladies of Asia—the Strand Hotel in Rangoon, Raffles in Singapore, and the E&O in Penang. There are others, for certain, such as the Oriental Hotel in Bangkok and the Manila Hotel in Manila, to name but two, but I mention these three in particular because all have something in common.

They were founded over a hundred years ago by the three enterprising Starkies brothers from Armenia. And they are all in the headlines again, or at least two of them are.

The much neglected Strand hasn't seen a coat of paint in over 40 years, but nonetheless, she stands much as she did when the Starkies brothers founded her. The Raffles in Singapore closed its doors ten months ago for extensive renovations—and rumour has it that it may never see completion. And now the E&O, it has just been announced, is about to see some drastic changes too.

If you plan to visit Penang, this may be your one remaining chance to see the last of the original Starkies Brothers' hotels. I just paid the hotel a nostalgic visit, and came away saddened. But I hope I'm wrong. Some great hotels have managed change rather well—Bangkok's Oriental Hotel, which has the accolade of being voted by business travellers as the "best hotel in the world" for nine consecutive years, and the Manila Hotel in Manila, which survived heavy naval shelling in World War II and major renovations in 1976. Maybe the E&O will somehow manage it too.

Super glass and concrete hotels have their place in our modern society, granted, but old hotels have their place too. Who doesn't like hotels that have history? What better pleasure is there than to walk down long dark corridors that echo with the voices of great names, names of those who have walked there before you? Imagine the stories they have to tell.

Their stories, unfortunately, do not come from subtle whispers. They come from study and research found in dusty archives and boring old record books. But once the homework is done, the old hotels speak out. That's what I discovered about the E&O Hotel. It has a great voice yearning to be heard. The E&O doesn't want to suffer the neglect of its sister the Strand in Rangoon, nor the fate of the Raffles in Singapore. But, unless precaution is taken, it may happen.

The E&O, the owners have announced, is to be upgraded with new wings, shopping centres and plazas, and a new car park. Does that mean the old has to be sacrificed to make room for the new?

Were the Starkie Brothers alive today, what would they think? No doubt, they would be in accord with the plans. Making changes was their raison d'etre from Day One when they founded the first hotel where the E&O stands today. In fact, hadn't there been changes, the E&O wouldn't exist at all. It just might be that their methods differed.

The Starkies came from Armenia, a disputed strip of land between Turkey and Russia. The Russians and Turks fought long and hard in the 19th century, each claiming the territory as their own. Armenians by the scores were driven from their homeland and many came east. They settled in small communities in places like Calcutta, Rangoon and the Straits Settlement (Penang, Malacca and Singapore), where they engaged in business.

Martin Starkies, an engineer, found Penang to his liking and settled there in 1869. In 1880 he was joined by his brother Togran. Records show that they opened a hotel facing the Esplanade and named it the Eastern Hotel, and the following year opened a second hotel, the Oriental, on a plot of land facing the sea.

Both hotels prospered, but to grow, the brothers saw the need to expand, except that, even then, land was at a premium. The only solution was to combine the two hotels into the Eastern and Oriental, or the E&O as it became known. The date was in 1885. Five years later, a younger brother, Arshak, came to Penang to take over management of the hotel.

Under the charge of the younger, energetic Arshak, expansion became the order of the day. In 1903, when the hotel boasted having 80 rooms, he added a large ballroom that was soon the talk of the East. The E&O became the centre of life and the venue for the colonial world of Penang and neighbouring towns on the Malay mainland.

The grand and gracious E&O was in its heyday. Here major functions were held—state dinners, important weddings, the annual St. George's Day ball, banquets and concerts by visiting musicians. The first theatrical play in the Federation of the Malay States was held at the E&O. The high life was the theme for many of Somerset Maugham's short stories, and the E&O became immortalised.

Arshok was no doubt a shrewd and determined negotiator. He eventually succeeded in purchasing a section of land along the sea front, and here he added the Victory Annex in 1922.

The ballroom and dining room were also enlarged and redecorated the same year, and the hotel was now able to boast of having the "longest sea front of any hotel in the world"—842 feet.

From the street the E&O is not an imposing building; at a glance it even appears to be rather small. But like the great Chinese mansions of Malacca, it can be deceiving. Enter the lobby and walk beneath the great dome, and exit via the back door into the gardens which surround the swimming pool; continue along the path following the seawall to the far end of the grounds, and then look back. Only then can one fully appreciate the vastness and beauty of the hotel. Its old world charm shines through. You almost expect an English planter to be sitting at a table beneath a shady tree, drinking a tall gin, talking to a lady in an ankle-length brocaded dress. But then, at the E&O you might still be able to do that. Old timers continue to come out of the woodwork and make their appearance at the hotel.

Arshok's powerful personality continues to stalk the hotel. On the ground floor is the Grand Ballroom, recently redecorated, where it is said that the fun-loving hotelier waltzed around the dance floor with a drink balanced on the pate of his bald head. Then there's the Anchor Restaurant, done up with nets and shells like a waterfront eatery; the 1885 Cocktail Lounge with its cozy atmosphere; and the Starkies' Corner, a 24-hour coffee shop. Along the walls in the lobby and corridors are framed photographs of the Starkies Brothers and Penang taken when both the hotel and the town were young.

The view from the rooms above is superb. Immediately below are tropical gardens and a swimming pool. Old cannons, some brought by Francis Light when he founded Penang, rest in their embrasures, pointing out to sea. And the seawall makes a sweeping curve separating hotel from beach. And out beyond, where the sea meets the horizon, is the historic Strait of Malacca, with islands far to the north shimmering in a blue-grey mist. Junks and great sailing ships, like in times of old, still beat their way up the current to Thailand and Burma beyond.

Fort Cornwallis is but a short distance away and it is here that the recorded history of Penang began. When Francis Light took possession of Penang, with orders to found a trading settlement, he had three ships carrying 100 sepoys, 30 lascars, 15 artillery men and five British officers. The site he chose for his settlement was the area between Fort Cornwallis and where the E&O now stands.

The ground then was thick with jungle. The work of clearing away the undergrowth proved to be too arduous even for the tough sepoys and they protested. To induce them to work, Light loaded a cannon with silver dollars and fired it into the jungles. Before long the land was cleared and the first camp established.

On August 11,1786, the Union Jack was raised and the settlement was named Prince of Wales Island. Less than 100 years later, the two Starkies built the Eastern Hotel facing the Esplanade.

The Starkies family sold their interest to the E&O to the Choong family after the war, and in 1965 they in turn sold to the Chans. In 1973, a majority interest was bought by Jack Chia, MPH of Singapore. But the Chans still retain an interest and the son Donny Chan, is the general manager.

When I was very young, I read everything by Somerset Maugham, and I believed that everything he wrote was fiction, that he imagined the events he wrote about and his people were unreal and the places made up. Then many years later I was in Penang, riding in my first trishaw, going from the waterfront to Fort Cornwallis. The driver made a turn in the road and suddenly it was there, the E&O Hotel.

It was as though I opened up the pages of a Maugham novel and I was back in my school days. But this was real. And Maugham's world, like the E&O, was real. Let's hope it remains real after its upgrading, and that it doesn't become a mere replica of something past. There's enough of that already in Asia. Jack Chia, do your thing. Keep Maugham and the E&O alive.

The rumour about Raffles Hotel in Singapore not opening it's doors again was false. Raffles did open it doors. However, unlike The Oriental in Bangkok, it did not recapture its old glory but nonetheless, in spite of all its alabaster and guided tours, it's still a fine hotel. And who would ever have believed, the Strand in Rangoon went through a facelift and is as splendid today as she ever was. And I was wrong about the E&O. She's had a few alterations, like new furniture in the lobby, and a fresh coat of paint, but little else. She remains much as she always was—a great lady in her fine evening dress and shining jewelry sitting back contented to see the world about her changing.

Chapter 30
WHAT BECAME OF ALL THOSE GREAT BARS IN ASIA

Before the days of tourists, it was seaman who brought back tales of Asia, and being sailors, they told about the fabulous bars. Those days, and bars, are gone, as I reported for the Post *on February 20, 1989.*

Whatever happened to all those old bars and saloons that flourished in Asia a couple of decades ago? We are reminded every time we see an old movie, or when we read accounts by writers who roamed Asia back then.

Or it could be from the old timers who have tales to tell. We have to admit, those were the days when a man could get a drink in the surroundings he knew.

But were such places only fiction, something we read or heard?

Perhaps some were, but not all of them. I remember when I was in China as a young marine after World War II. In those free-wheeling days all the ports in China had their share of rambunctious waterfront bars—Shanghai, Tsingtao, Tiensin. In any one of these ports you were certain to find an ABC Bar (American-British-Chinese), a New York Bar or a Little San Francisco.

Some were duzzies, run mostly by white Russians, with swinging doors, taxi dancers and live music. They served White Horse Whisky and Hubba Hubba vodka by the bottle, without ice. The vodka cost one dollar a bottle, and you had to pay 10 cents for a ticket to dance, or a dollar for a lady to sit at your table for an hour. Then you didn't have to pay her to dance.

After the war China's days were numbered, and so were the bars. Sailors, expatriates, war profiteers and an increasing number of foreign travellers called tourists found watering holes elsewhere, mainly in Southeast Asia. Hong Kong, Manila, Penang, Kuala Lumpur, Singapore, and, of course, Bangkok, all in time took their places and added sparkle to the lure of Asia. The age of bars and saloons reached its peak during the Vietnam War; it ended when the hostilities ended.

When it comes to bars, Asia is a strange place. In Europe and America, bars and saloons have a knack for survival. I can think of hundreds of establishments that have flourished for decades, and they'll be around longer than most of us. Harry's New York Bar in Paris is one. It's an institution, where Ernest Hemingway and F. Scott Fitzgerald chug-a-lugged in the roaring '20s, and where you can still have a stein of beer and a hotdog (Harry introduced hotdogs to Paris), right in the very heart of Paris. There's another Harry's in Venice but in name only.

Hussongs Cantina in Baja, Mexico, just across the border from California, had been around since the end of the last century, and it still stacks them in. Sometimes the place is five deep at the bar, as they stand on the sawdust-covered floor. And the Buena Vista overlooking the waterfront in San Francisco isn't about to close its doors. Irish coffee started here.

But in Asia bars do the disappearing act. Only a few, a very few, manage to linger on. Occasionally imitations will spring up, bearing the name of an old establishment, but they're only bad copies. It's much like Bugis Street in Singapore. That infamous Bugis Street (one of the few tourist attractions Singapore had left after the city decided to go modern) was torn down, and in it's place today you find "Bugis Street Centre," "Bugis Street Restaurant," "Bugis Street Square," and a half dozen more Bugis Street Something-or-Other. But they are all fakes, none which can even remotely compete with the old place where sailors came to swill down bottles of beer and dance on tables in the streets, along with transvestites.

Some of the modern-day bars we find in Asia are like meteors. They appear suddenly, glow brightly for a short spell and then fizz out in a flash. This often seems to be the case in Bangkok. There was a time, not so long ago, when the city had some great bars where everyone went to meet friends and drink. No one thought they would ever end. But they did. (Remember Sam Scott? And Maurice Rocco?)

One of the best bars in Bangkok 20 or more years ago was the Bamboo Bar at the old Oriental Hotel. The most popular place in town, it was located in what they call today the Author's Wing. After working hours the place was jampacked, a gathering spot for expatriates, journalists, tourists and GIs seeking a respite from the war in Vietnam. Sultry Australian songstress Shirley Simmons sang there for years, and entertained thousands of homesick GIs with "I Left My Heart in San Francisco."

A bar that has survived the ravages of time is Club 99 on Silom Road. Thus, I have to make it Number One for Bangkok. There are others that I equally like in town, but most of them haven't been around long enough to be placed into the "enduring bars" category.

But let's go beyond Bangkok. Let's begin with Singapore.

Singapore had a longtime reputation among seaman as a "good liberty town." But with independence in 1966, the new order was keen on creating a new image. Rowdiness was out, along with all traces of colonialism. They succeeded, and as a consequence, they destroyed Singapore's best tourist attractions.

A bar in Singapore that reached world fame was Bill Bailey's Coconut Grove off Orchard Road. The first Grove opened on the East Coast in 1935, but Japanese bombers used it for practice and made a direct hit. And poor Bill, he had to change his residence.

He was given quarters in Changi Prison for the duration of the war.

Bill managed to survive starvation and a brutal beating, and when the war ended he still didn't go home, not Bill Bailey. He opened another Coconut Grove, off Orchard Road. Times were hard but he never gave up, and no amount of singing— "Old Bill Bailey, won't you come home"—could make him change his mind.

The second Grove was in an old Chinese mansion, with piano and fanback chairs. Hotelier Franz Schutzman, when he was GM of Raffles Hotel in the '50s, told how he took clients from Raffles to meet Bill and to listen to his yarns. In latter years the Grove became the unofficial foreign corespondents' press club. Then came urban renewal; bulldozers leveled it to the ground and in its place today is a 14-storey highrise.

Until just a few years ago, the Pub on Orchard Road had all the prerequisites for a good English pub, with heavy wooden-panelled walls and brass rails, but like Bill Bailey's, it had to come down to make room for glass and concrete highrises.

There were others too, like the Boots and Saddle, a real Western bar, with the occasional barroom fight to give it authenticity. But the government didn't care for rowdy Western bars, no matter how many tourists and oil men it attracted. They not only closed the doors but they bulldozed the building flat to the ground.

What continues to be a fovourite hangout in Singapore today is the Raffles Hotel, one of Asia's oldest hotels. Nightly, the Long Bar is jammed, with tourists who come by bus loads for a quick Singapore Sling and a look at what Singapore used to be. GM Roberto Peragas, a one-man historian of the old Raffles, boasts that the Long Bar serves 2,000 Singapore Slings in any one day of the week.

But one doesn't have to be a part of the tourist scene to enjoy a drink at Raffles. Across the hall is the Author's Bar, an old English-style pub without a dart board. It rings with the atmosphere of Somerset Maugham, who did, actually, sit in a leather arm chair and drink his gin and bitters nightly, according to Franz Schutzman. One waiter at the Author's Bar still remembers serving Mr Maugham when he made his sentimental journey to Singapore in 1961.

Kuala Lumpur almost suffered the same fate as Singapore but somebody up there stopped them before it was too late. A few years back the old Selangor Club was doomed to destruction, but at the last minute the old colonial institution was given a reprieve. It would have been a tragedy to see it go.

The Tudor-style Selangor Club was built and opened back in 1884 long before there was any other permanent structures in the city. (Kuala Lumpur was founded in 1864.) It became a friendly place where members could refresh themselves, talk, read the months-old London newspapers (the club subscribed to 27 "home" newspapers), play cards or just loaf. The club house is still there, a landmark in the centre of town, but without 27 newspapers.

While the Selangor Club is private and you must know someone to have a drink at the bar, the old Coliseum Cafe & Bar on Batu Road is open to the public. It hasn't changed much in the past 60 years. The decor, the menu, the aging waiters, and even a few old patrons, are all the same.

The Coliseum caters to expatriates and has been their refuelling station for half a century. It's still the favourite for planters, tin miners and local officials. Occasionally a curious passing tourist will enter the swinging doors and find himself in another era.

The bar is separate from the dining room. It looks much like an English pub with dart board, bulletin board, a coat and hat rack in the corner and a brass rail around the counter. The bar also serves as front desk for the hotel rooms upstairs. Keys hang on a rack behind the bar. Old timers talk about past days when they had to hang their sidearms and solar topees on racks before ordering their drinks.

North of Kuala Lumpur is Penang, one of the oldest towns in Asia. It has a lot of the old world charm and nostalgia, especially when you go to the E&O Hotel for a drink, one of the three oldest hotels in Asia. The E&O is a sister to Raffles in Singapore and Strand Hotel in Rangoon.

For an unusual bar in Penang, and a truly sailor's bar, there is the Hong Kong Bar on Chuila Street. It's a place where you literally get yourself into the picture. When you step inside and order a drink, a pretty Chinese girl will appear with a camera and flash.

First impulse is to say no, that you don't want to have a photo taken. But she will tell you that she wants your picture. What you may not know is that it goes on record. The girls at the Hong Kong Bar have photographed virtually every customer who has stepped through the front door. The albums add up to many dozens. They are carefully numbered by the volume.

The unique collection is also cross-indexed. It takes only two minutes to find any photograph, by either name or date, and for seamen, their ship's names. The idea of keeping such a record of everyone who enters was the brainchild of its owner, Tan Phoon Kee. He started the bar in 1953, and from the very beginning it was a seaman's bar, with photographs of naval ships on the wall, all signed and autographed.

Both Manila and Cebu in the Philippines were considered to be excellent liberty ports, ever since the US Navy steamed into Manila Bay at the turn of the century. Many of the crusty bars were owned and operated by ex-GIs who, like Bill Bailey, never went home.

One ex-GI who did just that was Eddie Woolbright. While others failed, Eddie succeeded. His famous bar and restaurant is still there on the waterfront in Cebu— Eddie's Log Cabin Bar and Restaurant.

From the outside, it looks like a rundown godown. Step inside and it's what the name says, a log cabin. Wagon wheel overhead, old posters on the walls, brand marks burned into the beams, and an excellent Western menu. Eddie, who married a zillion times and has nine daughters, came out with the military in World War II and stayed on.

Another place where expats gather and drink in Cebu is the Magellan Hotel, my second favourite hotel in the Philippines. It has atmosphere.

My favourite water hole in Manila is the Manila Hotel. It was actually built by the US Army Corps of Engineers in 1912 for "a place for Americans to stay." It has since been the gathering place for travellers who want something more than a place to bed down. It has class, charm and charisma. Some world travellers class the Manila as one of the world's 10 best hotels. It's lobby bar ranks up at the top.

Then we come to Hong Kong, once the night owl's paradise of the Orient. In 1948, when I first went to Hong Kong as a young marine, it was a sailor's town, with only four or five bars. But what excitement these few bars had to offer! Everybody was out for a good time, bar girls and sailors alike, and nothing else mattered.

Twenty to 30 years ago, the town peaked out as Asia's best night spot. Hong Kong got much of its fame and reputation from Wanchai District, where Suzie Wong did her tricks and Richard Mason wrote about her. But the old Wanchai District isn't what it used to be in the days when Suzie Wong reigned, and back when Hong Kong was an R&R centre for GIs escaping the war in Vietnam.

Today Wanchai's bar scene has gone downhill, all the way to the bottom. Most of the bars are girlie bars, designed to take money away from big spenders. There are a couple of solid drinking bars, and a few old-fashioned pubs with dart boards, like the

Old China Hand and Horse and Groom, still exist.

Not drinking pubs but two that are still big attractions are Bottoms-Up and the Red Lips Bar. Located on Locke Road, they have somehow survived redevelopment in the area. Red Lips, they say, is the oldest bar in the colony but some of the old timers disagree. They say it only looks that way, since the girls are the same ones since the bar opened. The rumours are that it too will soon disappear under the wrecker's hammer.

Most of the action today in Hong Kong is on the Kowloon side. A good pub here is Blacksmith's Arms at 16 Minden Avenue. There are several very good Australia-style bars, the Kangaroo and Ned Kelly's Last Stand, the latter having some good jazz.

One of the latest trends in bars in Hong Kong is the Japanese style hostess bar. Unlike their counterparts in Tokyo, however, these are huge places with as many as a hundred geishas. The biggest is Club Volvo which has a Rolls Royce to transport customers to their tables.

Kathmandu is not what you would actually call a night owl's town but there is a bar there that is one of the best in Asia. It's called the Rum Doodle. It might not sound that great but it is. The name is a spoof on mountaineering. Nightly it's jam packed with trekkers and climbers.

Atmosphere is the key at Rum Doodle. On the walls are paper cutouts of foot prints, scribbled with autographs of all the world's great mountain climbers for all to see, from Edmund Hillary to Barry Bishop. The drinks are superb.

What Asia needs is more Rum Doodles.

I should give readers an up-date on the Asian bars I mentioned. The Oriental Hotel in Bangkok has a new Bamboo Bar which should not be confused with the old one. They are not the same. Nor is the famous Long Bar in Raffles Hotel in Singapore similar to the old one. It is in name only. In Penang you will find little has changed at the E&O Hotel, and the waitresses at Hong Kong Bar continue to snap your picture when you enter, and keep it on file. I can't vouch for Hong Kong for the situation there changes daily, and recently when I went to Kathmandu, anxious to take friends to the Rum Doodle, it was closed. How sad, especially when I said what Asia needs is more bars like the Rum Doodle. And so too has Club 99 in Bangkok closed its doors. Sorry.

Divers on Schooner *So Fong* bring up the name plate from the *HMS Repulse*, sunk by Japanese bombers in the opening days of World War II.

Chapter 31
DIVING ON A MONSTER OF THE DEEP

American yachtsman Bill Mathers and 10 divers set out to find the HMS Repulse, the mighty British battleship which was sunk along with the HMS Prince of Wales by Japanese torpedo bombers on the Malay coast during the opening days of World War II. The search took place on the anniversary of the sinking, and I was fortunate to be on that diving expedition and wrote about it for the Post, *published April 14, 1985.*

I had never seen the sea so calm, and like the scene in Coleridge's epic poem, we were that "painted ship upon a painted ocean." The sky was lacquered blue with only puffs of cirrus clouds high above. The horizon all around us seemed to float. The Malaysian tropical sun beat down unrelentingly and heated the decks where the awning didn't reach. Our 80-foot schooner *So Fong* rode gently on the swells, held to the bottom 180 feet below by a light one-inch nylon line. Conditions were perfect, but still, it was all so eerie, even foreboding.

While divers and assistants pulled their equipment across the deck, adjusting straps and checking dials and gauges, I couldn't help looking up at the sky, searching through the puffs of clouds to the blue, listening for the distant sound of motors. But I was looking into the past and not the present, for here in this very same spot, 43 years before, at 10:15 am on Wednesday, December 10, 1941, two mighty British warships escorted by three swift destroyers were steaming on an easterly course when they were spotted by a Japanese reconnaissance plane that had been searching for them. What followed was a nightmare for the British Navy and the Western powers.

The ships were the battleship *HMS Prince of Wales* and the battle cruiser *HMS Repulse*. It was the third day of the war that Japan had started in the Far East, and the two capital ships with their destroyer escorts had left Singapore the evening before and headed up the coast in a last-minute effort to intercept and stop the Japanese invasion of southern Thailand and Malaya. Ninety minutes later, after Midshipman Masame Hoashi spotted the British ships and radioed his sighting to Admiral Sadaichi Masunaga in Saigon, the mighty *Prince of Wales* and *Repulse* were at the bottom of the South China Sea sunk by Japanese torpedo planes.

Now after she had lain untouched in its watery grave for more than four decades, we had located the *Repulse* and were about to dive upon her.

There's no mystery as to how these two ships were sunk, but what is a matter of great interest is that they were left to lie, untouched, exactly as they went down, without any attempt by private company or even government to salvage them. For certain, few divers have ever seen them. The fact that the British government has declared both vessels a war grave has much to do with it; but perhaps another important reason is the vast dangers involved in reaching them.

"A storm can form in minutes in this area," explained Bill Mathers, one of the few men to have dived on the *Repulse*. Bill made his dive 10 years before when he was part of a BBC camera crew attempting to film a documentary about the sinking.

Mathers explained the other dangers involved. Once a diver is on the bottom, fierce and treacherous currents could force him to miss the support line. He would then be swept down range, and attempts to find him might prove to be futile.

The length of time divers can spend at such a depth is another concern. After 15 or 17 minutes they could start to suffer from nitrogen narcosis, a state of euphoria where they lose the power to reason. There is also the fear of being sucked into the hull upon reaching the wreck or there is the possibility of getting lost when fine sediment is kicked up and blocks out visibility. Then there's the need to compress on the way to the surface, and there's always the threat of a shark attack.

Despite such dangers, many divers and adventurers who live in Southeast Asia have the desire, whether it be openly or secretly, to dive on *Repulse*. (*Prince of Wales* is in deeper water and much more difficult to reach.) Logistics, though, remain the major problem. There is the need to assemble qualified divers, to arrange boats and equipment, to choose a time when the currents are not strong and to possess the navigational ability and equipment to find the wreck.

One devoted Englishman who had that desire and was determined to take up the challenge was Derek Potter, an expatriate who lived in Singapore. Well-experienced in diving and engineering work, Derek had actually been trying for years to organise a diving expedition on the *Repulse*. He had gone so far as to charter a salvage yacht, and had spent a week fruitlessly trying to locate the site. Having retired from his position as a diving company executive, he was determined to make one last try before embarking on a world cruise. He gathered together an impressive group of divers, including Bill Mathers whose experience with the *Repulse* was needed. Also Bill owned the 80-foot schooner *So Fong* which he had turned into a diver-research vessel.

Others included Mike Ballentyne, a New Zealand veteran diver and certainly one of the most experienced divers in Asia; Willy Bullock, New Zealand, a professional oil field diver with one of the largest companies in the world. Henrik Nimb, Danish, a Singapore-based diving instructor. Dorian Ball, South African, an instructor with the Singapore Aquanaughts; Adrian Dale, UK, consultant marine engineer and experienced yacht master; John Horseburgh, UK, who has dived on many wrecks off the English coast; Martin Rush, UK, Tanglin Club diving instructor; Jim Russel, Canadian, experienced diver; Mike Slade, New Zealand, a sub-sea inspector; Bob Taylor, US, an underwater photographer; and Murray Wilkey, New Zealand, a diving company executive. Including Bill Mathers and his first mate, I made up the 14th member of the expedition.

Jobs and positions were assigned. Mike Ballentyne was the dive master in charge of operations, and under him were three dive leaders, Martin Rush, Henrik Nimb and John Horseburgh. One dive leader was to be on deck at all times. Every detail was organised all precautions were considered.

Derek, who is also a keen yachtsman, owns his own sailing yacht, *Tai Shan*, which he outfitted with satellite-navigation gear, depth-sounder and magnetometer. The plan called for Derek and diver Adrian Dale to set sail from Singapore aboard *Tai Shan* to try to locate the *Repulse,* and for *So Fong* to follow two days later with its tons of equipment and the remaining divers. A dawn rendezvous at the site of the sinking was planned.

Late in October, just after dusk, *So Fong* lifted anchor and left Sembawang and sailed down the Johore Strait for the open sea. We followed the same course *Prince of Wales* and *Repulse* had taken when they left Singapore on their last voyage.

All the next day as we sailed northward aboard *So Fong* for our rendezvous with *Tai Shan,* we studied plans and diagrams of *Repulse*'s construction and her armament. Every bit of knowledge we could gain would help divers on the bottom and it became understandable why she was thought to be unsinkable. Her main armament consisted of six 15-inch guns in two double turrets forward and one aft, and the secondary armament consisted of nine 4-inch guns. She also carried ten 21-inch torpedo tubes. Her decks were lined with both .20- and .50-calibre machine guns and pom-poms.

Repulse measured 250 metres, and had a beam of 30 metres with a 10-metre draught. She weighed 36,800 tons fully loaded and had a top speed of 32 knots. Underwater bulges up to 4.5 metres wide were built outside the main hull to absorb the force of a torpedo hit. Her sides and flanks carried 22.5-cm armour plating; her decks 37.5-cm plating. We could only imagine this brooding hulk waiting for us at the bottom of the sea only a short distance away.

An hour before daybreak we picked up a dot on *So Fong's* radar screen. Could this be Derek Potter's *Tai Shan*?

It seemed unlikely as we had been unable to make radio contact since leaving Singapore. The seas had become turbulent during the night and perhaps Derek sailed *Tai Shan* to the lee of one of the islands for shelter. Nevertheless, at first light we lined the deck, every eye scanning the horizon ahead. Then a mast came into view and as we drew closer we could see the *Tai Shan* riding at anchor. We had underestimated Derek Potter. He wasn't about to let a little bad weather stop him a second time. He and Adrian saw us coming, too, and so excited were they that they climbed into their engine-powered dinghy and headed out to greet us. The exuberant look on Derek's face told the story. They had found *Repulse*.

So Fong was soon alive with human vibrations as both Derek and Adrian spoke excitedly of their discovery.

"Our sat nav guided us to the location," Derek explained. "We lowered the magnetometer and began the final search. Then..."—he threw up his hands—"It always happens. A late afternoon storm came in from the south. Forty-knot winds kept blowing us away from the wreck. We tried something and it worked. We lowered an anchor on 180 feet of line to the sea bed. It seemed to help."

The gale raged all night while the two-man crew of *Tai Shan* slept below. When dawn came and the winds subsided, they made an alarming discovery. *Tai Shan* dragged four miles during the night.

"We hauled in the anchor and re-established the sat nav before motoring back to our previous position," Adrian explained.

After circling the site with magnetometers and echo-sounders in operation, they lowered a grappling hook. "I could feel it scraping over something solid," Derek said. But was it *Repulse*? "I knew it was the wreck when I saw an oil slick rising to the surface." After 43 years the wreck still leaks oil.

With *Tai Shan* grappled to the wreck, the two divers kitted up for their first look underwater. It was to be an experience they would never forget.

"We descended slowly down the anchor line," Derek began, with everyone hanging on his every word. "Slowly we began to see the enormous dark shape of the hull take form. Four long fingers like a dead man's hand reached up from the bottom. We were above the stern. Soon four propellers came into view."

As they continued down the line, they could see the ship was lying over at an angle of about 140 degrees with most of the guns and superstructure underneath. "So abundant was the marine life that at times our view was blocked," Derek said. "Schools of barracuda" —he stretched out his arms indicating a metre—" and a 12-foot shark passed right by us."

The water was so clear, when they looked up they could see *Tai Shan* floating 180 feet above them. After checking the grappling hook, the two divers returned to the surface and awaited the arrival of *So Fong,* due the following morning.

We were more excited than ever now. Ballentyne went over the details. He laid out a plan of *Repulse* and explained the divers' approach. Each diver had to memorise the plan.

"Remember her gun positions," he stressed. "You can get your bearings from her gun positions."

Although the atmosphere aboard *So Fong* was charged with excitement, it was also tempered by tension. Each diver seemed lost in his own private thoughts.

Conditions were ideal: the current was mild and visibility good. The sky was clear. Still, with everything in our favour, the thought of descending into the strange and mysterious world below lay heavy on each man's mind. But it wouldn't be long now.

With all the details fresh in everyone's mind, especially the locations of the torpedo holes, divers made their final preparations. Before the dives could be started, two divers had secured *So Fong* to the bottom, by attaching a line to *Repulse* amid ships. The line would further serve as the divers' support line.

Two divers at a time then dropped below the surface. Using NTL tables, they made their descent and had 17 minutes on the bottom. Decompression was in two stages, 10 minutes at 20 feet and 20 minutes at 10 feet. Divers had to spend at least five hours on deck before they could begin their second dive.

Derek was right: that first view of *Repulse* is overpowering, even frightening. At 30 feet the faint outline unfolds. At 60 feet she begins to take shape and form. You can make out details. But now as you drop lower the hull begins to take over, to dominate the ocean floor.

It's impossible to see the ship in its entirety. You begin to concentrate on one feature, maybe a torpedo hole. Everything you've heard or read before about *Repulse* may have not seemed real, until now. All the horrors of how that mighty ship sank into this dreadful grave suddenly registers upon you. You can almost hear someone pounding inside the hull, until you realise it's your own pulse beat gone wild.

Each diver returned to the deck of *So Fong* with his own impressions. One diver marvelled at the torpedo holes that had ripped through her tough sides. Another was impressed by the four huge propellers that project from the stern. "You can still see her rudder jammed hard to port," Ballentyne emphasised.

Most divers commented on the trailing fishing lines and nets that had been lost by Malay fisherman over the years and how these added to the eeriness and the overall effect. They told of schools of fish often in such numbers that they blocked out the light; of the large barracuda, mantarays and the occasional shark, cautious wary. Teak was still on the decks, and the entire floor of the ocean was littered with shell casings. Derek reported finding aeroplane engines still in their crates amidships.

A few divers commented on the strange crackling sound that they picked up near the bottom. And there was even laughter when a diver told how he poked his head into a torpedo hole and saw a four metre shark basking inside. "The problem was, I couldn't turn around fast enough," he joked.

Everyone agreed that *Repulse* remains in remarkably good condition despite her long years at the bottom of the sea. The torpedoes that sent her there had sliced effortlessly through her armoured sides and had left them twisted and gnarled.

Derek Potter and Jim Russel did the longest survey by going against the current along the hull from the stern to the bow. "We had to pull ourselves along," Derek said, "We held on at the bow where the current was like a wind storm. We could see the 14-inch gun turret and the anchors still in place." Bill Mathers located *Repulse's* heavy brass name-plate, and with the use of an air bag he and Willy Bullock brought it to the surface. It is now in a museum in London.

Just before dusk, on the day the first dive, tragedy almost struck—in the form of a storm. The South China Sea is a notorious region for fast-forming storms. Within minutes winds can reach 80 kph, and seas can develop chops of up to two metres. All divers were aboard when the storm stuck but it did not pass without mishap.

The winds hit *So Fong* head on. She pulled hard at her mooring line. Her bow dropped deep into the water then flashed high into the air.

I was below deck in the main cabin, reading about *Repulse,* when suddenly someone began shouting.

"We're going to crash! We're going to crash!

I rushed on deck to find that our mooring line had parted and we were drifting back upon *Tai Shan.* Although it was dusk I could still see the vessel's mast just a few metres from our stern. The next second we collided, the stern of *So Fong* striking *Tai Shan* on her port quarter.

Another violent thrust of the sea, and *So Fong's* over-hanging stern would slice *Tai Shan* open and send her to the same fate as *Repulse* 180 feet below us. But the quick actions of the crew prevented the disaster. While a few hands were attempting to fend off, Adrian made a daring leap from *So Fong* aboard *Tai Shan*, started the engine and was able to break away. *Tai Shan* was spared. By morning, the sea was again calm.

Each diver made two dives a day during the two days that followed, and one night dive. With the main cabin light reflecting on the damp faces of weary divers, we talked about the ill-fated *Repulse* and the horror that entombed some 540 sailors on the bottom below us. And later when we turned in and lay in our bunks, we could imagine helpless voices calling out on that bleak December day, calling out to help that never came.

After the third day of diving on *Repulse*, the last diver unhooked our mooring line and we drifted downwind from the wreck. We remained there for the longest time, each man looking blankly at the sea. Our thoughts were there in the deep. We couldn't help wondering what might have happened if the British fleet had not been spotted by that Japanese reconnaissance plane. Could the mighty *HMS Prince of Wales* and *HMS Repulse* have played a significant role in stopping the Japanese invasion of southern Thailand and Malaya? Could they then have steamed to the Philippines and helped the US stop the Japanese there? Could they have turned the tide at the beginning of the war?

Maybe, but they didn't.

On April 4, 1986, William Mathers arrived in Bangkok after being released from Vietnam where he was held captive in solitary for nine months, awaiting execution. He was charged with violating Vietnam's territorial waters and spying. Mathers was sailing his schooner So Fong *from Thailand to Hong Kong when he was stopped and boarded on the high seas by armed Vietnamese fishermen. Mathers was put into prison in Saigon where he was held. He was finally released, but fined US$10,000, and* So Fong *and all its equipment (worth $300,000) were confiscated. Bill went on to make other discoveries, including a Manila galleon sunk in a storm off the coast of Saipan. His story about the discovery appeared in* National Geographic, *and I wrote about him and his discovery in detail in my book* At Home in Asia.

Chapter 32
A LOOK AT BEAUTY AS SEEN THROUGH ASIAN CULTURES

Dr. Dato Shahrum has been a friend for thirty years, since I began writing travel and adventure for the Post. *He has been a source of much of my information, and I liked nothing better that to sit in his cluttered office in the basement of the National Museum in Kuala Lumpur and talk with him about exciting things in our past. Although the following article, published on March 15, 1993, is about a specific exhibition that Dr. Shahrum staged, it discusses a subject that is ever lasting—beauty.*

Dr. Dato Shahrum, the past curator of the National Museum in Kuala Lumpur, has over the years put on some astounding exhibitions, some that have brought the public to a startling halt. He believes that museums should be something more than stuffy archives—they should be alive. As a result, he has done such zany things like staging the history of music—with popular Malay singers and even rock bands that performed in the museum. For the history of pugilistics, he set up an arena in the museum and had staged actual boxing matches. And he has had on show everything from snake charmers to live elephants walking around the museum.

Then just a year ago, Dr. Shahrum put together a most remarkable exhibition on the human skull, which could well have been labeled "The Art of Dying." He carried visitors on head hunting expeditions into the jungle of Borneo after the Dyaks to dining with New Britain cannibal tribes in New Guinea.

This year Dr. Shahrum has outdone himself. Forced into retirement last year by government law, and now adviser to the Ministry of Culture, he spent a year and a half, and nearly half a million ringgit (Malay dollars), on an exhibition that opened in July last year and will run until December. It could well top all others he has out on. The new exhibition is on beauty.

"But what is beauty?" Dr. Shahrum asks. "If you ask a Thai beauty queen or any of the hilltribe people around Mae Hong Song, you will get a different answer." This in essence is what the exhibition is all about. It is true to the adage: beauty is in the eyes of the beholder.

The exhibition is called "Enduring Beauty" and as the brochure states, it "aims to create an awareness of cross-cultural and cross-temporal perspectives of beauty." It deals not with such things as women's changing styles, make up or hair fashions but with permanent bodily alterations such as head deformation, dental mutilation, tattooing, scarification, foot-binding, the wearing of labrets in the lip, ear and nose ornamentation, the use of corsets, the wearing of coils around the neck and modern cosmetic surgery.

The exhibition has been named Enduring Beauty, according to Dr. Shahrum, because of the dual meaning of the word 'enduring' which signifies something lasting or permanent and also means to undergo pain or suffering.

The numerous transformations of the natural body as portrayed in this exhibition involve varying degrees of pain. It illustrates the French proverb that "one must suffer to be beautiful."

When viewed in the eyes of different cultures, beauty is a difficult concept to define, which becomes apparent when viewing the exhibits. However, it is evident that beauty lies in the eyes of the beholder and one must keep in mind that these eyes are culturally conditioned.

The exhibition covers an immense time span, from pre-historic days to the present. We may wonder why our ancestors violated the human body as they did, until we look objectively at the practices used by some of the youth today, namely he so called "skin heads." Dr. Shahrum calls this exhibit "Modern Primitive." Multiple ear piercing, nose rings, tattooing of shaven heads, they all, as shown in the exhibit, have become membership badges for adolescent urban rebels.

The exhibit also features innumerable societies in nearly every country of the world and illustrates that every society creates its own idea of beauty as well as methods to attain it. Dr. Shahrum travelled what amounted to be several times around the world to gather information and in many cases to purchase objects to put on display. His wanderings took him to Africa, Central and South America, the northwest coast of North America, China, Assam in India, northern Thailand and dozens of other areas, some of which were quite remote.

Dr. Shahrum gives much credit to the success of the exhibition to his wife, Maureen. She helped with the research and painstakingly wrote most of the descriptions that appear on each of the exhibit dispays. "A focus on the body's alterations can be understood as an endeavour to put on a new skin, a cultural as opposed to natural skin," she wrote in the museum booklet that accompanies the exhibition. "The changes created are an embodiment of a particular society's cultural code and beauty is but a cultural construct."

Mrs. Shahrum then explains that in some traditional societies the customs associated with bodily alterations are closely linked to social status and rites of passage such as puberty and betrothal.

In some cultures it is the men, not the women, who are the most elaborately adorned and transformed, whereas in others, it is the norm for the women to be subject to the greatest bodily alterations.

The exhibition does not ridicule societies for their interpretation of beauty, but rather it shows that even in western society, for example, body alterations are practiced which are accepted norms, and often which we give no thought to as being "odd." Dr. Shahrum gives the examples of corsets. For this he turns to Hollywood.

"I spent days in the shops in Hollywood looking for posters," he said as he pointed out movie advertisements of such notable films as "Gone with the Wind," "The Great Train Robbery," "The Great Waltz," "The Girl from the Golden West" and "The Outlaw."

Early Greeks used corsets, and it's still the practice of the men in the Itaburi tribe in Papua New Guinea to wear them. In the 15th century, knights in armour going off to battle outfitted their wives with iron corsets, and only they held the keys.

Also on display is a photograph of a young lady who holds the record in the *Guinness Book of World Records* for having the smallest known waist, some 13 inches.

There's even a photograph of Joan Collins wearing a corset.

As Dr. Shahrum led me through the museum, he stopped at each display, with some comment to make about it. He points to a collection of lip rings under glass. "This is beautiful, from the Congo, what I didn't have to do to get it." He then has an anecdote to tell. Other visitors stop to listen. When he lingered too long, he had an audience.

"Men have taken to wearing earrings today, but it's not anything new," he said as we stopped in front of a display of earrings with photographs above. He then points to a painting. "You see not only pirates of yesteryear wore earrings, but William Shakespeare did as well." In deed, the painting shows Shakespeare wearing a ring in his left ear. Then Dr. Shahrum laughs. "Some people accuse me of painting in the ring, but I assure you it's real."

Some of the displays are real shockers, like the Chinese custom of foot binding. Dr. Shahrum had to go through the archives in

Nanking to find many of the photographs he uses to illustrate the ancient practice. Some photos show the shapes of the deformed feet, while others illustrate how the binding was done. He has a collection of shoes, some only inches long.

The section on tattooing is equally as remarkable, with tattoos from Maori face carvings of New Zealand to the current tattooing methods employed among the Thais.

Many of the photos Dr. Shahrum took himself. There is an excellent coloured photo of a hilltribe girl in Mae Hong Song which depicts how she must sleep while wearing neck rings, rings which, he explains, never come off.

For other photographs Dr. Shahrum and his staff had to look though countless publications, some that dated back to the 1920s.

The museum is open every day. Nowhere else can you discover so clearly what the human race doesn't go through to attain beauty as seen by various cultures.

The exhibition does not mean that Dr. Shahrum is hanging up his hat and going into retirement. Not the man who habitually wears a bow tie—he has 400 in his private collection—and who has won the prestigious Magsaysay Award for his contribution to society. "The next one, ah," he says with a sigh, "that will be an exhibition." He was about to tell me, and then says "No, you had better wait and see. It's a surprise."

Maybe, but it would have to be pretty sensational to beat Enduring Beauty.

The wreck of a B-29 bomber that Stephens found on New Britain Island in New Guinea.

Chapter 33
A FORTUNE WAITING IN WORLD WAR II WRECKS

No other article I wrote for the Bangkok Post *had more reader response than this one that appeared on August 29, 1982. It wasn't only treasure divers looking for leads but war veterans as well who remembered the war and the sites that I mentioned.*

Ned Johnson did it as a lark. He wasn't serious, only drunk. He came out of the New Guinea Club in Rabaul late one night with a few too many beers under his belt and staggered towards his Land Rover. With each step he became more and more and more annoyed that he had to park so far way, for the whole parking lot was jampacked with war surplus jeeps and semi-trucks, road scrapers, a couple of bulldozers and other assortment of wheeled generators and machinery intended for the front lines.

But there weren't any more front lines. Japan had just surrendered and the war was over. For two weeks Ned Johnson had been shouting at the authorities to clear up the mess. The U.S. military dumped their supplies in Rabaul until a decision was made about its disposal.

So in his stubborn, drunken mood, Ned Johnson decided to play a joke on the authorities. From his Land Rover he took a can of white paint and a brush and proceeded to go around the lot defacing the government property. In big bold letter he wrote SOLD on the vehicles, and on some he painted his own name. He wasn't afraid of the authorities, he said to himself. Feeling satisfied with his prank, he climbed into his Land Rover and drove the two hour track back to his plantation on New Britain.

Ned awoke with a big headache the next morning. He couldn't remember much that happened the night before, nor did he really care. The long war had played havoc to his plantation and he had much work to do to put it back in order.

A week later a government vehicle with two police officers arrived at Ned's plantation. One was the Superintendent of Police, the other a black Kanaka corporal.

The senior officer was obviously annoyed that he had to make the long drive. "You're in a bit of trouble," he began. "All that equipment at the New Guinea Club. I'm afraid we're going to have to fine you unless—"

Ned suddenly remembered. What a stupid thing to do, to put his own name on that junk heap. But he wasn't going to give in. "Unless what?" he snapped back.

The officer was blunt. "Unless you get it the hell out of there immediately. You bought it, now you get rid of it!"

And so Ned Johnson got into the construction business and became a millionaire overnight. He can attribute it to a can of white paint and the follies of war.

Ned Johnson was but one of many thousands of post war profiteers and adventurers who made a fortune from war surplus material. But the irony is that it's not over; there are fortunes still there waiting to be picked up.

I have spent the last five years sailing my schooner around Southeast Asia and the South Pacific, touching upon many islands that were battle sites during World War II. We came upon airstrips with bombers and fighters still on the runways; harbours with hundreds of wrecked ships and vessels, some in water so shallow you could see them below the surface; caves filled with rusting arms, helmets and mess gear; heavy brass cannons hidden in lonely mountain outposts; and still at other islands the military simply walked off when it was all over and left everything behind.

There are obstacles, of course, to salvaging much of what remains. The biggest one is ownership. Nearly every island chain in the Pacific has become independent since the war and they have set up rigid rules protecting their islands and the people who inhabit them. I can think of one case in particular.

The place is Lorengau, the port capital of the island Manus north of New Guinea. We dropped anchor in Seeadler Harbour and along with a rusted freighter we were the only two ships there. Through my binoculars I studied the slumbering quiet little port basking in the tropics. I really had to stretch my imagination to picture the place as it was 35 years before. Lorengau then was one of the most important deep water ports in the South Pacific.

It was this small and almost unknown island that General Douglas MacArthur pointed a finger to on the map and said, "Here we begin our offensive." Soon after two marine divisions stormed ashore and within five days of bloody fighting retook the island from the Japanese forces. Then came the changes.

At Manus, the US Government assembled one of the greatest naval establishments in history. One writer who was there at the time described it: "Overnight Lorengau became a city larger than Sacramento. It had stores worth half a billion dollars. MacArthur was preparing for the invasion of Leyte and in the roadstead I saw 26 carriers, dozens of battle ships and actually hundreds of lesser craft."

Others who had been there reported seeing no less than a thousand ships at anchor at any one time. There were post exchanges by the score, dozens of movie houses, fuel depots, electric power plants, two dry cleaners and three huge laundries, a radio station telephone exchange, miles of paved roads, six airfields and storage sheds that filled acres of ground. What happened to it all? Today the island is back to jungle.

"You yanks walked off and left it all," an Australian District Officer explained when I went ashore. "What you couldn't sell, you bulldozed into the sea." He pointed out to a jetty. "Most expensive seawall in the world."

The bulk of the incredible wealth, however, was sold lock, stock and barrel to Chinese wholesalers at 10 cents to the dollar and carried off to make fortunes in Hong Kong.

But it wasn't only the Chinese who had the mind for making a fortune from the war. The District Officer drove me to a hidden storage pit that is worth a gold mine. He explained how it was discovered.

When New Guinea got its independence from Australia a few years back, most of the land was divided among the islanders. One native went out to look at the land given to him which was heavily overgrown by jungle. He stumbled across some corrugated tin which he uncovered. It would make good siding for his house. When he pulled the tin out he noticed it was a covering for a deep pit of sorts, and when he checked farther he saw a wooden crate which he opened.

Inside was a washing machine, perfectly preserved. But he had no need for a washing machine or anything else he saw. And most likely he would have said nothing about his discovery except people started asking about the new tin that appeared on his house. Eventually the story reached the authorities and the District Officer went to check. What he found was more than a washing machine.

No one knows the facts, and probably no one ever will, but what may have happened was when the America had to withdraw from the islands when the war ended, they were ordered to destroy supplies and equipment they couldn't carry with them. Most likely it was an enterprising officer who had some other ideas. He bulldozed a huge pit a hundred feet long, 15 deep and 20 wide. That makes a pretty deep hole in the ground. Then into this pit he drove trucks and jeeps, loaded with engines and generators and tools. Each and every item was preserved in thick grease. He then took some 10-inch "I" beams, laid them across the top, and covered this with corrugated tin. When this was done he covered the roof with several feet of earth.

The officer no doubt intended to return one day and claim his treasure, but, obviously, he never did. In any event, the location of the site was forgotten. But the incredible part of the story is that the Melanesian whose property the niche is on, refuses to uncover it. He is aware that he has a fortune on his land but the knowledge of it alone is sufficient enough to make him happy. No one can force him to look beyond.

The District Officer pointed out that this was just one case in many. "Anyone who wants to go to the trouble can dig up a fortune," he said. He told about a mountain of treasure above Lorengau. He explained how the Japanese had dug in and moved all their installations underground, with their guns pointed towards Seeadler Harbour. Rather than try to blast them out, a U.S. Naval commander gave orders to a See Bee Company to come in from behind and bulldoze the top of the mountain over on the Japanese, which they did. No one has bothered to uncover the caves.

A similar situation happened at Santo in the New Hebrides. Overnight the port became another Lorengau and grew into a great naval base. The war ended and the French who had possession of the islands refused to pay 10 cents on the dollar, knowing well the Americans would not take everything back. Instead, with tears in their eyes, the French watched the U.S. Military drive their tanks and jeeps and trucks into the sea. At Santo, I anchored next to a seawall a mile long, and all along its base the sea lapped at old engine blocks, heavy axles and truck beds. The loss had to be staggering.

Who would ever expect Bora Bora, reputed to be the most beautiful island in the world, to once be a military stronghold. It was. In early 1942, some 5,000 U.S. Marines and sailors arrived aboard two cruisers, two destroyers, four cargo ships, one tanker and two transports. There were no docks or port facilities. They built them. Bora Bora had no roads, electricity or water supply. A month later they had them all. And three months after the Americans arrived, the first airstrip in the South Pacific was completed. It was carved out of a coral reef and is still used to this day.

All Polynesian women between 15 and 50 were moved to a neighbouring island and for recreation the marines were given volleyball courts and baseball diamonds. Their concrete foundations can still be seen today. I anchored my schooner in a bay where the marines first landed—the docks have disappeared—and an outrigger with a native aboard came to greet us. The man introduced himself, Louis Picaro, retired school master, ex-radio operator for the Americans during the war.

"Naval guns are still there in the hills," Louis said and pointed to the ridge high above us. "There are six installations in all." He also told us where there is still surplus material in bunkers deep in one valley.

We found the bunkers, Quonset huts, actually. They were dug into the ground and covered over. What was so surprising was to find everything so well preserved. Steel doors opened on their hinges, and it was possible to unscrew nuts from bolts that held the trusses together with bare fingers. The corrugated tin, like that we had seen in New Guinea, was in excellent condition with no rust or corrosion. Manufacturers can produce top quality material when they want to.

It took some doing but we found two of the cannons. We had to cut away the underbrush so we could get photographs. At the base of one gun scratched in the concrete footing was the inscription: April 21, 1942, SHAFFER SM 3/C and W.E. HOBSEN SM 3/C BOBCAT.

BOBCAT was the code name for the operation. In June 1946 the Americans sailed away. They left behind a tremendous inventory. Again the French refused to buy any material, even at a ridiculously low price. Tons and tons of material including whole structures were thrown into the sea. Water purification and electrical plants were abandoned. The only thing salvaged was the telephone exchange which was sent to Papeete on Tahiti. Many of the untouched wrecks still remain in the harbour.

One of the biggest surprises I had was on Bouganville in the Solomons. We anchored in a quiet cove and a black Kanaka who lived on the shore insisted that he had something to show me of great value. I was only mildly interested but went along mostly to please him. My curiosity waned quickly after trying to keep up with him after an hour in the dense jungle. But then suddenly the earth beneath me became hard. It was a tarmac—a runway. The edge of the field was overhanging with tree limbs trailing thorny creepers, but as we pressed deeper the jungle gave way and there before me was a sight so astounding I found myself breathless. A squadron of perhaps a dozen B-29 bombers were posed as though ready for take-off.

I climbed into the cockpit of one plane, and it still had that electrical smell of a new plane about it. I was afraid to touch any dials or switches for fear that the engines might start. A few planes did, in fact, still have fuel in the tanks.

On the remote atoll called Tongareva in the northern Cook Islands I did find another landing strip. This one was kept up by the islanders, although a plane had not landed in years. An old timer took me to the lagoon at the edge of the runway and pointed to the shallow water. During the war a bomber was making an emergency landing during the night when the generators failed and the lights went out. The natives hastily lit beach fires but the pilot misjudged and crashed into the lagoon. It wasn't a violent crash and the plane more or less settled calmly to the bottom. It's still there, almost intact. We found the skeleton of another plane that crashed on land. The natives use the plane's skin for making fishing lures. Some of the engine parts are as good as new.

North of Tongareva is an interesting island—Christmas Island. It was discovered by Captain Cook and down through the ages went uninhabited, until this century when the Ellis Islanders moved in. The island made headlines 25 years ago when Great Britain used the atoll for her atomic tests. Methods were primitive then. Bombs were exploded from a tower and natives were told to sit on the beach with their heads lowered on their knees and not to look up until they were told to.

In the lagoon at Christmas Island I saw more fish than I have seen at any other place in the Pacific. Giant parrot and coral fish, huge rays that come gliding by and lobster waiting to be picked up from the bottom. But no one would dare. Sailing directions warn that sealife might be radioactive. The natives eat their fish from cans.

I took my motorbike and attempted to motor around the atoll. It's the world's largest, stretching some 60 miles across. The roads were excellent but monotonous. After 20 miles I gave up. But along that 20 miles were rows of abandoned barracks and warehouses. The copper wire alone from the fallen electric lines could make one enough money to retire for life. In two warehouses in London, the island capital, I saw an organ still in its crate, dozens of diesel engines unpacked, building supplies and garden tools and everything a native population doesn't need, most of it surplus.

The greatest war prize a native could have on any island across the Pacific is to possess a jeep. A jeep and they are king. On Lou Island, a very lush volcanic island north of New Guinea, the natives there came aboard when we anchored and asked if we could repair the jeep they had. We took our tool kit from the schooner and I went with the engineer to see what we could do.

It seems the Americans had landed on the island but when they withdrew the clever natives managed to hide one prized jeep which they maintained down through the years. We saw the vehicle. It was in remarkably good shape. Where they got the gas to run it, I didn't know. They had one road on the island, six miles long between two villages. It was dirt, but well used. They now waited for me and the engineer to get the machine running again.

We stepped up to the old war vintage jeep, put down our bag of tools and opened the hood. We did a double take. We couldn't believe it. There was no engine. And judging by the look of things, there never had been. What the islanders had been doing was pushing the vehicle between the two villages. We had a hard time explaining that we couldn't get it to run like it had been when the marines were on the island. We lost face among them.

Over the last several years the lagoon at Truk Island in the Caroline Islands has become famous for scuba divers. It was here the Japanese navy was bottled up and sunk. A place I think which is even more spectacular is Rabaul on the island of New Britain. Rabaul was one of the most important targets in the Pacific war. The Japanese captured the all-important port two days after they bombed Pear Harbour. Immediately they began constructing one of the toughest, most formidable bastions ever built. It was virtually impregnable. The combined Allied Forces were unable to recapture Rabaul in spite of dropping more than 20,000 tons of bombs on the place.

The Japanese surrendered only when the war ended. The Australians and Americans came ashore and to their astonishment they found 90,000 Japanese, both civilians and military, living in an amazing subterranean world. In connecting underground caverns were 360 miles of caves into which ships and even submarines were pulled when air attacks threatened them.

I spent many exciting days exploring some of these caves. No attempt has been made to cover them up or conceal them. They are ignored by the locals. Each cave I explored offered something different. Some had steel helmets by the thousands; others rusted mess gear and canteens, a few contained smashed medical supplies; one had crates of engine parts, and still others were locker-box full of files, ledgers, records and books—all eaten through by white ants.

Some Allied bombers did, however, find success. Records show that more than 400 known wrecks lay at the bottom of the bay, including an American submarine. The submarine entered the port during the war and for some mysterious reason never came out. Only a mere handful of these wrecks have been explored by divers.

My crew met several weekend divers and dove with them on a few wrecks. One Australian engineer and his 16-year-old son had been working the harbour for three years. He told me, off the record, he had earned enough to retire for life from bringing up brass shell casings and selling them to the Chinese. He was an avid underwater photographer and showed me hundreds of photos of sunken vessels, including a Japanese Zero in shallow water and virtually intact.

Not far south of Rabaul begin the Solomon Islands, the scene of some of the heaviest fighting in the Pacific war. As I mentioned, entire air fields were lost and forgotten, and in some bays entire navies went to the bottom. In the Malacca Strait there are endless World War II wrecks, including submarines. Indonesian waters are a graveyard of wrecks.

But the salvage diver, the adventurer, doesn't have to look to World War II wrecks to earn a living. There was hardly an island or an atoll that we did visit where there wasn't at least one Korean or Taiwanese fishing boat up on the reef. Some large islands had two or three. If the islands were inhabited, the natives, of course, picked the cargos clean—but the ships themselves with all their valuable equipment and gear remain.

These are the modern wrecks. Think of all those prior to World

War II. The Chinese were trading in these waters for 5,000 years before European nations made the scene. How many of their ships were wrecked, with priceless cargo?

The list in endless.

Stephens, boarding a Thai Airways International aircraft, has his own ideas about jet lag.

Chapter 34
HOW TO CONQUER JET LAG

This article appeared on June 12, 1989, under the title "Ignore Jet Lag and Enjoy Your Flight." Not too long ago someone remarked to me that I see a lot of movies. I had to think about it. I have to agree, I am more or less caught up on the latest movies, and yet I seldom go to the cinema. Then I realised, I see all the latest movies the airlines have to offer.

How marvelous, I tell myself. Somehow I save a day. My THAI B747 touches down in Seattle. It's a bright Monday morning, and a wall clock at immigration shows that it's 10:30 a.m. Most remarkable, especially when I consider that at exactly 8:30 a.m., on the same Monday morning, only two hours earlier by the clock, I had left Bangkok.

But when I look down at my watch, I wonder if my recent Oriental Avenue purchase from a guy on the street is trustworthy. (A good gold Rolex for $45.) It reads 1:30 a.m., Tuesday morning. I begin my calculations. The watch is correct; it is that time in Bangkok. But shouldn't I be sleepy at 1:30 in the morning? Not always. Sometimes do I stay up late in Bangkok, usually when I'm showing visitors the night life at Patpong.

But I'm not in Bangkok. I am in Seattle and my destination is Portland, Oregon, a little more than 150 miles south of Seattle. Since it's day, and there are things to see, I decide to hire an AVIS car and drive. At the airport I produce a credit card and a neat little blonde in a red uniform leads me to a small compact Ford Falcon. She hands me the keys and smiles.

But for some reason she's looking at me strangely. I tell her I know all about Ford Falcons, and slide in behind the driver's wheel. Except there's no driver's wheel. It takes me a second. In America they put drivers' wheels on the wrong side. How embarrassing. I should know that, but what I don't realise is that jet lag is beginning to set in. It sneaks up on you.

I take off, leaving rubber behind. Again, I should know these big American cars have power. I reach the super eight-lane highway, where people drive on the wrong side of the road, and turn south. The clock on the dash says it's noon now, and I should be hungry, but I'm not. My watch tells me it's 3 a.m. in Bangkok. No wonder. I never eat at 3 a.m. I try to imagine I'm still on a late night in Patpong, but it doesn't help anymore. Everyone has gone home. My eye lids become heavy laiden and I have to rub the back of my neck.

I have to face it. I am an exhausted refugee from another time zone who is beginning to feel the effects. The time zone has defeated me. I was sure I would be the winner this time. I had done all the things I should have done, all those things the experts tell you to do to beat jet lag. I ate little aboard the jet, I drank lots of juices, I kept away from hard liquor and I walked around as much as I could. I even did arm and toe exercises.

It didn't do any good. It was now nearing two in the afternoon and I need to get some rest. To make matters worse, a light rain begins to fall, and I long for the cool feeling of fresh sheets and a place to lie down after 26 hours in an upright chair.

A few hours' rest will do it. I find a Motel 6 and check in. "Just for a few hours," I tell the front desk.

I awake from my nap and feel much better now. What a few hours won't do! I look at my watch, and it's 11 o'clock. Is that 11:00 a.m. or 11:00 p.m.? I am completely befuddled and rush to throw open the window curtain, only to discover it's dark outside. The only light comes from distant traffic moving up and down Interstate 5 and the red glow of the Motel 6 sign suspended high in the darkness on two poles.

Good lord, I'm in America and it's the middle of the night. I can't sleep now even if I wanted to. I shower and get dressed. Outside the rain has stopped.

Two hours later I reach Portland, but I can hardly drive up to my friend's home at 5 a.m. I find a 24-hour coffee shop and sit with the truckers until dawn, casual like, as though I'm a driver of one of the 10-wheelers parked outside. They talk in loud voices in a language that's hard to follow. They banter back and forth.

With the sun coming up, I drive to my friend's house.

"Welcome to America," he shouts. At last! Words I had been waiting to hear. I had travelled from Singapore to Bangkok, then took a 17 hour marathon journey across the biggest ocean in the world, crossed the International Date Line, arrived in America and drove another half day. How nice, my friend and his wife are excited to see me. That's what friends are all about.

We have a gargantuan breakfast, as they can do only in America, and they plan the day's events. I look at my wristwatch. It's bed time back in Bangkok. My head nods, and my friends suggest I take a little nap. I lie down, and when I awake they are going to bed. "You were so fast asleep," they said, "we didn't want to wake you."

I have been tortured by the time zone syndrome. I have no alternative but to go to bed too, and lay awake all night hoping sleep will over take me. It does, finally, at dawn.

I really don't know how airline pilots and cabin attendants can do it. They always seem refreshed and relaxed. I made up my mind. On my return flight to Bangkok I'd do it my way.

My flight leaves a little past noon. I go to the Business Class lounge and have a drink as I wait. I watch the CNN news. My flight is departing and I go aboard. We take off.

The FASTEN SEAT BELT sign goes off and I order a double martini. An hour out and it's lunch. I have red wine with my meal and cognac afterwards. The table is cleared and I listen to the classical music channel. I have a cold Singha beer, and when the movie comes on I watch Michael Caine and Ben Kingsley in "Without a Clue." I have a second cold beer.

I change to gin and tonic before dinner, and can't decide if I should have fish or veal. I take some of both, with white wine with the fish, and red with the veal. Benedictine with my desert.

"A refill, Sir?"

"Yes, please."

A moment later. "Hot coffee, Sir."

"Yes, certainly, don't mind if I do." I settle back, and while others sleep, I watch a video, about stunt men. It shows how a man leaps off a tall building on to an air bag a couple hundred feet below. I learn something.

We fuel stop in Tokyo, fifty minutes. Everyone must get off the plane. I take a seat at the bar and see sake on the shelf behind the bar. If you are in Japan, drink what the Japanese drink. Why not. I have a warm sake.

Dinner aboard is soon after takeoff. Champagne before, Bordeaux red with, Camus Napoleon after. I go for the satay noodles with the braised beef. I don't want to miss the movie, "Running on Empty." The movie ends and Charlie Chaplin comes on. He's in a gold rush, in a building that's about to tumble over a cliff. When the movie ends, I listen to Hungarian Rhapsody No 4 and then a little Country 'n Western—"Don't You Get Tired of Hurting Me."

Two hours before we arrive in Bangkok and lights go on. Hot towels are brought out. Immigration cards. Some passengers cover their heads. I don't have that trouble. I stayed awake after the last movie and read all the time. It's late evening, almost midnight, and time for snacks. I have a coffee and cake.

Don Muang is aglow in the dark. We come to a landing and disembark. Immigration has improved and only a few passengers are stopped for customs. A taxi ride and I am back home. I turn in, sleep well, and I am ready to begin work at my typewriter after morning coffee.

I have finally learned the secret of time zone travel. But before I tell you, let me quote from a newspaper article I cut it out and stuck it in my briefcase when I was in Seattle. It was written by a disgruntled travel writer. "There is a misconception," the author wrote, "among people who haven't travelled to distant places of the world that there is something magical, mystical and adventuresome about airplane travel. Having travelled to the farthest place there is, I'll report that long-distance airplane travel in economy class on a 747 is a death times four, as the rock 'n roll poet Norman Greenbaum used to say.

"Nor does it give any sense of achievement. It's just practical, daunting and dull, leaving you on arrival with no sense of where you are or how you got there."

This is rubbish. Flying like travelling aboard ship is what you make of it. My advice is to enjoy your flight, every minute of it. Eat, drink, watch movies, listen to music, and enjoy yourself. Airlines today do all they can to please passengers, so why not take advantage of what they give. After all, flying is part of the fun of travelling.

And as for jet lag, there's one solution, and only one solution—ignore it. And don't worry. Be happy.

Zamboanga's City Hall was originally a fort built by the U.S. Army when they took over the Philippines in 1899.

Chapter 35
OFF THE BEATEN TRACK: A TALE OF THREE PORTS

The following article on three exciting ports of Southeast Asia appeared on June 22, 1987. There are places far off the tourist track.

Want to get off the beaten path in Southeast Asia, to the rambunctious days of yesterday? There are such paces, and I have in mind three ports, three exciting ports. And what can be more exciting that the of Chittagong, Sandakan, and Zambonga? Just the very mention of their names can send anyone seeking adventure to the ticket office.

What is it about a name? Are these ports only names in fancy gazetteers? Hardly. They are real and like their names they have a mystique about them. For those who haven't seen them, the closest thing is to watch the late TV shows of old Gary Cooper and Humphrey Bogart movies that have their settings in the Far East: a seething tropical waterfront filled with intrigue—hotel lobbies with cane chairs, revolving ceiling fans and uncertain characters moving about; and strong cigars, coffee-eyed women and rum in tall glasses. This, without frills, is the three ports.

Let's look at Chittagong. I first saw Chittagong when I was making an overland jeep trip from Europe to Singapore. That was twenty years ago, but I understand the place hasn't changed, except Bangladesh then was called East Pakistan, and Dhaka is the new spelling for Dacca.

When I arrived in Dacca I discovered I couldn't drive through Burma to reach Thailand. I had no other choice but to drive south from Dacca to Chittagong and ship my jeep from there to Penang or Singapore. I went to the U.S. Embassy for information on Chittagong. The consul gave me the embassy report for their Foreign Service officers: "Chittagong, East Pakistan's largest port, is a small town, hot, with malaria and a variety of tropical diseases. There is no entertainment or nightlife, except for trips over weekends and holidays to Dacca, 160 miles north."

Nevertheless, the drive from Dacca to Chittagong was packed with interest, and with excitement far more than I intended. The road skirted the Assam border. River barges with huge triangular sails moved slowly up the rivers and looked like picture post cards. The road was narrow and straight, with little vehicular traffic, and followed a rail line. I caught up with a coal-burning train pulling a dozen cars, when abruptly it stopped. The engineer, fireman, guards, and everyone aboard, they all suddenly leaped from the train and took cover in a ditch. I could see puffs of smoke coming from the forest beyond. Rifle fire! Someone in the forest was shooting at the train. I drove the jeep down over the bank and also took cover. Presently, a platoon of soldiers came running down the road. I then heard more shooting. In twenty minutes it was over, and again I was headed south. It could have been a Humphrey Bogart movie, except I saw the bullet holes.

Darkness came when I was 10 miles from Chittagong. I stopped to eat at a small roadside stall. The Muslim keeper spoke English and asked where I was going. He suggested the resthouse in Chittagong. He pointed to a man in a white robe and said if I carried him, he could show me how to get to the rest house. I agreed, and it was fortunate that I did. I could never have found my way. Chittagong was a congestion of ox-drawn carts and oil burning trucks rumbling over rutted streets and railroad tracks. Rickshaws pushed in and out between the lines of traffic. It was unlike any town I had ever seen.

We found the resthouse, right out of Kipling, and I took a room on the second floor. Nine boys, I counted them, came to my aid and unloaded the jeep, and of course, nine boys held their hands out in the end. It was worth the nine rupees.

I asked about food, and was told most of the restaurants were closed, but one room boy knew "a place where I could eat." He brought along a friend and we started off in the jeep, turned down a mud road that actually was a watershed and parked at a dead end. The friend stood guard while the first boy led me across a bamboo bridge—with one pole serving as a guideline and another pole to walk upon. In the dark we came to a railroad track where, as it happened, a slow-moving passenger train was en route. We ran after the train, jumped aboard, squeezed through the crowded compartment and jumped out on the other side.

We hurried down a wide avenue through a very primitive village and came to the waterfront. River boats were tied together. We jumped from one to the other until we came to the end boat, the largest one. We darted through the engine room past sleeping bodies and climbed a ladder. On the second level we encountered a man dressed in white. The room boy spoke to him and we were then led to a dining room—the captain's.

I said to the man in white: "Do you think the captain will mind?

"I am the captain," he said. I paid him five rupees and dined on soup, curried fish, chicken and mango for desert. I skipped the coffee. When I returned to the resthouse I was anxious to jot down my notes. Some day, I thought, I might want to recommend a place to eat in Chittagong. I just have.

That was Chittagong. I decided to do some exploring before I shipped off my jeep. I headed south to one of the world's longest beaches, Cox's Bazaar, some 90 miles in length. A beautiful beach, but awfully boring, with no one on it. Next I drove to nearby Chittagong hilltribes, not unlike those in northern Thailand. In one village I met an Englishman married to a hilltribe princess. He kept me entertained for two days with stories, and he proved that Humphrey Bogart characters are still alive in Asia.

Then we come to Sandakan in Borneo. Sandakan came as a pleasant surprise. I never expected to go there. A few years back I was sailing in the central Philippines aboard my schooner *Third Sea* when we received warning that a typhoon was approaching. We hastily looked at the Sailing Directions: "Borneo, noted by early sailors as 'land below the wind.' Free of typhoon. Sandakan, a safe, deep-water port on the northeast coast of Sabah." We sailed for Sandakan.

In Sandakan, Sabah's big, busy boom town, people call the huge logs bobbing up and down in the Sulu Sea "floating money." Logs float down wide rivers from timber forest surrounding the harbour where they pass through the hands of Chinese merchants and are then lifted onto massive freighters bound for Japan. This was our introduction Sandakan as we sailed into the wide port and anchored in front of the Sandakan Yacht Club. That night we were struck by winds so violent that even with the engine running we dragged halfway across the harbour. So much for the Sailing Directions and 'the land below the wind.'

But we liked the town. It was obvious that Sandakan prospers like a mini-Hong Kong, with the clatter of mahjong tiles and the wail of Chinese opera. Once the capital of north Borneo, during World War II it was heavily bombed and levelled to its very foundations. After the war it was completely rebuilt into a modern town with new trimmings.

Sandakan has some interesting sights. Located 24 km away is the Sepilok Sanctuary, the world's largest orangutan community. Orangutans which lived in captivity and were abandoned by their owners are sent here for rehabilitation. They actually have to be taught to live in the forest again.

And 32 km from Sandakan across the bay are the hallowed

Gomatang Caves, which are rich in the birds' nests used to make birds' nest soup. Sandakan is also a great starting point for jungle exploration. Dyaks live not too far inland.

Finally, there is Zamboanga. Among all three ports, Zamboanga is my favourite. It spells adventure, and it's about as far away as you can go and still be somewhere. It's a town few tourists ever visit.

For those who don't have a deck beneath their feet, getting there, actually, is not as difficult or complicated as one might expect. From Manila to Zamboanga is but two hours by air or 24 hours by local inter-island ferry.

Accommodation in Zambo, as the people call their town, is plentiful and varied. For anyone who wants to go first class there are new and modern hotels, and for the budget-minded, several second-class hotels plus four inns and five lodging houses. I like to sit in any one of the waterfront establishments in a wicker fanback chair and watch the world pass by.

A number of things make Zambo exciting. At first appearance it's the old-world architecture, which is part Spanish and part American, and added to this is the Oriental touch. The parks, central plaza and the fort are direct imports from Spain, although they came 400 years ago; the government buildings are American from the days when General "Black Jack" Pershing was governor, and the oriental influence reigns from the Muslim Moros who built the mosques and sail the colourful prows through the straits.

Zamboanga's location is another thing. Situated at the southern tip of Mindanao, on the eastern shore of the Moro Gulf and the Celebes Sea, the port has been the scene of endless historic naval battles and skirmishes over the last four centuries. Time has not changed the waterfront. Trading boats from the Sulu Islands, including contraband vessels, rusted freighters, passenger ferries from up north, cruise ships, yachts, government launches and patrol boats, and colourful sailing craft from as far as Borneo—they all make up the waterfront.

And then there are the people of Zamboanga. Christian Filipinos bear Chinese-Malay features but answer to Spanish names. There are the Moros, or the Muslims from the Sulu Islands. A proud race who continue to resist authority from the Manila government, they live by their own code of ethics, and many still believe that by killing a Christian they win a quick transit to Paradise. They fought the Spaniards, they fought the Americans, and they continue to do battle against the Philippine Constabulary. Some of the most colourful of these tribesmen from the Sulu are the Badjaos, often called sea gypsies.

The Badjaos were the first people to call the place Zamboanga, or land of the fragrant flowers. In 1635, the Spanish moved in, kept the name, and fortified the town against possible attack by the Portuguese, British, Dutch and the Sulu pirates. They built a fort and named it Fort Real Fuerza de Nuestra Señora del Pilar de Zaragoza, which, fortunately, was shortened to Fort Pilar. It was captured by the US cavalry in 1899 and held by the Japanese in 1942. The ruins still stand today.

The strongest American influence is seen in the massive, greystone city hall located in the city centre. Its enormous gates were designed so that a company of mounted cavalry could ride through six abreast. The building was originally built to serve as provisional army headquarters and as quarters for staff officers. There are a few old-timers who still recall the gala functions that went on within the walks before World War II.

The Americans also took pride in building parks and the first 18-hole golf course in the country. The Pasonanca Park was designed and laid out by General Pershing in 1912 and completed in 1916. At an elevation of 500 feet above sea level it's often called "The Little Baguio of the South." The Filipinos are famous for giving second names to things and people.

A late addition to the tourist attractions in Zamboanga is the "Tree House". The tourist office tries to promote it, and it's not a bad gimmick for individuals (or couples who are married) who want to live for a night or two on a tree-top, and for free. But Zamboanga really doesn't need a gimmick to attract visitors. Its attractions are its streets, its small restaurants and the raucous waterfront.

Morning is the best time to visit the market at the waterfront where a dozen races come to sell their wares, which include everything from fish to fruit and flowers. Walk through the market area and along the seawall to the main docks. Here, where Sulu trading boats and freighters tie up, there is a large enclosed area called the "barter traders." Much of the trade here is in contraband, smuggled in from Hong Kong and Borneo.

Also one of the best markets in Southeast Asia for seashells is Zamboanga. The blue and emerald-green seas of the Philippines abound in giant clams, black and finger coral, turtles and shellfish of varied hues and sizes. Fishermen and traders bring them to Zamboanga to sell.

In every sense of the word, Zamboanga is the division between East and West. It's the line of demarcation. In the narrow Basilan channel the Orient ends on one shore and the great South Pacific begins at the other.

Many travellers are frightened away from the southern Philippines because of the civil disturbances between the rebel Muslims and the central government. It's a condition that has existed for 400 years, and it's one that is likely to continue. I can't recommend visiting the Sulu Islands to the south or venturing inland on Mindanao itself. The political situation in Zamboanga changes with the tide, and the only sure way is to check with the tourist office in Manila. The government doesn't want to lose tourists, and won't authorise anything that isn't safe.

And if Zamboanga happens to be closed to tourists, there's always Sandakan, or even Chittagong.

I returned to Chittagong since I wrote this article, and found that nothing has changed, although I couldn't find the resthouse this time. That doesn't mean it's not there, however. And in Sandakan I joined a safari into the neighboring jungles looking for wild elephants. We didn't find them, but we could hear them in the distance. And the Sepilok Sanctuary is still the home for lost orangutans.

Chapter 36
DON'T THROW AWAY ALL THOSE OLD POSTCARDS

The following article appeared on January 26, 1987. I've added to my postcard collection since then.

I never could understand people who sent post cards. And I never really did enjoy receiving them. If someone had something to say, why not say it properly in a letter? Also, it seemed the only time I ever heard from some people was when they were travelling, and it was as if they were trying to tell me they were doing something I couldn't.

I must admit, however, I did go through a post card sending phase but for a different reason. A number of years ago I was back home visiting, and met an old grammar school chum, a man who had never travelled more than fifty miles from home, and most likely never would. But he was interested in places, and he asked if I would send him a card every now and then—"You know, from all those foreign places."

So I began sending him cards from everywhere I went. But I took my card sending a step further. The messages I wrote on the cards were in the language of the country I was in. And it was always the very same message that I wanted translated into that language—"Having a wonderful time wish you were here." Nothing else, not even my signature. If I passed through Tahiti, I then had the message written in Tahitian. And when I went to Singapore, it was written in Chinese; in Japan, Japanese. Over the years the countries mounted up. And since I didn't give my return address, I never got an answer or a thank you. My amusement, imagining my friend receiving the cards, was reward enough.

Sometimes, I admit, I had a very difficult time explaining to the person doing the writing that it really didn't matter if the addressee couldn't understand Chinese or Japanese or whatever language it was, and "having a wonderful time" might translate "time good me have" but nevertheless, off the cards went. One day I will go back, and I'm curious what friends will have to say. Maybe the cards annoyed him, and he threw them away, or worse, he may have died long ago and the post office threw them away.

Just as my friend may have been annoyed, I, too, found this business of sending post cards annoying. How many times has it happened this way: You check out of your hotel, a taxi is waiting with the meter running, and the person you are travelling with wants to stop at a rack in the lobby and buy post cards? "Wait, just five minutes," she says.

Then there is all this fuss about choosing the right post card. What's the difference? You send them to different people anyway. Why not pick a dozen you like and save yourself the agony?

But waiting while people choose post cards is only half the problem. They have to post them. The hotel where they bought the cards is always out of stamps, or else the clerk who sells the stamps has the key and has just gone for a coffee break. The taxi driver will take you to the post office, but it's five dollars out of the way to the airport. And your friend argues, what good are post cards if they aren't mailed in the country in which they are bought? You just can't win, so you have to join them, which is what I did. Overnight, more or less, I became an avid post card devotee, and sender.

It happened when I stopped at the Thai International office in Bangkok and sat talking to Vicky Chanvinij while waiting to see her boss. I have to admit, sometimes I go to THAI just to see

Vicky. She's my source of information when I want to know something about, say, the intricacies of Thai culture. She always seems to have the right answers. And she's nice to talk to.

This time when I mentioned that I was interested in early Thai embassies in Europe, Vicky said she could help. "I have to read my cards," she said.

"Vicky, I'm serious!" I replied.

"So am l," she answered. And then she explained the cards she mentioned were not what I thought. Hers were a collection of some 500 cards her husband's family had, cards posted by a grandfather who travelled extensively in Europe at the turn of the century. "Post cards," she said with conviction, "are a great documentation of history. Sometimes it may be all we have." Later she brought some of the cards to her office for me to see. How right she was! Here was history in pictures that you don't find in history books.

Sometimes you have to stumble over a thing before you know it exists. I was this way about post cards. I may have known they existed, but I never stopped to realise their value.

I remembered talking to Roberto Peragaz, general manager of the Raffles Hotel in Singapore. Mr Peragaz is forever coming up with old menus or photographs of the famous hotel, all from a bygone era, perhaps sixty or maybe seventy years ago. He uses them to publicise the hotel, and guests love it. I asked him how he did it.

"Post cards," he answered without hesitation. "You see, my biggest source of historical information comes from post cards. Most often the cards come from guests who once stayed here; they send them to me."

He showed me his collection. A menu dated 1912, old horse and carriages in front of the hotel, an elderly English lady in Victorian dress sitting in a rickshaw, also in front of the hotel; the Palm Court dining room shot from inside; one of the early suites with ceiling fan and mosquito net; and he had many street scenes of Singapore, about the time the motorcar was introduced.

Post cards! When I think about all those post cards I've thrown away over the years. But it's never too late, they say. I've even got into the habit now of sending myself post cards, ones I really like.

Post cards really are the spirit of travel. It's not an ego trip we are on, to prove we have been someplace; we simply want to tell people we are there. It's the cheapest and most economical way (no words wasted) to let people know we exist and care.

Post cards can be many things. They can be artistic, beautiful works of art. Some can be strictly informative, others funny or even spicy and others still can have specific messages to tell. And in later years, many of these cards can become quite valuable. Like stamp collectors, there are post card collectors. You can even join a post card club.

And for publishers, post cards can mean big business, and a profitable one. Competition is usually keen, so very often publishers hire the finest photographers they can afford to work for them.

Having become a keen post card enthusiast, I sometimes become vexed, however, when I study a rack of cards and find they are misleading. Post cards can give a wrong impression. For example, I recently saw cards of the Singapore River, jam-packed with sampans and river boats. There hasn't been a boat on the river in three years. They were all removed. And it always irks me when I see a Tahitian, in a bright red sarong, a flower behind his ear, tossing a fish net out over the water. Tahitians may toss nets all right, but they are generally wearing baggy frayed shorts, without flowers beind their ears. They hardly make good post card material.

In San Francisco I found a stamp shop that also deals in old post cards. The owner, Helen Wong, an American Chinese, explained that random acquisition is not the way to begin collecting cards. It's specialisation, even in post cards. Potential collectors should work on series of cards—automobiles, cities around the world, animals, monuments, statues, just about anything. Surprisingly, cards with "artistic" themes actually have little value. Similarly, she explained that a post card taken of dancers on Bali fifty years ago would not have much re-sale value today. Balinese dancers look much the same today as they did then.

The worth of any card need not be the subject matter, that is the picture or drawing: it can be the stamp, the postmark or even the addressee. With old cards, where the writing is clear, you find history encapsulated, an instant of time preserved, more valuable to the historian and researcher than a thousand printed words.

I asked Helen Wong if each and every post card is worth keeping.

"Ordinarily glossy picture post cards are not. They do become valuable if you've got in the foreground either people—so that you can clearly see the clothes they are wearing, the style of the era—or dateable objects such as motorcars, motorbikes or buses. They also become worth something if you can plainly see a shop front and signs—then a post card becomes a historical document. And it's worth keeping."

So go through all those dusty shoe boxes and look for old post cards. You may have a valuable collection tucked away somewhere. Or you can start sending post cards to your family for keeping. In sixty or seventy years, they too may be worth something. But even better, they make good memories and can be fun saving. That's what's most important!

Roberto Peragaz is no longer the general manager of Raffles Hotel in Singapore; he moved on to the new Cockpit Hotel on Orchard Road. But Helen Wong still owns and operates her stamp-and-post card shop in San Francisco.

Also by Harold Stephens

Who Needs a Road
Discover the Orient
Destination Singapore
Wander with the Wind
Turn South at the Equator
Malaysia
Asian Portraits
Asian Adventure
At Home in Asia
The Last Voyage: the Story of Schooner Third Sea

Thousands have come to know Asia through Harold Stephens' books, and magazine and newspaper articles. One of Asia's best and most enduring writer/adventures, Stephens has for thirty years served as travel writer for the *Bangkok Post* and travel correspondent for Thai Airways International. From its jungles, to its mountains, from its vibrant cities to its empty seas, few have experienced Asia the way Harold Stephens has.

In this his latest book you will find a collection of his articles that appeared in the *Post* over the years, from diving on wrecks to climbing mountains, and from interviews with interesting people to living the free life in Southeast Asia.